15-MINUTE
GERMAN
LEARN IN JUST 12 WEEKS

Sylvia Goulding

Penguin
Random
House

REVISED EDITION
DK LONDON
Senior Editor Ankita Awasthi Tröger
Senior Art Editor Clare Shedden
Illustrators Peter Bull Art Studio and Dan Crisp
Managing Editor Carine Tracanelli
Managing Art Editor Anna Hall
US Editor Heather Wilcox
US Executive Editor Lori Hand
Production Editor Kavita Varma
Senior Production Controller Poppy David
Jacket Design Development Manager Sophia MTT
Associate Publishing Director Liz Wheeler
Art Director Karen Self
Publishing Director Jonathan Metcalf

DK DELHI
Project Editor Nandini D. Tripathy
Senior Art Editor Ira Sharma
Project Art Editor Anukriti Arora
Assistant Art Editor Sulagna Das
Managing Editor Soma B. Chowdhury
Senior Managing Art Editor Arunesh Talapatra
Jacket Designer Juhi Sheth
Senior Jacket Designer Suhita Dharamjit
Senior Jackets Coordinator Priyanka Sharma-Saddi
DTP Coordinators Pushpak Tyagi
DTP Designers Rakesh Kumar, Mrinmoy
Mazumdar, Vikram Singh
Hi-res Coordinator Neeraj Bhatia
Production Editor Vishal Bhatia
Production Manager Pankaj Sharma
Pre-production Manager Balwant Singh
Senior Picture Researcher Sumedha Chopra
Picture Research Manager Taiyaba Khatoon
Creative Head Malavika Talukder

**Language content for Dorling Kindersley by
g-and-w publishing.
Additional translations for 2023 edition by
Andiamo! Language Services Ltd.**

This American Edition, 2023
First American Edition, 2005
Published in the United States by DK Publishing
1745 Broadway, 20th Floor, New York, NY 10019

Copyright © 2005, 2012, 2018, 2023
Dorling Kindersley Limited
DK, a Division of Penguin Random House LLC
23 24 25 26 27 10 9 8 7 6 5 4 3 2 1
001–334018–Aug/2023

A catalog record for this book
is available from the Library of Congress.
ISBN 978-0-7440-8080-3

Printed in China

For the curious
www.dk.com

MIX
Paper | Supporting
responsible forestry
FSC™ C018179

This book was made with Forest
Stewardship Council™ certified
paper – one small step in DK's
commitment to a sustainable future.
**For more information go to
www.dk.com/our-green-pledge**

Contents

How to use this book

Twelve themed chapters are broken down into five daily 15-minute lessons, allowing you to work through four teaching units and one practice unit each week. The lessons cover a range of practical themes, including leisure, business, food and drink, and travel. A reference section at the end contains a menu guide and English-to-German and German-to-English dictionaries.

Warm up
Each day starts with a warm-up that encourages you to recall vocabulary or phrases you have learned previously.

Instructions
Each exercise is numbered and introduced by instructions that explain what to do. In some cases, additional information is given about the language point being covered.

Text styles
Distinctive text styles differentiate German, English, and the pronunciation guide.

Audio
This icon indicates that you should listen to audio recordings in order to do the exercise. See page 7 for details of how to access and use the audio app.

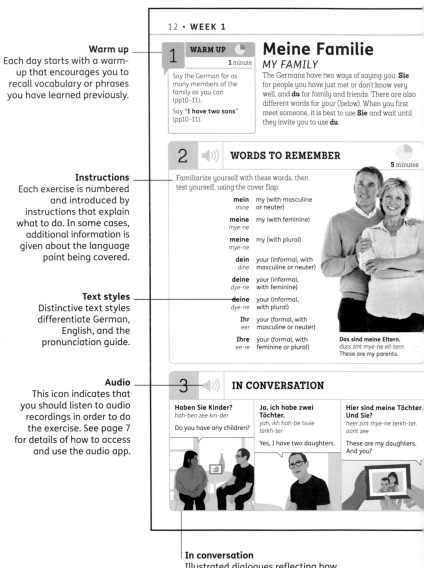

12 · **WEEK 1**

1 WARM UP
1 minute

Say the German for as many members of the family as you can (pp10–11).

Say "**I have two sons**" (pp10–11).

Meine Familie
MY FAMILY

The Germans have two ways of saying *you*: **Sie** for people you have just met or don't know very well, and **du** for family and friends. There are also different words for *your* (below). When you first meet someone, it is best to use **Sie** and wait until they invite you to use **du**.

2 WORDS TO REMEMBER
5 minutes

Familiarize yourself with these words, then test yourself, using the cover flap.

mein *mine*	my (with masculine or neuter)
meine *mye-ne*	my (with feminine)
meine *mye-ne*	my (with plural)
dein *dine*	your (informal, with masculine or neuter)
deine *dye-ne*	your (informal, with feminine)
deine *dye-ne*	your (informal, with plural)
Ihr *eer*	your (formal, with masculine or neuter)
Ihre *ee-re*	your (formal, with feminine or plural)

Das sind meine Eltern.
duss zint mye-ne ell-tern
These are my parents.

3 IN CONVERSATION

Haben Sie Kinder?
hah-ben zee kin-der

Do you have any children?

Ja, ich habe zwei Töchter.
yah, ikh hah-be tsvie terkh-ter

Yes, I have two daughters.

Hier sind meine Töchter. Und Sie?
heer zint mye-ne terkh-ter. oont zee

These are my daughters. And you?

In conversation
Illustrated dialogues reflecting how vocabulary and phrases are used in everyday situations appear throughout the book.

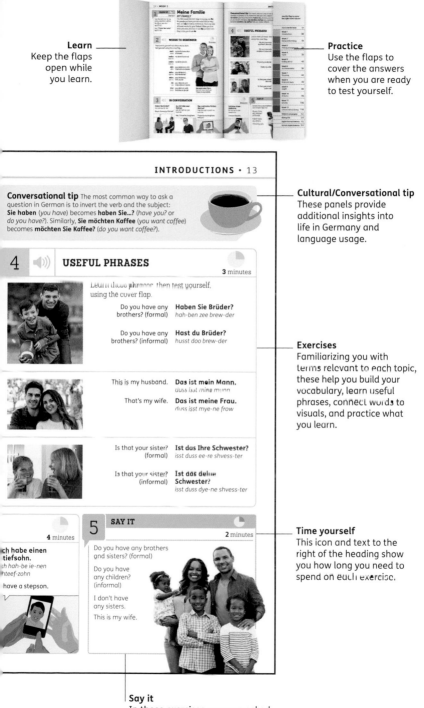

Learn
Keep the flaps open while you learn.

Practice
Use the flaps to cover the answers when you are ready to test yourself.

Conversational tip The most common way to ask a question in German is to invert the verb and the subject: **Sie haben** (you have) becomes **haben Sie...?** (have you? or do you have?). Similarly, **Sie möchten Kaffee** (you want coffee) becomes **möchten Sie Kaffee?** (do you want coffee?).

Cultural/Conversational tip
These panels provide additional insights into life in Germany and language usage.

4 USEFUL PHRASES

3 minutes

Learn these phrases, then test yourself using the cover flap.

Do you have any brothers? (formal)	**Haben Sie Brüder?** *hah-ben zee brew-der*
Do you have any brothers? (informal)	**Hast du Brüder?** *husst doo brew-der*
This is my husband.	**Das ist mein Mann.** *duss isst mine munn*
That's my wife.	**Das ist meine Frau.** *duss isst mye-ne frow*
Is that your sister? (formal)	**Ist das Ihre Schwester?** *isst duss ee-re shvess-ter*
Is that your sister? (informal)	**Ist das deine Schwester?** *isst duss dye-ne shvess-ter*

Exercises
Familiarizing you with terms relevant to each topic, these help you build your vocabulary, learn useful phrases, connect words to visuals, and practice what you learn.

4 minutes

ch habe einen tiefsohn.

ch hah-be ie-nen hteef-zohn

have a stepson.

5 SAY IT

2 minutes

Do you have any brothers and sisters? (formal)

Do you have any children? (informal)

I don't have any sisters.

This is my wife.

Time yourself
This icon and text to the right of the heading show you how long you need to spend on each exercise.

Say it
In these exercises, you are asked to apply what you have learned, using different vocabulary.

»

Review

At the end of every week's lessons, a practice unit lets you test yourself on what you have learned so far. A recap of selected elements from previous lessons helps reinforce your knowledge.

Test yourself
Use the cover flap to conceal the answers while you review.

Reference

This section appears at the end of the book and brings together all the words and phrases you have learned over the weeks. While the menu guide focuses on food and drink, the dictionary lists German translations of common words and phrases.

Dictionaries
Mini-dictionaries provide ready reference from English to German and German to English for 2,500 words.

Menu guide
Use this guide as a reference for food terminology and popular German dishes.

PRONUNCIATION GUIDE

Many German sounds will already be familiar to you, but a few require special attention. Take note of how these letters are pronounced:

ch pronounced from the back of the throat, as in the Scottish *loch*

j pronounced *y* as in *yes*

r rolled, produced from the back of the throat

s pronounced either *s* as in *see* or *z* as in *zoo*

sch pronounced *sh* as in *ship*

ß a special character that represents a double *ss*

v pronounced *f* as in *foot*

w pronounced *v* as in *van*

z/tz pronounced *ts* as in *pets*

German vowels can be tricky, with the same vowel having a number of different pronunciations. Watch out also for these combinations that may look like familiar English sounds, but are pronounced differently in German:

au as the English *now*

ee as the English *lay*

ei as the English *high*

eu as the English *boy*

ie as the English *see*

Below each German word or phrase, you will find a pronunciation transcription. Read this, bearing in mind the tips above, and you will achieve a comprehensible result. But remember that the transcription can only ever be an approximation and that there is no real substitute for listening to native speakers.

HOW TO USE THE AUDIO APP

The free audio app accompanying this book contains audio recordings for all numbered exercises on the teaching pages, except for the Warm Up and Say It exercises (look out for the audio icon). There is no audio for the practice pages.

To start using the audio with this book, download the **DK 15 Minute Language Course** app on your tablet or smartphone from the App Store or Google Play and select your book from the list of available titles. Please note that this app is not a stand-alone course, but is designed to be used together with the book to familiarize you with the language and provide examples for you to repeat aloud.

There are two ways in which you can use the audio. The first is to read through the 15-minute lessons using just the book, then go back and work with the audio and the book together. Or you can combine the book and the audio from the start, pausing the app to read the instructions on the page.

You are encouraged to listen to the audio and repeat the words and sentences out loud until you are confident you understand and can pronounce what has been said. Remember that repetition is vital for language learning. The more often you listen to a conversation or repeat an oral exercise, the more the new language will sink in.

SUPPORTING AUDIO
This icon indicates that audio recordings are available for you to listen to.

FREE AUDIO APP

1 WARM UP
1 minute

The Warm Up panel appears at the beginning of each topic. Use it to reinforce what you have already learned and to prepare yourself for moving ahead with the new subject.

Guten Tag
HELLO

In formal situations, Germans greet each other with a handshake. They are addressed with the titles **Herr** (for men) and **Frau** (for women) and their last name. The title **Fräulein** (*miss*) is no longer in use. Young people may greet each other with a kiss on each cheek.

2 ◀))) WORDS TO REMEMBER
2 minutes

Familiarize yourself with these words by reading them aloud several times, then test yourself by concealing the German on the left with the cover flap.

Guten Tag *goo-ten tahk*	Good day/Hello
Guten Abend/Nacht *goo-ten ah-bent/nukht*	Good evening/night
Bis bald/morgen *biss balt/mor-gen*	See you soon/tomorrow
Auf Wiedersehen/Tschüss *owf vee-der-zay-en/tchews*	Goodbye (formal/informal)
Danke *dun-ke*	Thank you

Hallo!
hal-loe
Hi!

3 ◀))) IN CONVERSATION: FORMAL
3 minutes

Guten Tag. Ich heiße Martina Li.
goo-ten tahk. ikh high-se mar-teen-a lee

Hello. My name's Martina Li.

Guten Tag. Michael Brand, freut mich.
goo-ten tahk. mikh-ah-ail brant, froyt mikh

Hello. Michael Brand, pleased to meet you.

Freut mich.
froyt mikh

Pleased to meet you.

4 🔊 PUT INTO PRACTICE

3 minutes

Read the German on the left and follow the instructions to complete this dialogue. Then, test yourself by concealing the German on the right with the cover flap.

Guten Abend, Herr Gohl.
goo-ten ah-bent, hair goel

Guten Abend.
goo-ten ah-bent

Good evening, Mr. Gohl.
Say: Good evening.

Ich heiße Ilse Gerlach.
ikh high-se ilze gair-lakh

Freut mich.
froyt mikh

My name is Ilse Gerlach.
Say: Pleased to meet you.

Cultural tip

In addition to proper names, all nouns start with a capital letter in German—for example, **der Tag** (*the day*), as in the greeting **Guten Tag** (*good day*). This tradition began in the Middle Ages and became a rule in the late 19th century.

5 🔊 USEFUL PHRASES

3 minutes

Learn these phrases by reading them aloud several times, then test yourself by concealing the German on the right with the cover flap.

What's your name? **Wie heißen Sie?**
vee high-sen zee

My name is Thomas. **Ich heiße Thomas.**
ikh high-se toe-mass

Pleased to meet you. **Freut mich.**
froyt mikh

6 🔊 IN CONVERSATION: INFORMAL

3 minutes

Also, bis morgen?
ull-zoe, biss mor-gen

So, see you tomorrow?

Ja, auf Wiedersehen.
yah, owf vee-der-zay-en

Yes, goodbye.

Tschüss. Bis bald.
tchews. biss balt

Goodbye. See you soon.

Die Verwandten
RELATIVES

Many German terms for family relationships are similar to the English terms—for example, father/**Vater**, daughter/**Tochter**, etc. Spouses are often referred to by the shortened terms **mein Mann** or **meine Frau**. Common collective nouns for family members include **Kinder** (*children*), **Enkelkinder** (*grandchildren*), and **Geschwister** (*siblings*).

---

1 WARM UP
1 minute

Say "**hello**" and "**goodbye**" in German (pp8–9).

Now say "**My name is...**" (pp8–9).

Say "**Mr.**" and "**Mrs.**" (pp8–9).

---

2 🔊 MATCH AND REPEAT
5 minutes

Look at the people in this scene and match their numbers to the vocabulary list on the left. Then, test yourself by concealing the German on the left, using the cover flap.

❶ **der Vater**
dair fah-ter

❷ **die Mutter**
dee moot-ter

❸ **die Schwester**
dee shvess-ter

❹ **der Bruder**
dair broo-der

❺ **die Tochter**
dee tokh-ter

❻ **der Sohn**
dair zoen

❼ **die Großmutter**
dee groes-moot-ter

❽ **der Großvater**
dair groes-fah-ter

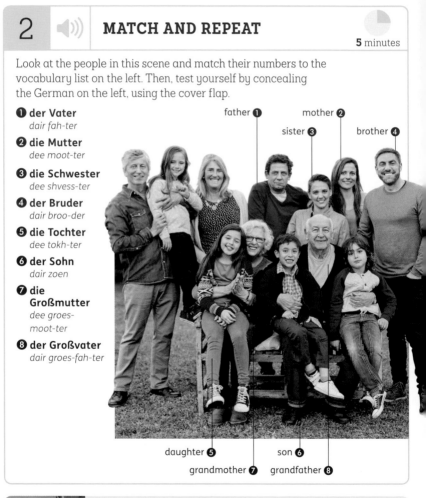

father ❶ mother ❷
sister ❸ brother ❹
daughter ❺ son ❻
grandmother ❼ grandfather ❽

Conversational tip In German, things are masculine, feminine, or neuter, taking a different form of *the* according to gender: **der**, **die**, and **das**, respectively. The word for *a/an*, **ein**, also changes according to gender: **das ist ein Mann** (*that is a man*), but **das ist eine Frau** (*that is a woman*). Genders of words have to be memorized individually.

3 WORDS TO REMEMBER:
RELATIVES

4 minutes

Familiarize yourself with these words, then test yourself, using the cover flap.

die Ehefrau **der Ehemann**
dee ay-afrow *dair ay-amunn*
wife husband

Ich bin verheiratet.
ikh bin fer-hye-rah-tet
I'm married.

children	**die Kinder** *dee kin-der*
brother-in-law/ sister-in-law	**der Schwager/ die Schwägerin** *dair shvar-ger/ dee shvay-ge-rin*
half-brother/ half-sister	**der Halbbruder/ die Halbschwester** *dair hulp-broo-der/ dee hulp-shvess-ter*
stepson/stepdaughter	**der Stiefsohn/ die Stieftochter** *dair shteef-zohn/ dee shteef-tokh-ter*
stepfather/stepmother	**der Stiefvater/ die Stiefmutter** *dair shteef-fah-ter/ dee shteef-moot-ter*
I have two sons.	**Ich habe zwei Söhne.** *ikh hah-be tsvie zer-ne.*

4 WORDS TO REMEMBER:
NUMBERS

3 minutes

Familiarize yourself with these words, then test yourself, using the cover flap. Note that plurals are formed by adding an **en**, **e**, **er**, or **s** to the end of the word and using a number or the plural definite article, as in **eine Frau/zwei Frauen** (one woman/two women), **ein Tag/drei Tage** (one day/three days), **ein Kind/ vier Kinder** (one child/four children), **ein Auto/fünf Autos** (one car/five cars). In some cases, the main vowel changes to a vowel with an umlaut, as in **der Mann/die Männer** (man/men).

one	**eins** *ients*
two	**zwei** *tsvie*
three	**drei** *drie*
four	**vier** *feer*
five	**fünf** *fewnf*
six	**sechs** *zeks*
seven	**sieben** *zee-ben*
eight	**acht** *akht*
nine	**neun** *noyn*
ten	**zehn** *tsayn*

5 SAY IT

2 minutes

One sister.
Three sons.
Two children.

1 WARM UP

1 minute

Say the German for as many members of the family as you can (pp10–11).

Say "**I have two sons**" (pp10–11).

Meine Familie
MY FAMILY

The Germans have two ways of saying *you*: **Sie** for people you have just met or don't know very well, and **du** for family and friends. There are also different words for *your* (below). When you first meet someone, it is best to use **Sie** and wait until they invite you to use **du**.

2 WORDS TO REMEMBER

5 minutes

Familiarize yourself with these words, then test yourself, using the cover flap.

mein *mine*	my (with masculine or neuter)	
meine *mye-ne*	my (with feminine)	
meine *mye-ne*	my (with plural)	
dein *dine*	your (informal, with masculine or neuter)	
deine *dye-ne*	your (informal, with feminine)	
deine *dye-ne*	your (informal, with plural)	
Ihr *eer*	your (formal, with masculine or neuter)	
Ihre *ee-re*	your (formal, with feminine or plural)	

Das sind meine Eltern.
duss zint mye-ne ell-tern
These are my parents.

3 IN CONVERSATION

Haben Sie Kinder?
hah-ben zee kin-der

Do you have any children?

Ja, ich habe zwei Töchter.
yah, ikh hah-be tsvie terkh-ter

Yes, I have two daughters.

Hier sind meine Töchter. Und Sie?
heer zint mye-ne terkh-ter. oont zee

These are my daughters. And you?

Conversational tip The most common way to ask a question in German is to invert the verb and the subject: **Sie haben** (*you have*) becomes **haben Sie...?** (*have you?* or *do you have?*). Similarly, **Sie möchten Kaffee** (*you want coffee*) becomes **möchten Sie Kaffee?** (*do you want coffee?*).

4 USEFUL PHRASES

3 minutes

Learn these phrases, then test yourself, using the cover flap.

Do you have any brothers? (formal)	**Haben Sie Brüder?** *hah-ben zee brew-der*
Do you have any brothers? (informal)	**Hast du Brüder?** *husst doo brew-der*
This is my husband.	**Das ist mein Mann.** *duss isst mine munn*
That's my wife.	**Das ist meine Frau.** *duss isst mye-ne frow*
Is that your sister? (formal)	**Ist das Ihre Schwester?** *isst duss ee-re shvess-ter*
Is that your sister? (informal)	**Ist das deine Schwester?** *isst duss dye-ne shvess-ter*

4 minutes

Ich habe einen Stiefsohn.
ikh hah-be ie-nen shteef-zohn

I have a stepson.

5 SAY IT

2 minutes

Do you have any brothers and sisters? (formal)

Do you have any children? (informal)

I don't have any sisters.

This is my wife.

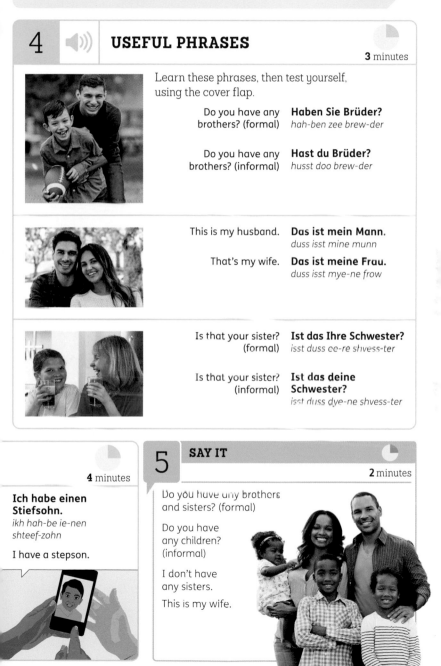

1 WARM UP
1 minute

Say "**See you soon**" (pp8–9).

Say "**I am married**" (pp10–11) and "**I have a wife**" (pp12–13).

Sein und haben
TO BE AND TO HAVE

German verbs have more forms than English ones, so learn them carefully. The verbs **sein** (*to be*) and **haben** (*to have*) are used in many expressions, often differently from English. For example, in English, you say *I'm hungry*, but in German, you say **ich habe Hunger** (literally *I have hunger*).

2 🔊 SEIN: TO BE
5 minutes

Practice **sein** (*to be*) and the sample sentences, then test yourself, using the cover flap.

ich bin *ikh bin*	I am
du bist *doo bisst*	you are (informal singular)
er/sie/es ist *air/zee/ess isst*	he/she/it is
wir sind *veer zint*	we are
ihr seid *eer ziet*	you are (informal plural)
Sie sind/sie sind *zee zint*	you are (formal singular or plural)/they are

Ich bin Engländerin.
ikh bin ang-lan-darin
I'm English.

Ich bin müde. *ikh bin mew-de*	I'm tired.

Ist sie glücklich? *isst zee glewk-likh*	Is she happy?

Wir sind Deutsche. *veer zind doitche*	We're German.

3 HABEN: TO HAVE

5 minutes

Practice **haben** (*to have*) and the sample sentences, then test yourself, using the cover flap.

Haben Sie Brokkoli?
hah-ben zee brokolee
Do you have any broccoli?

I have	**ich habe** *ikh hah-be*
you have (informal singular)	**du hast** *doo husst*
he/she/it has	**er/sie/es hat** *air/zee/ess hut*
we have	**wir haben** *veer hah-ben*
you have (informal plural)	**ihr habt** *eer hahpt*
you have (formal singular or plural)/they have	**Sie haben/sie haben** *zee hah-ben*

He has a meeting.	**Er hat eine Besprechung.** *air hut ie-ne be-shpre-khoong*
Do you have a cell phone?	**Haben Sie ein Smartphone?** *hah-ben zee ine smart-fon*
They have a half brother	**Sie haben einen Halbbruder.** *zee hah-ben ie-nen hulp-broo-der*

4  NEGATIVES

4 minutes

The most common way to make a sentence negative in German is to put **nicht** (*not*) in front of the word that is negated, much as in English: **wir sind nicht verheiratet** (*we are not married*). Note the following special negative constructions: *not a/not any* becomes **kein/keine**, *not ever/never* becomes **nie**, and *not anywhere/nowhere* becomes **nirgendwo**. Read these sentences aloud, then test yourself, using the cover flap.

das Fahrrad
duss fahr-raht
bicycle

Ich habe kein Auto.
ikh hah-be kine ow-to
I don't have a car.

I'm not tired.	**Ich bin nicht müde.** *ikh bin nikht mew-de*
He's not married.	**Er ist nicht verheiratet.** *air isst nikht fer-hye-rah-tet*
We don't have any children.	**Wir haben keine Kinder.** *veer hah-ben kye-ne kin-der*

Antworten *Answers*
(Cover with flap)

How many?

❶ **drei**
drie

❷ **neun**
noyn

❸ **vier**
feer

❹ **zwei**
tsvie

❺ **acht**
akht

❻ **zehn**
tsayn

❼ **fünf**
fewnf

❽ **sieben**
zee-ben

❾ **sechs**
zeks

Hello

❶ **Guten Tag. Ich heiße...**
goo-ten tahk. ikh high-se...

❷ **Freut mich.**
froyt mikh

❸ **Ja, und ich habe zwei Söhne. Und Sie?**
yah, oont ikh hah-be tsvie zer-ne. Oont zee?

❹ **Auf Wiedersehen. Bis morgen.**
owf vee-der-zay-en. biss mor-gen

Wiederholung
REVIEW AND REPEAT

1 HOW MANY?
2 minutes

Say these numbers in German, then test yourself, using the cover flap.

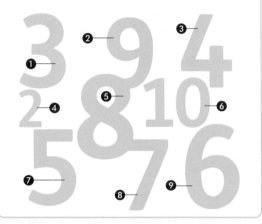

2 HELLO
4 minutes

You meet someone in a formal situation. Join in the conversation, replying in German, following the numbered English prompts.

Guten Tag. Ich heiße Luisa.
❶ Hello. My name is... [your name].

Das ist mein Mann, Theo.
❷ Pleased to meet you.

Sind Sie verheiratet?
❸ Yes, and I have two sons. And you?

Wir haben drei Töchter.
❹ Goodbye. See you tomorrow.

3 BE OR HAVE

5 minutes

Fill in the blanks with the correct form of **haben** (*to have*) or **sein** (*to be*).

❶ Das _____ mein Mann.
❷ Sie (she) _____ müde.
❸ Wir _____ Deutsche.
❹ _____ Sie eine Besprechung?
❺ Sie (she) _____ eine Schwägerin.
❻ Ich _____ kein Handy.
❼ _____ du glücklich?
❽ Ich _____ verheiratet.

Be or have

❶ ist
isst

❷ ist
isst

❸ sind
zint

❹ haben
hah-ben

❺ hat
hut

❻ habe
hah-be

❼ bist
bisst

❽ bin
bin

4 RELATIVES

4 minutes

Name these family members in German.

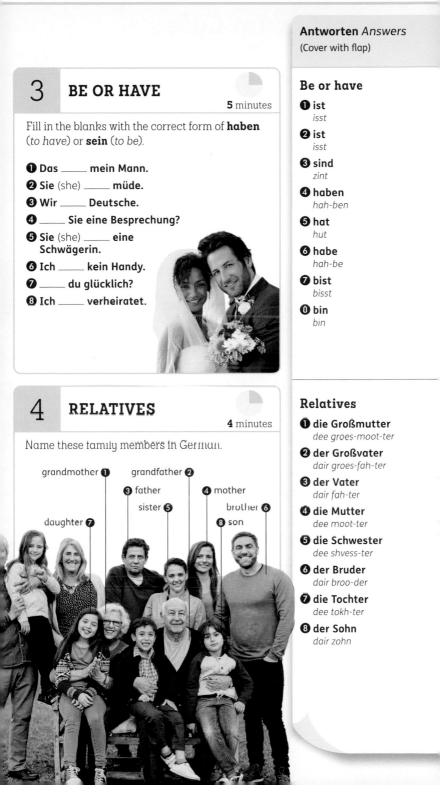

grandmother ❶   grandfather ❷
❸ father   ❹ mother
sister ❺   brother ❻
daughter ❼   ❽ son

Relatives

❶ die Großmutter
dee groes-moot-ter

❷ der Großvater
dair groes-fah-ter

❸ der Vater
dair fah-ter

❹ die Mutter
dee moot-ter

❺ die Schwester
dee shvess-ter

❻ der Bruder
dair broo-der

❼ die Tochter
dee tokh-ter

❽ der Sohn
dair zohn

1 WARM UP
1 minute

Count to ten (pp10–11).

Say "**hello**" and "**goodbye**" (pp8–9).

Ask "**Do you have a brother?**" (pp12–13).

Im Café
IN THE CAFÉ

In a German café, the busiest time is the afternoon, when people stop for **kaffee und kuchen** (*coffee and cake*). Savory dishes are usually available, but the emphasis is on pastries and cakes. Most cafés offer table service, and it is usual to tip the server, but a good rounding-up will be enough.

2 🔊 MATCH AND REPEAT

Familiarize yourself with these words, then test yourself, using the cover flap.

der Kaffee *dair kuf-fay*	coffee
der Kaffee ohne Milch *dair kuf-fay oh-ne milkh*	black coffee
der schwarze Tee *dair shvar-tse tay*	black tea
das Gebäck *duss ge-beck*	pastry
das Sandwich *duss zent-vitch*	sandwich
der Zucker *dair tsook-ker*	sugar

ein Stück Kuchen
ine shtewck koo-khen
slice of cake

der Milchkaffee
dair milkh-kuf-fay
coffee with hot milk

3 🔊 IN CONVERSATION

Ich hätte gern eine Tasse Tee mit Milch.
ikh het-te gairn ie-ne tuss-se tay mit milkh

I would like a cup of tea with milk, please.

Sonst noch etwas?
zonsst nokh et-vuss

Anything else?

Haben Sie Kuchen?
hah-ben zee koo-khen

Do you have any cake?

Cultural tip A standard coffee is usually served with milk and sugar on the side. Tea drinkers should specify whether they want herbal or black tea and whether they want it with *milk* (**mit Milch**) or *lemon* (**mit Zitrone**).

5 minutes

der Tee mit Milch
dair tay mit milkh
tea with milk

4 📢 USEFUL PHRASES

5 minutes

Learn these phrases, then test yourself, using the cover flap.

Ich hätte gern eine Tasse Kaffee, bitte.
ikh het-te gairn ie-ne tuss-se kuf-fay, bit-te

I'd like a cup of coffee, please.

Sonst noch etwas?
zonsst nokh et-vuss

Anything else?

Ja, ein Teilchen, bitte.
yah, ine tile-khen, bit-te

Yes, a Danish pastry, please.

Was macht das?
vuss mukht duss

How much is that?

4 minutes

Ja, selbstverständlich.
yah, zelpst-fer-shtend-likh

Yes, certainly.

Danke. Was macht das?
dun-ke. vuss mukht duss

Thank you. How much is that?

Acht Euro, bitte.
akht oy-roe, bit-te

Eight euros, please.

1 WARM UP
1 minute

Say "**I'd like**" (pp18–19).

Say "**I don't have a brother**" (pp14–15).

Ask "**Do you have pastries?**" (pp18–19).

When do you use "**der**" and "**die**" (pp10–11)?

Im Restaurant
IN THE RESTAURANT

There are a variety of eating places in Germany. A **Café** (pp18–19) will offer hot and cold drinks, small plates, and cakes. A **Gaststätte** serves local or international dishes, while a **Gasthof** offers a more homey style of cooking. You'll get regional specialities in a **Ratskeller**, usually located in the basement of a historic town hall, while a **Weinstube** has local wine and snacks.

2 🔊 MATCH AND REPEAT
5 minutes

Match the numbered items to the list, then test yourself, using the cover flap.

❶ **Untertasse**
dee unter-tuss-se

❷ **die Tasse**
dee tuss-se

❸ **das Glas**
duss glahss

❹ **die Gabel**
dee gah-bell

❺ **das Messer**
duss mess-ser

❻ **der Löffel**
dair lerff-fel

❼ **der Teller**
dair tell-ler

❽ **die Serviette**
dee zair-vee-ett-te

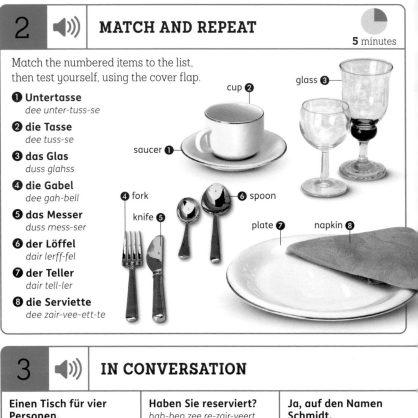

cup ❷ · glass ❸ · saucer ❶ · fork ❹ · knife ❺ · spoon ❻ · plate ❼ · napkin ❽

3 🔊 IN CONVERSATION

Einen Tisch für vier Personen.
ie-nen tish fewr feer pair-zoe-nen

A table for four.

Haben Sie reserviert?
hah-ben zee re-zair-veert

Do you have a reservation?

Ja, auf den Namen Schmidt.
yah, owf dayn nah-men shmitt

Yes, in the name of Schmidt.

4 🔊 WORDS TO REMEMBER

3 minutes

Familiarize yourself with these words, then test yourself, using the cover flap.

Ich esse mit meiner Familie zu Mittag.
ikh ess-se mit mye-nair fuh-mee-lee-ye tsoo mit-tahk
I'm having lunch with my family.

menu	**die Speisekarte** *dee shpie-ze-kar-te*
wine list	**die Weinkarte** *dee vine-kar-te*
appetizers	**die Vorspeisen** *dee for-shpie-zen*
main courses	**die Hauptgerichte** *dee howpt-ge-rikh-te*
desserts	**der Nachtisch** *dair nahkh-tish*
breakfast	**das Frühstück** *duss frew-shtewk*
lunch	**das Mittagessen** *duss mit-tahk-ess-sen*
dinner	**das Abendessen** *duss ah-bent-ess-sen*

5 🔊 USEFUL PHRASES

2 minutes

Learn these phrases, then test yourself, using the cover flap.

What do you have for dessert?	**Was haben Sie zum Nachtisch?** *vuss hah-ben zee tsoom nahkh-tish*
May I have the bill, please?	**Könnte ich bitte die Rechnung haben?** *kern-te ikh bit-te dee rekh-noong hah-ben*

4 minutes

Welchen Tisch möchten Sie?
vel-khen tish merkh-ten zee

Which table would you like?

Am Fenster, bitte.
um fens-ter, bit-te

Near the window, please.

Selbstverständlich. Folgen Sie mir.
zelpst-fer-shtend-likh. fol-gen zee meer

Of course. Follow me.

Die Gerichte
DISHES

Say "**I am tired**" and "**We have children**" (pp14–15).

Ask "**Do you have a fork?**" (pp20–21).

Say "**I'd like a black coffee**" (pp18–19).

Germany is famous for its sausages and meat dishes as well as its sauerkraut and dumplings. Today's restaurants, however, offer a wide selection of international dishes. Although German cuisine is traditionally meat-based, many restaurants now offer vegetarian dishes.

---

2 🔊 **MATCH AND REPEAT**
4 minutes

Match the numbered items to the list, then test yourself, using the cover flap.

❶ **das Gemüse**
duss ge-mew-ze

❷ **das Obst**
duss opst

❸ **der Käse**
dair kay-ze

❹ **die Nüsse**
dee news-se

❺ **die Suppe**
dee zoop-pe

❻ **das Geflügel**
duss ge-flew-gel

❼ **die Nudeln**
dee noo-deln

❽ **der Fisch**
dair fish

❾ **die Meeresfrüchte**
dee mair-es-frewkh-te

❿ **das Fleisch**
duss fliesh

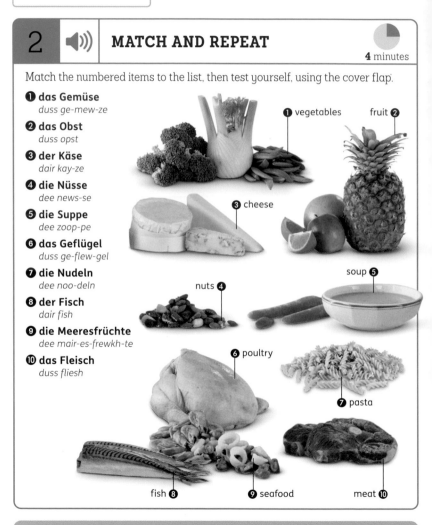

❶ vegetables fruit ❷

❸ cheese

soup ❺

nuts ❹

❻ poultry

❼ pasta

fish ❽ ❾ seafood meat ❿

Cultural tip In most restaurants at lunchtime, you will usually have the choice of eating a **Tagesgericht** (*dish of the day*) or of choosing **à la carte** from the menu.

3 WORDS TO REMEMBER:
COOKING METHODS

3 minutes

Familiarize yourself with these words, then test yourself, using the cover flap.

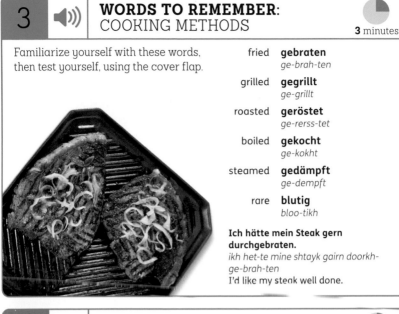

fried	**gebraten** *ge-brah-ten*
grilled	**gegrillt** *ge-grillt*
roasted	**geröstet** *ge-rerss-tet*
boiled	**gekocht** *ge-kokht*
steamed	**gedämpft** *ge-dempft*
rare	**blutig** *bloo-tikh*

Ich hätte mein Steak gern durchgebraten.
ikh het-te mine shtayk gairn doorkh-ge-brah-ten
I'd like my steak well done.

4 WORDS TO REMEMBER:
DRINKS

3 minutes

Familiarize yourself with these words, then test yourself, using the cover flap.

das Wasser mit Kohlensäure
duss vuss-ser mit koe-len-zoy-re
fizzy water

water	**das Wasser** *duss vuss-ser*
still water	**das Wasser ohne Kohlensäure** *duss vuss-ser oe-ne koe-len-zoy-re*
wine	**der Wein** *dair vine*
fruit juice	**der Fruchtsaft** *dair frookht-zufft*

5 USEFUL PHRASES

2 minutes

Learn these phrases, then test yourself, using the cover flap.

I am a vegetarian. **Ich bin Vegetarier/Vegetarierin.**
ikh bin vay-ge-tah-ree-er/vay-ge-tah-ree-er-in

I am allergic to nuts. **Ich bin allergisch gegen Nüsse.**
ikh bin ull-lair-gish gay-gen news-se

What is "Spätzle"? **Was ist "Spätzle"?**
vuss isst shpets-le

6 SAY IT

2 minutes

What is "Sauerbraten"?
I'm allergic to seafood.
I'd like a fruit juice.

1
WARM UP
1 minute

What are "**breakfast**," "**lunch**," and "**dinner**" in German (pp20–21)?

Say "**I**," "**you**" (informal, singular), "**he**," "**she**," "**it**," "**we**," "**you**" (formal, plural), "**they**" (pp14–15).

Mögen
TO WANT

In this section, you will learn the present tense of a verb that is essential to everyday conversation—**mögen** (*to want*)—as well as a useful polite expression, **ich hätte gern** (*I would like*). Remember to use this form when requesting something because **ich möchte** (*I want*) may sound too forceful.

---

2 🔊 **MÖGEN**: TO WANT

6 minutes

Practice **mögen** (*to want*) and the sample sentences, then test yourself, using the cover flap.

ich möchte *ikh merkh-te*	I want
du möchtest *doo merkh-test*	you want (informal singular)
er/sie/es möchte *air/zee/ess merkh-te*	he/she/it wants
wir möchten *veer merkh-ten*	we want
ihr möchtet *eer merkh-tet*	you want (informal plural)
Sie möchten/ sie möchten *zee merkh-ten*	you want (formal singular or plural)/ they want

Möchtest du Wein? *merkh-test doo vine*	Do you want some wine?
Sie möchte ein neues Auto haben. *zee merkh-te ine noy-es ow-to hah-ben*	She wants a new car.
Wir möchten in Urlaub fahren. *veer merkh-ten in oor-lowp fah-ren*	We want to go on vacation.

Ich möchte Bonbons haben.
ikh merkh-te bom-bongs hah-ben
I want some candy.

Conversational tip In German, you don't need to say *some* in sentences like *we want some popsicles*— **wir möchten Eis am Stiel haben**. A handy term for *some* is **ein paar**, generally used only when you want to imply *some* but not *all*, as in **ich habe nur ein paar Bonbons gegessen** (*I've eaten only some of the candy*).

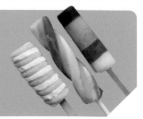

3 🔊 POLITE REQUESTS

4 minutes

It is polite to use the expression **ich hätte gern** (*I would like*) to explain what you would like. Practice the sample sentences, then test yourself, using the cover flap.

I'd like a beer.

Ich hätte gern ein Bier.
ikh het-te gairn ine beer

I'd like a table for tonight.

Ich hätte gern einen Tisch für heute Abend.
ikh het-te gairn ie-nen tish fewr hoy-te ah-bent

I'd like the menu.

Ich hätte gern die Speisekarte.
ikh het-te gairn dee shpie-ze-kar-te

---

4 🔊 PUT INTO PRACTICE

4 minutes

Complete this dialogue, then test yourself, using the cover flap.

Guten Abend. Haben Sie reserviert?
goo-ten ah-bent. hah-ben zee re-zair-veert

Good evening. Do you have a reservation?

Say: No, but I would like a table for three.

Nein, aber ich hätte gern einen Tisch für drei Personen.
nine, ah-ber ikh het-te gairn ie-nen tish fewr drie per-zoe-nen

Welchen Tisch möchten Sie?
vel-khen tish merkh-ten zee

Which table would you like?

Say: Near the window, please.

Am Fenster, bitte.
um fens-ter, bit-te

Wiederholung
REVIEW AND REPEAT

Antworten *Answers*
(Cover with flap)

At the table

❶ **die Nüsse**
dee news-se

❷ **der Zucker**
dair tsook-ker

❸ **die Meeresfrüchte**
dee mair-es-frewkh-te

❹ **das Fleisch**
duss fliesh

❺ **das Glas**
duss glahss

1 AT THE TABLE

Name these items in German.

❶ nuts

sugar ❷

❸ seafood

meat ❹

glass ❺

This is my…

❶ **Das ist mein Ehemann.**
duss ist mine ay-emunn

❷ **Hier ist meine Tochter.**
heer ist mye-ne tokh-ter

❸ **Meine Kinder sind müde.**
mye-ne kin-der zint mew-de

2 THIS IS MY…

4 minutes

Say these sentences in German.
Use **mein** or **meine**.

❶ This is my husband.
❷ Here is my daughter.
❸ My children are tired.

I'd like…

❶ **Ich hätte gern einen Milchkaffee.**
ikh het-te gairn ie-nen milkh-kuf-fay

❷ **Ich hätte gern Kuchen.**
ikh het-te gairn koo-khen

❸ **Ich hätte gern einen Tee mit Milch.**
ikh het-te gairn ie-nen tay mit milkh

3 I'D LIKE…

3 minutes

Say you'd like these items in German.

❶ coffee with hot milk   cake ❷   ❸ tea with milk

4 minutes

6 pasta

7 cheese

knife 8

9 napkin

10 beer

At the table

❻ **die Nudeln**
dee noo-deln

❼ **der Käse**
dair kay-ze

❽ **das Messer**
duss mess-ser

❾ **die Serviette**
dee zair-vee-ett-te

❿ **das Bier**
duss beer

4 RESTAURANT

4 minutes

You arrive at a restaurant. Join in the conversation, replying in German, following the numbered English prompts.

Guten Tag.
❶ Hello. I would like a table for six.

Haben Sie reserviert?
❷ Yes, in the name of Tröger.

Folgen Sie mir, bitte.
❸ I'd like the menu, please.

Möchten Sie die Weinkarte?
❹ No. Fizzy water, please.

Bitte schön.
❺ I don't have a glass.

Restaurant

❶ **Guten Tag. Ich hätte gern einen Tisch für sechs Personen.**
goo-ten tahk. ikh het te gairn ie-nen tish fewr zeks pair-zoe-nen

❷ **Ja, auf den Namen Tröger.**
yah, owf dayn nah-men trer-ger

❸ **Ich hätte gern die Speisekarte, bitte.**
ikh het-te gairn dee shpie-ze-kar-te, bit-te

❹ **Nein. Wasser mit Kohlensäure, bitte.**
nine. vuss-ser mit koe-len-zoy-re, bit-te

❺ **Ich habe kein Glas.**
ikh hah-be kine glahss

1 WARM UP
1 minute

Say **"He is"** and **"They are"** (pp14–15).

Say **"He is not"** and **"They are not"** (pp14–15).

What is German for **"the children"** (pp10–11)?

Die Tage und die Monate
DAYS AND MONTHS

In German, the days of the week and months of the year are all masculine. **Die Woche** (*week*) is feminine. You use **im** with months: **im April** (*in April*), and **am** with days: **am Montag** (*on Monday*). You also use **am** with **Wochenende** (*weekend*).

2 ◀)) WORDS TO REMEMBER: DAYS
5 minutes

Familiarize yourself with these words, then test yourself, using the cover flap.

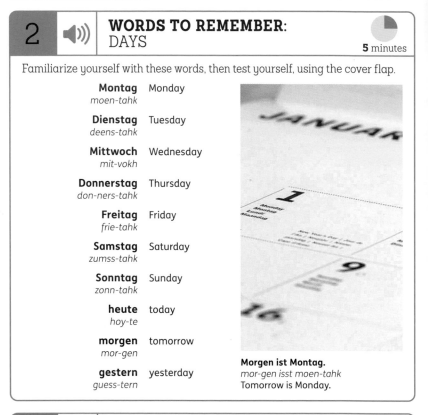

Montag *moen-tahk*	Monday
Dienstag *deens-tahk*	Tuesday
Mittwoch *mit-vokh*	Wednesday
Donnerstag *don-ners-tahk*	Thursday
Freitag *frie-tahk*	Friday
Samstag *zumss-tahk*	Saturday
Sonntag *zonn-tahk*	Sunday
heute *hoy-te*	today
morgen *mor-gen*	tomorrow
gestern *guess-tern*	yesterday

Morgen ist Montag.
mor-gen isst moen-tahk
Tomorrow is Monday.

3 ◀)) USEFUL PHRASES: DAYS
2 minutes

Learn these phrases, then test yourself, using the cover flap.

Die Besprechung ist am Dienstag.
dee be-shpre-khoong isst am deens-tahk

The meeting is on Tuesday.

Ich arbeite sonntags.
ikh ar-bie-te zonn-tahks

I work on Sundays.

4 🔊 WORDS TO REMEMBER: MONTHS

5 minutes

Familiarize yourself with these words, then test yourself, using the cover flap.

Unser Hochzeitstag ist im Juli.
oon-zair hokh-ziets-tahk isst im yoo-lee
Our wedding anniversary is in July.

Weihnachten ist im Dezember.
vie-nahkh-ten isst im day-tsem-bair
Christmas is in December.

January	**Januar**	*yunn-oo-ahr*
February	**Februar**	*fay-broo-ahr*
March	**März**	*mairts*
April	**April**	*ah-prill*
May	**Mai**	*mie*
June	**Juni**	*yoo-nee*
July	**Juli**	*yoo-lee*
August	**August**	*ow-goosst*
September	**September**	*zep-tem-bair*
October	**Oktober**	*ok-toe-bair*
November	**November**	*noe-vem-bair*
December	**Dezember**	*day-tsem-bair*
month	**der Monat**	*dair moenut*
day	**der Tag**	*dair tahk*

5 🔊 USEFUL PHRASES: MONTHS

2 minutes

Learn these phrases, then test yourself, using the cover flap.

My children are on vacation in August.
Meine Kinder haben im August Ferien.
mye-ne kin-der hah-ben im ow-goosst fay-ree-en

My birthday is in June.
Mein Geburtstag ist im Juni.
mine ge-boorts-tahk isst im yoo-nee

Die Zeit und die Zahlen
TIME AND NUMBERS

Germans use the 12-hour clock in everyday conversation and the 24-hour clock in official contexts, such as timetables. Note that in German, half past five is expressed as **halb sechs** (literally *half six*).

---

1 | **WARM UP** | **1** minute

Count in German from 1 to 10 (pp10–11).

Say "**I have a reservation**" (pp20–21).

Say "**The meeting is on Wednesday**" (pp28–29).

---

2 ◀))) | **WORDS TO REMEMBER:** TIME | **4** minutes

Familiarize yourself with these words, then test yourself, using the cover flap.

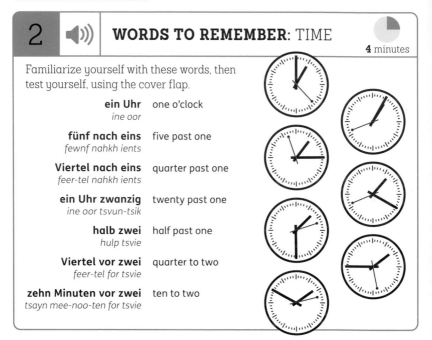

ein Uhr *ine oor*	one o'clock
fünf nach eins *fewnf nahkh ients*	five past one
Viertel nach eins *feer-tel nahkh ients*	quarter past one
ein Uhr zwanzig *ine oor tsvun-tsik*	twenty past one
halb zwei *hulp tsvie*	half past one
Viertel vor zwei *feer-tel for tsvie*	quarter to two
zehn Minuten vor zwei *tsayn mee-noo-ten for tsvie*	ten to two

---

3 ◀))) | **USEFUL PHRASES** | **2** minutes

Learn these phrases, then test yourself, using the cover flap.

Wie spät ist es? *vee shpayt isst es*	What time is it?
Wann möchten Sie frühstücken? *vunn merkh-ten zee frew-shtewk-ken*	What time do you want breakfast?
Die Besprechung ist um 12 Uhr. *dee be-shpre-khoong isst oom tsverlf oor*	The meeting is at noon.

4 🔊 WORDS TO REMEMBER: HIGHER NUMBERS

6 minutes

In German, apart from numbers like 20, 30, 40, 50, etc., units are said before tens, so 21 is **einundzwanzig** (literally *one-and-twenty*), 32 is **zweiunddreißig** (*two-and-thirty*), and so on.

Familiarize yourself with these words, then test yourself, using the cover flap.

Ich habe viele Bücher.
ikh hah-be fee-le bew-kher
I have many books.

Ich habe kontaktlos fünfundachtzig Euro bezahlt.
ikh hah-be konn-tuckt-lows fewnf-oont-akht-tsik oy-roe be-tsahlt
I've paid eighty-five euros by contactless payment.

eleven	**elf**
	elf
twelve	**zwölf**
	tsverlf
thirteen	**dreizehn**
	drie-tsayn
fourteen	**vierzehn**
	feer-tsayn
fifteen	**fünfzehn**
	fewnf-tsayn
sixteen	**sechzehn**
	zekh-tsayn
seventeen	**siebzehn**
	zeep-tsayn
eighteen	**achtzehn**
	akh-tsayn
nineteen	**neunzehn**
	noyn-tsayn
twenty	**zwanzig**
	tsvun-tsik
thirty	**dreißig**
	drie-ssik
forty	**vierzig**
	feer-tsik
fifty	**fünfzig**
	fewnf-tsik
sixty	**sechzig**
	zekh-tsik
seventy	**siebzig**
	zeep-tsik
eighty	**achtzig**
	akh-tsik
ninety	**neunzig**
	noyn-tsik
hundred	**hundert**
	hoon-dairt
three hundred	**dreihundert**
	drie-hoon-dairt
thousand	**tausend**
	tow-zent
ten thousand	**zehntausend**
	tsayn-tow-zent
two hundred thousand	**zweihunderttausend**
	tsvie-hoon-dairt-tow-zent
one million	**eine Million**
	ie-ne mill-ee-oen

5 SAY IT

2 minutes

twenty-five

sixty-eight

eighty-four

ninety-one

five to ten

half past eleven

What time is lunch?

1 WARM UP
1 minute

Say the days of the week in German (pp28–29).

Say "**It's three o'clock**" (pp30–31).

What's the German for "**today**," "**tomorrow**," and "**yesterday**" (pp28–29)?

Die Termine
APPOINTMENTS

Business in Germany is generally conducted more formally than in Britain or the United States. Business associates generally call each other by their title and last name and use the formal form of *you*, **Sie**. Appointments are usually set using the 24-hour clock—for example, **fünfzehn Uhr** (*3pm*).

2 🔊 USEFUL PHRASES
5 minutes

Learn these phrases, then test yourself, using the cover flap.

Können wir uns morgen treffen? *kernen veer oons mor-gen treff-fen*	Can we meet tomorrow?
Mit wem? *mit vaym*	With whom?
Wann haben Sie Zeit? *vunn hah-ben zee ziet*	When do you have time?
Es tut mir leid, ich bin beschäftigt. *es toot meer liet, ikh bin be-sheff-tikht*	I'm sorry, I am busy.
Wie wär's mit Donnerstag? *vee vairs mit don-ners-tahk*	How about Thursday?
Das passt mir gut. *duss pusst meer goot*	That's good for me.

Willkommen.
vil-komm-men
Welcome.

der Händedruck
dair hen-de-drook
handshake

3 🔊 IN CONVERSATION

Guten Tag. Ich habe einen Termin.
goo-ten tahk. ikh hah-be ie-nen terr-meen

Hello. I have an appointment.

Mit wem, bitte?
mit vaym, bit-te

With whom, please?

Mit Dieter Frenger.
mit dee-ter fren-ger

With Dieter Frenger.

4 🔊 PUT INTO PRACTICE

5 minutes

Complete this dialogue, then test yourself, using the cover flap.

Können wir uns am Donnertsag treffen?
kernen veer oons am don-ners-tahk treff-fen

Shall we meet on Thursday?

Es tut mir leid, da bin ich beschäftigt.
es toot meer liet, dah bin ikh be-sheff-tikht

Say: Sorry, I'm busy.

Wann haben Sie Zeit?
vunn hah-ben zee ziet

When do you have time?

Dienstagnachmittag.
deens-tahk-nahkh-mit-tahk

Say: Tuesday afternoon.

Das passt mir gut.
duss pusst meer goot

That's good for me.

Um wie viel Uhr?
oom vee-feel oor

Ask: At what time?

Um sechzehn Uhr, wenn es Ihnen passt.
oom zekh-tsayn oor, venn ess ee-nen pusst

At four o'clock, if that's good for you.

Das passt mir gut.
duss pusst meer goot

Say: It's good for me.

4 minutes

Sehr gut. Um wie viel Uhr?
zair goot. oom vee-feel-oor

Very good. What time?

Um fünfzehn Uhr, aber ich bin etwas verspätet.
oom fewnf-tsayn oor, ah-ber ikh bin et-vuss fer-shpay-tet

At three o'clock, but I'm a little late.

Kein Problem. Setzen Sie sich, bitte.
kine pro-blaym. zet-sen zee zikh, bit-te

Don't worry. Sit down, please.

1 WARM UP
1 minute

Say "**I'm sorry**" (pp32–33).

What is the German for "**I'd like an appointment**" (pp32–33)?

How do you say "**With whom?**" in German (pp32–33)?

Am Telefon
ON THE TELEPHONE

The emergency number for the **Rettungsdienst** (*ambulance*) and **Feuerwehr** (*fire department*) is 112, while for the **Polizei** (*police*), it is 110. You can call free of charge from any cell phone or landline in the country. To make direct international calls from Germany, dial the access code 00, then the country code, area code (omit the initial 0), and the phone number. The country code for Germany is 49.

2 🔊 MATCH AND REPEAT

Match the numbered items to the list, then test yourself, using the cover flap.

❶ **die Ohrhörer**
dee ohr-her-er

❷ **die Kopfhörer**
dee kopf-her-er

❸ **das Telefon**
duss tay-lay-foen

❹ **das Smartphone**
duss smart-fon

❺ **das Ladegerät**
duss lah-de-ge-rayt

❻ **die SIM-Karte**
dee seem-kar-te

❼ **der Anrufbeantworter**
dair un-roof-bay-unt-vor-ter

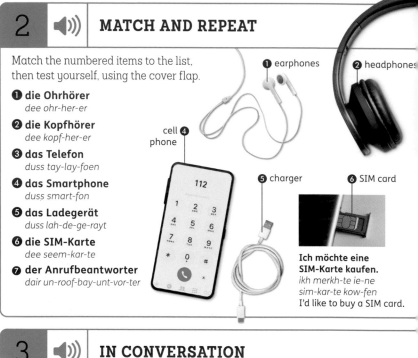

❶ earphones ❷ headphones

cell ❹ phone

❺ charger ❻ SIM card

Ich möchte eine SIM-Karte kaufen.
ikh merkh-te ie-ne sim-kar-te kow-fen
I'd like to buy a SIM card.

3 🔊 IN CONVERSATION

Hallo. Elke Rubin am Apparat.
hul-lo. el-ke roo-been umm up-pa-raht

Hello. Elke Rubin speaking.

Guten Tag. Ich möchte bitte Peter Harnisch sprechen.
goo-ten tahk. ikh merkh-te bit-te peeter har-neesh shpre-khen

Hello. I'd like to speak to Peter Harnisch.

Mit wem spreche ich?
mit vaym shpre-khe ikh

May I know who's calling?

5 SAY IT
2 minutes

I'd like to speak to Mr. Braun.

Can I leave a message for Gaby?

Can she call me back on Wednesday, please?

4 minutes

❸ telephone

answering machine ❼

4 🔊 USEFUL PHRASES
4 minutes

Learn these phrases, then test yourself, using the cover flap.

I'd like the number for Monika.

Ich möchte Monikas Nummer bitte.
ikh merkh-te monikas num-mer bit-te

I'd like to speak to Rita Wolbert.

Ich möchte mit Rita Wolbert sprechen.
ikh merkh-te mit ree-ta vol-bert shpre-khen

Can I leave a message?

Kann ich eine Nachricht hinterlassen?
kunn ikh ie-ne nahkh-rikht hin-ter luss-sen

Sorry, I have the wrong number.

Es tut mir leid, ich habe mich verwählt.
ess toot meer liet, ikh hah-be mikh fer-vaylt

4 minutes

Mit Norbert Lorenz von der Druckerei Knickmann.
mit nor-bert loe-rents fon dair drook-er-ie knick-munn

Norbert Lorenz of Knickmann Printers.

Es tut mir leid. Es ist besetzt.
ess toot meer liet. ess isst be-zetst

I'm sorry. The line is busy.

Würden Sie ihn bitten, mich anzurufen?
vewr-den see een bit-ten, mikh un-tsoo-roo-fen

Can he call me back, please?

Wiederholung
REVIEW AND REPEAT

Antworten *Answers*
(Cover with flap)

Telephones

❶ **das Smartphone**
das smart-fon

❷ **das Telefon**
duss tay-lay-foen

❸ **der Anrufbeantworter**
dair un-roof-bay-unt-vor-ter

❹ **die Kopfhörer**
dee kopf-her-er

❺ **die SIM-Karte**
dee sim-kar-te

When?

❶ I have an appointment on Monday, May 20.

❷ My birthday is in September.

❸ I work on Fridays.

❹ They don't work in August.

Time

❶ **ein Uhr**
ine oor

❷ **fünf nach eins**
fewnf nahkh ients

❸ **Viertel nach eins**
feer-tel nahkh ients

❹ **ein Uhr zwanzig**
ine oor tsvun-tsik

❺ **halb zwei**
hulp tsvie

❻ **zehn Minuten vor zwei**
tsayn mee-noo-ten for tsvie

---

1 TELEPHONES

Name these items in German.

❶ cell phone

❷ telephone

❸ answering machine

headphones ❹

---

2 WHEN?

2 minutes

What do these sentences mean?

❶ Ich habe einen Termin am Montag, den zwanzigsten Mai.

❷ Mein Geburtstag ist im September.

❸ Ich arbeite freitags.

❹ Sie arbeiten nicht im August.

---

3 TIME

3 minutes

Say these times in German.

❶ ❷ ❸

❹ ❺ ❻

3 minutes

5 SIM card

4 MATH

4 minutes

Say the answers to these problems in German.

1 10 + 6 = ?
2 14 + 25 = ?
3 66 − 13 = ?
4 40 + 34 = ?
5 90 + 9 = ?
6 46 − 5 = ?

Math
1 sechzehn
zekh-tsayn
2 neununddreißig
noyn-oont-drie-ssik
3 dreiundfünfzig
drie-oont-fewnf-tsik
4 vierundsiebzig
feer-oont-zeep-tsik
5 neunundneunzig
noyn-oont-noyn-tsik
6 einundvierzig
ine-oont-feer-tsik

5 I WANT...

3 minutes

Fill in the blanks with the correct form of **mögen** (*to want*).

1 ＿＿ Sie einen Kaffee?
2 Sie (*singular*) ＿＿ in Urlaub fahren.
3 Wir ＿＿ einen Tisch für drei Personen.
4 Du ＿＿ ein Bier.
5 Ich ＿＿ Bonbons.
6 Er ＿＿ Obst.

I want...
1 möchten
merkh-ten
2 möchte
merkh-te
3 möchten
merkh-ten
4 möchtest
merkh-test
5 möchte
merkh-te
6 möchte
merkh-te

1 WARM UP
1 minute

Count to 100 in tens
(pp10–11, pp30–31).

Ask "**At what time?**"
(pp30–31).

Say "**It's half-past one**"
(pp30–31).

Am Fahrkartenschalter
AT THE TICKET OFFICE

On German trains, children under the age of 6 travel free, while children ages 6–14 years go free if traveling with a fare-paying adult and pay half fare if not. There are also other concessions—for example, for senior citizens, groups, and weekend travel.

2 WORDS TO REMEMBER
3 minutes

Familiarize yourself with these words, then test yourself, using the cover flap.

der Bahnhof station
dair bahn-hoef

der Bahnsteig platform
dair bahn-shtiek

das Schild sign
duss shilt

der Fahrplan timetable
dair fahr-plahn

die Fahrkarte ticket
dee fahr-kar-te

eine einfache single ticket
Fahrkarte
ie-ne ine-fa-khe fahr-kar-te

eine Rückfahrkarte return ticket
ie-ne rewck-fahr-kar-te

erster/zweiter Klasse first/second
airs-ter/tsvie-ter kluss-se class

der Zug **der Fahrgast**
dair tsook *dair fahr-gust*
train passenger

Der Bahnhof ist überfüllt.
dair bahn-hoef isst ew-ber-fewllt
The station is crowded.

3  IN CONVERSATION

Zwei Fahrkarten nach Berlin, bitte.
tsvie fahr-kar-ten nahhk bair-leen, bit-te

Two tickets for Berlin, please.

Rückfahrkarten?
rewck-fahr-kar-ten

Return?

Ja. Muss ich die Sitze reservieren?
yah. mooss ikh dee zit-se re-zair-vee-ren

Yes. Do I need to reserve seats?

4 USEFUL PHRASES

5 minutes

Learn these phrases, then test yourself, using the cover flap.

Der Zug hat zehn Minuten Verspätung.
dair tsook hut tsayn mee-noo-ten fer-shpay-toong
The train is ten minutes late.

How much is a ticket to Cologne?	**Was kostet eine Fahrkarte nach Köln?** *vuss kos-tet ie-ne fahr-kar-te nahkh kerln*
Can I pay by credit card?	**Kann ich mit Kreditkarte zahlen?** *kunn ikh mit kray-deet-kar-te tsah-len*
Do I have to change trains?	**Muss ich umsteigen?** *mooss ikh oomm-shtie-gen*
Which platform does the train leave from?	**Von welchem Bahnsteig fährt der Zug ab?** *fon vel-khem bahn-shtiek fairt dair tsook up*
Are there concessions?	**Gibt es Ermäßigungen?** *geept ess er-mays-si-goong-en*
What time does the train for Dresden leave?	**Wann fährt der Zug nach Dresden ab?** *vunn fairt dair tsook nahkh dres-den up*

Cultural tip Most large railway stations have ticket offices and **Fahrkartenautomaten** (*automatic ticket machines*) that accept credit and debit cards, cash, and payments via mobile and digital wallets.

5 SAY IT

2 minutes

Which platform does the train for Leipzig leave from?

Three return tickets to Hamburg, please.

---

4 minutes

Nein. Dreihundert Euro, bitte. *nine. drei-hoon-dairt oy-roe, bit-te*	**Nehmen Sie Kreditkarten?** *nay-men zee kray-deet-kar-ten*	**Ja. Der Zug fährt auf Bahnsteig zehn ab.** *yah. dair tsook fairt owf bahn-shtiek tsayn up*
No. Three hundred euros, please.	Do you accept credit cards?	Yes. The train leaves from platform ten.

1 WARM UP
1 minute

How do you say "**train**" in German? (pp38–39).

What does "**Von welchem Bahnsteig fährt der Zug ab?**" mean (pp38–39)?

Ask "**When are you free?**" (pp32–33).

Gehen und nehmen
TO GO AND TO TAKE

Gehen (*to go*) and **nehmen** (*to take*) are essential verbs in German and often form a part of many useful expressions. Note that these verbs are not always used in the same way as in English and that you need to learn phrases individually.

2 ◀))) GEHEN: TO GO
6 minutes

Practice **gehen** (*to go*) and the sample sentences, then test yourself, using the cover flap.

ich gehe *ikh gay-e*	I go
du gehst *doo gayst*	you go (informal singular)
er/sie/es geht *air/zee/ess gayt*	he/she/it goes
wir gehen *veer gay-en*	we go
ihr geht *eer gayt*	you go (informal plural)
Sie gehen/sie gehen *zee gay-en*	you go (formal singular or plural)/ they go

Wo gehen Sie hin? *voe gay-en zee hin*	Where are you going?
Ich gehe nach Bonn. *ikh gay-e nahkh bonn*	I'm going to Bonn.
Wie geht es Ihnen? *vee gayt ess ee-nen*	How are you?

Ich gehe zum Brandenburger Tor.
ikh gay-e tsoom brun-den-boor-ger tor
I'm going to the Brandenburg Gate.

Conversational tip German has no equivalent of the English present continuous tense (which uses the *-ing* ending)—it uses the same verb form for both the present and the present continuous. For example, **ich gehe nach Hamburg** means both *I am going to Hamburg* and *I go to Hamburg*. The same is true of other verbs—for example, **wir nehmen den Zug** means both *we are taking the train* and *we take the train*.

3 NEHMEN: TO TAKE

6 minutes

Practice **nehmen** (*to take*) and the sample sentences, then test yourself, using the cover flap.

Ich nehme die Straßenbahn jeden Tag.
ikh nay-me dee shtrahs-sen-bahn yay-den tahk
I take the tram every day.

I take	**ich nehme** *ikh nay-me*
you take (informal singular)	**du nimmst** *doo nimmst*
he/she/it takes	**er/sie/es nimmt** *air/zee/ess nimmt*
we take	**wir nehmen** *veer nay-men*
you take (informal plural)	**ihr nehmt** *eer naymt*
you take (formal singular or plural)/ they take	**Sie nehmen/ sie nehmen** *zee nay-men*

I don't want to take a taxi.	**Ich möchte kein Taxi nehmen.** *ikh merkh-te kine tuck-see nay-men*
Take the first on the left.	**Nehmen Sie die erste Straße links.** *nay-men zee dee airs-te shtrahs-se links*
He'll have the roast venison.	**Er nimmt den Rehbraten.** *air nimmt dayn ray-brah-ten*

4 PUT INTO PRACTICE

2 minutes

Complete this dialogue, then test yourself, using the cover flap.

Wo gehen Sie hin?
vöe gay-en zee hin
Where are you going?

Say: I'm going to the station.

Ich gehe zum Bahnhof.
ikh gay-e tsoom bahn-hoef

Möchten Sie die U-Bahn nehmen?
merkh-ten zee dee oo-bahn nay-men
Do you want to take the metro?

Say: No, we want to go by bus.

Nein, wir wollen den Bus nehmen.
nine, veer vol-len dayn booss nay-men

Taxi, Bus und Bahn
TAXI, BUS, AND RAIL

In cities, it's relatively easy to find a taxi, but in smaller places, you may need to book in advance. Cities and larger towns may have **U-Bahn** (*underground*), **S-Bahn** (*suburban train*), or **Straßenbahn** (*tram*) networks. With buses and the underground, you will usually need to buy and validate your ticket before starting your journey.

2 🔊 WORDS TO REMEMBER
4 minutes

Familiarize yourself with these words, then test yourself, using the cover flap.

der Bus *dair booss*	bus
der Reisebus *dair rye-se-booss*	motor coach
der Busbahnhof *dair booss-bahn-hoef*	bus station
die Bushaltestelle *dee booss-hal-te-shtel-le*	bus stop
der Fahrpreis *dair fahr-priess*	fare
das Taxi *duss tuck-see*	taxi
der Taxistand *dair tuck-see-shtunt*	taxi stand
die U-Bahnstation *dee oo-bahn-shta-tsee-oen*	underground station

Hält der Bus Nummer 120 hier?
helt dair booss noom-mer hoon-dairt-tsvun-tsik heer
Does the number 120 bus stop here?

3 🔊 IN CONVERSATION: TAXI
2 minutes

Zum Flughafen, bitte.
tsoom flook-hah-fen, bit-te

The airport, please.

Jawohl, kein Problem.
yah-voel. kine pro-blaym

Yes, no problem.

Können Sie mich bitte hier absetzen?
ker-nen zee mikh bit-te heer up-zet-sen

Can you drop me here, please?

4 USEFUL PHRASES

4 minutes

Learn these phrases, then test yourself, using the cover flap.

I'd like a taxi to the cathedral.

Ich hätte gern ein Taxi zum Dom.
ikh het-te gairn ine tuck-see tsoom doem

Please wait for me.

Bitte warten Sie auf mich.
bit-te vahr-ten zee owf mikh

How long is the journey?

Wie lange dauert die Fahrt?
vee lan-ge dow-airt dee fahrt

How do you get to the museum?

Wie komme ich zum Museum?
vee kom-me ikh tsoom moo-zay-oom

When is the next bus?

Wann fährt der nächste Bus?
vunn fairt dair nekh-ste booss

Cultural tip All taxis in Germany have meters. You can hail a taxi in the street when the lights are switched on, board one at a taxi stand, or call for a taxi from your hotel or private address. Round up the fare to tip the driver.

6 SAY IT

2 minutes

Do you go near the railway station?

The bus station, please.

When's the next coach to Kiel?

5 IN CONVERSATION: BUS

2 minutes

Fahren Sie zum Museum?
fah-ren zee tsoom moo-say-oom

Do you go to the museum?

Ja. Das kostet einen Euro neunzig.
yah. duss kos-tet ie-nen oy-roe noyn-tsik

Yes. That's one euro, ninety.

Können Sie mir sagen, wann wir da sind?
ker-nen zee meer zah-gen, vunn veer dah zind

Can you tell me when we arrive?

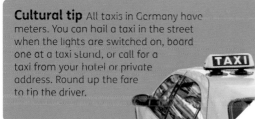

1 WARM UP
1 minute

Say "**I have...**" (pp14–15).

Say "**my father**," "**my sister**," and "**my parents**" (pp16–17).

Say "**I'm going to Berlin**" (pp40–41).

Auf der Straße
ON THE ROAD

German **Autobahnen** (*highways*) are fast, but on many stretches, there is now a speed limit of 80 mph (130 kmph). **Autobahnen** are marked with the letter "A" on a blue sign, **Europastraßen** (*international expressways*) with "E" on a green sign, and **Bundesstraßen** (*main roads*) with "B" on a yellow sign.

2 ◀))) MATCH AND REPEAT

Match the numbered items to the list, then test yourself, using the cover flap.

❶ **der Kofferraum**
dair kof-fer-rowm

❷ **die Windschutzscheibe**
dee vint-shoots-shie-be

❸ **der Ladestecker**
dair lah-de-shtek-ker

❹ **die Ladesäule**
dee lah-de-soy-le

❺ **die Tür**
dee tew

❻ **der Reifen**
dair rie-fen

❼ **die Scheinwerfer**
dee shien-vair-fer

❽ **das Ladekabel**
duss lah-de-kah-bell

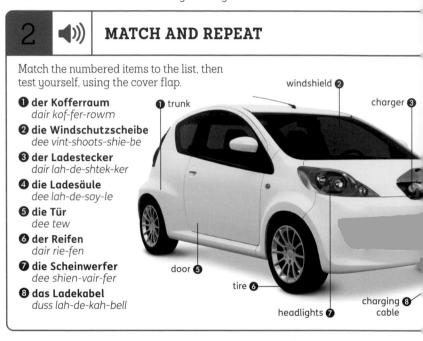

❶ trunk
windshield ❷
charger ❸
door ❺
tire ❻
headlights ❼
charging ❽ cable

Cultural tip At self-service stations, the pump shows the fuel being added and the money owed. At unmanned gas stations, you may need to authorize a card payment before the pump starts working. Electric cars can be charged at public charging stations, paid for by card or app, and could take up to half a day to fully charge.

3 ◀))) ROAD SIGNS

die Einbahnstraße
dee ine-bahn-shtrah-se
One-way

der Kreisverkehr
dair kries-fer-kair
Roundabout

Vorfahrt gewähren
for-fahrt ge-wair-en
Yield

4 🔊 USEFUL PHRASES

4 minutes

Learn these phrases, then test yourself, using the cover flap.

My turn signal isn't working. **Mein Blinker funktioniert nicht.**
mine blin-ker foonk-tsee-oe-neert nikht

Fill it up, please. **Volltanken, bitte.**
foll-tan-ken, bit-te

4 minutes

charging point/station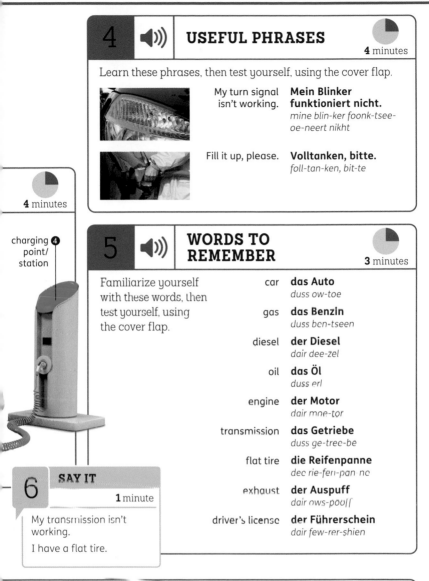

5 🔊 WORDS TO REMEMBER

3 minutes

Familiarize yourself with these words, then test yourself, using the cover flap.

car	**das Auto**	*duss ow-toe*
gas	**das Benzin**	*duss ben-tseen*
diesel	**der Diesel**	*dair dee-zel*
oil	**das Öl**	*duss erl*
engine	**der Motor**	*dair moe-tor*
transmission	**das Getriebe**	*duss ge-tree-be*
flat tire	**die Reifenpanne**	*dee rie-fen-pan-ne*
exhaust	**der Auspuff**	*dair ows-poolf*
driver's license	**der Führerschein**	*dair few-rer-shien*

6 SAY IT

1 minute

My transmission isn't working.

I have a flat tire.

2 minutes

die Vorfahrtstraße
dee for-fahrt-shtrah-se
Priority road

Einfahrt verboten
ine-fahrt fer-boe-ten
No entry

Parken verboten
par-ken fer-boe-ten
No parking

Wiederholung
REVIEW AND REPEAT

Transport

❶ **das Auto**
duss ow-toe

❷ **der Bus**
dair booss

❸ **das Taxi**
duss tuk-see

❹ **der Zug**
dair tsook

❺ **das Fahrrad**
duss fahr-raht

Go and take

❶ **gehe**
gay-e

❷ **geht**
gayt

❸ **nehme**
nay-me

❹ **gehen**
gay-en

❺ **nehmen**
nay-men

❻ **gehen**
gay-en

1 TRANSPORT

Name these forms of transport in German.

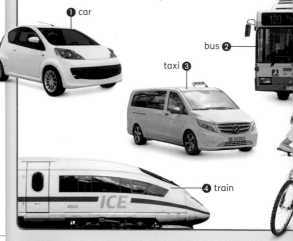

❶ car

bus ❷

taxi ❸

❹ train

2 GO AND TAKE

4 minutes

Fill in the blanks with the correct form of **gehen** (*to go*) or **nehmen** (*to take*).

❶ Ich _____ zum Bahnhof. (gehen)

❷ Wie _____ es dir? (gehen)

❸ Ich _____ den Rehbraten. (nehmen)

❹ Wir _____ nach Berlin. (gehen)

❺ _____ Sie die erste Straße links (nehmen)

❻ Wo _____ Sie hin? (gehen)

3 minutes

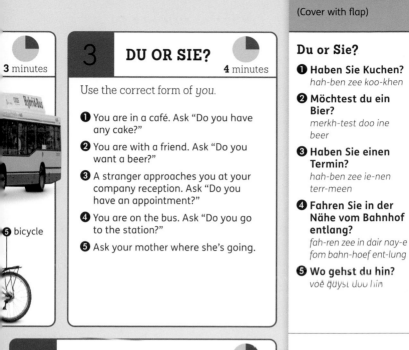

5 bicycle

3 DU OR SIE?

4 minutes

Use the correct form of *you*.

❶ You are in a café. Ask "Do you have any cake?"

❷ You are with a friend. Ask "Do you want a beer?"

❸ A stranger approaches you at your company reception. Ask "Do you have an appointment?"

❹ You are on the bus. Ask "Do you go to the station?"

❺ Ask your mother where she's going.

4 TICKETS

4 minutes

You are buying tickets at a railway station. Join in the conversation, replying in German, following the numbered English prompts.

Kann ich Ihnen helfen?
❶ I'd like two tickets to Berlin.

Rückfahrkarte oder einfach?
❷ Return, please.

Bitte schön. Dreihundert Euro, bitte.
❸ What time does the train leave?

Um dreizehn Uhr zehn.
❹ What platform does the train leave from?

Bahnsteig sieben.
❺ Thank you very much. Goodbye.

Du or Sie?

❶ **Haben Sie Kuchen?**
hah-ben zee koo-khen

❷ **Möchtest du ein Bier?**
merkh-test doo ine beer

❸ **Haben Sie einen Termin?**
hah-ben zee ie-nen terr-meen

❹ **Fahren Sie in der Nähe vom Bahnhof entlang?**
fah-ren zee in dair nay-e fom bahn-hoef ent-lung

❺ **Wo gehst du hin?**
voe gayst doo hin

Tickets

❶ **Ich hätte gern zwei Fahrkarten nach Berlin.**
ikh het-te gairn tsvie fahr-kar-ten nahkh bair-leen

❷ **Rückfahrkarte, bitte.**
rewck-fahr-kar-te, bit-te

❸ **Wann fährt der Zug ab?**
vunn fairt dair tsook up

❹ **Von welchem Bahnsteig fährt der Zug ab?**
fon vel-khem bahn-shtiek fairt dair tsook up

❺ **Vielen Dank. Auf Wiedersehen.**
fee-len dunk. owf vee-der-zay-en

In der Stadt
ABOUT TOWN

1 **WARM UP** 🕐
1 minute

Ask "**How do you get to the museum?**" (pp42–43).

Say "**I want to take the bus**" and "**I don't want to take a taxi**" (pp40–41).

Most German towns still have a market day and a thriving community of small shops. Even small villages tend to have a mayor and a town hall. Parking is usually regulated. Look out for blue parking zones where you can park your car for a limited time without charge.

---

2 🔊 **WORDS TO REMEMBER** 🕐 **4** minutes

Familiarize yourself with these words, then test yourself, using the cover flap.

die Tankstelle *dee tunk-shtel-le*	gas station
die Touristeninformation *dee too-ryss-ten-in-for-mah-tsee-oen*	tourist office
die Werkstatt *dee vairk-shtutt*	car repairs
das Schwimmbad *duss shvim-bad*	swimming pool
die Bibliothek *dee beeb-lee-o-tayk*	library

---

3 🔊 **MATCH AND REPEAT** 🕐 **4** minutes

Match the numbered locations to the list, then test yourself, using the cover flap.

❶ **das Rathaus**
   duss raht-hows

❷ **das Museum**
   duss moo-zay-oom

❸ **die Brücke**
   dee brew-ke

❹ **die Kunstgalerie**
   dee koonst-gal-le-ree

❺ **das Stadtzentrum**
   duss shtutt-tsen-troom

❻ **die Kirche**
   dee keer-khe

❼ **der Platz**
   dair pluts

❽ **der Parkplatz**
   dair park-pluts

church ❻

❺ town center

❶ town hall

❷ museum

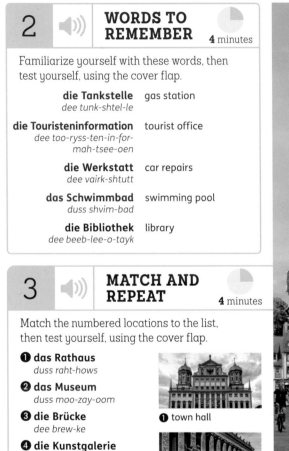

❸ bridge

❹ art gallery

4 USEFUL PHRASES

4 minutes

A useful expression for asking about public amenities is **es gibt** (*there is*). Notice that some words are often contracted in German—for example, **in dem** (*in the*) is contracted to **im**; **zu dem** (*to the*, masculine and neuter) becomes **zum**; and **zu der** (*to the*, feminine) contracts to **zur**.

Learn these phrases, then test yourself, using the cover flap.

Is there an art gallery in town?	**Gibt es eine Kunstgalerie in der Stadt?** *geept es ie-ne koonst-gal-le-ree in dair shtutt*
Is it far from here?	**Ist das weit von hier?** *isst duss viet fon heer*
There is a swimming pool near the bridge.	**Es gibt ein Schwimmbad bei der Brücke.** *es geept ien shvim-bad bie dair brew-ke*
There isn't a library.	**Es gibt keine Bibliothek.** *es geept kie-ne beeb-lee-o-tayk*

5 PUT INTO PRACTICE

2 minutes

Complete this dialogue, then test yourself, using the cover flap.

Kann ich Ihnen helfen?
kunn ikh ee-nen hel-fen

Can I help you?

Ask: Is there a library in town?

Gibt es in der Stadt eine Bibliothek?
geept es in dair shtutt ie-ne beeb-lee-o-tayk

Nein, aber es gibt ein Museum.
nine, ah-ber es geept ine moo-zay-oom

No, but there's a museum.

Ask: How do I get to the museum?

Wie komme ich zum Museum?
vee kom-me ikh tsoom moo-zay-oom

Es ist dort.
es isst dort

It's over there.

Say: Thank you very much.

Vielen Dank.
fee-len dunk

7 square

8 parking lot

1 WARM UP

1 minute

How do you say "**Near the station**" (pp42–43)?

Say "**Take the first on the left**" (pp40–41).

Ask "**Where are you going?**" (pp40–41).

Die Wegbeschreibung
FINDING YOUR WAY

In German, you use **gehen** (*to go*) when talking about going somewhere on foot, but **fahren** (*to drive*) when in a car. So, *go left* is **gehen Sie nach links** if you are on foot, but **fahren Sie nach links** if you are traveling in a car.

2 WORDS TO REMEMBER

Familiarize yourself with these words, then test yourself, using the cover flap.

die Ampel *dee um-pel*	traffic lights
die Hauptstraße *dee howpt-shtrah-se*	main road
die Straße *dee shtrah-se*	street/road
der Stadtplan *dair shtutt-plahn*	(city) map
die Online-Karten *dee on-line-kar-ten*	online maps
gegenüber *gay-gen-ew-ber*	across from

das Geschäft
duss ge-sheft
shop

Wir sind hier.
veer zint heer
We are here.

die Fußgängerzone
dee foos-geng-er-tsoe-ne
pedestrian zone

3 IN CONVERSATION

Gibt es ein Restaurant in der Stadt?
geept es ine res-to-rung in der shtutt

Is there a restaurant in town?

Ja, am Bahnhof.
yah, um bahn-hoef

Yes, near the station.

Wie komme ich zum Bahnhof?
vee kom-me ikh tsoom bahn-hoef

How do I get to the station?

5 SAY IT
2 minutes

Turn right at the end of the street.

It's across from the museum.

It's ten minutes by bus.

4 minutes

die Ecke
dee ek-ke
corner

der Brunnen
dair broon-nen
fountain

4 USEFUL PHRASES

4 minutes

Learn these phrases, then test yourself, using the cover flap.

go left/right	**gehen Sie nach links/rechts** *gay-en zee nahkh links/rekhts*
on the left side/ right side	**auf der linken Seite/ rechten Seite** *owf dair lin-ken zie-te/ rekh-ten zie-te*
first (street) on the left	**die erste (Straße) links** *dee airs-te (shtrah-se) links*
turn left at the main square	**gehen Sie am Hauptplatz nach links** *gay-en zee am howpt-pluts nahkh links*
(continue) straight	**geradeaus (weiter)** *ge-rah-de-ows (vieter)*
at the end of the street	**am Ende der Straße** *um en-de dair shtrah-se*
How do I get to the swimming pool?	**Wie komme ich zum Schwimmbad?** *vee kom-me ikh tsoom shvim-bad*

Ich habe mich verlaufen.
ikh hah-be mikh fer-low-fen
I'm lost.

4 minutes

Gehen Sie an der Ampel nach links.
gay-en zee un dair um-pel nahkh links

Go left at the traffic lights.

Ist es weit?
isst es viet

Is it far?

Nein, es ist fünf Minuten zu Fuß.
nine, es isst fewnf mee-noo-ten tsoo fooss

No, it's five minutes on foot.

Besichtigungen
SIGHTSEEING

1 WARM UP
1 minute

Say "**Is there a museum in town?**" (pp48–49).

How do you say "**At six o'clock**" (pp30–31)?

Ask "**What time is it?**" (pp30–31).

Most national museums and art galleries close one day a week and on public holidays. Larger museums tend to stay open all day and are open late once a week. Museums in smaller places may have more restricted opening hours and are often closed on Sundays. Shops are normally closed on Sundays, but some might remain open all weekend in tourist areas.

2 ◀)) WORDS TO REMEMBER
4 minutes

Familiarize yourself with these words, then test yourself, using the cover flap.

der Reiseführer *dair rye-ze-few-rer*	guide, guidebook, travel guide
die Eintrittskarte *dee ine-trits-kar-te*	entrance ticket
die Öffnungszeiten *dee erff-noongs-tsie-ten*	opening times
der Feiertag *dair fie-er-tahk*	public holiday
die Ermäßigung *dee er-mes-see-goong*	reduction/ discount

die Führung
dee few-roong
guided tour

Cultural tip Germany observes a number of religious holidays in addition to Christmas and Easter—for example, Whit Monday and Ascension Day. The May bank holiday is always celebrated on May 1, whatever day of the week it falls on. There are also additional regional holidays. The majority of public buildings and private offices close for public holidays.

3 ◀)) IN CONVERSATION

Sind Sie heute Nachmittag geöffnet?
zint zee hoy-te nahkh-mit-tahk ge-erff-net

Are you open this afternoon?

Ja, aber wir schließen um sechzehn Uhr.
yah, ah-ber veer shliee-sen oom zekh-tsayn oor

Yes, but we close at four o'clock.

Gibt es Zugang für Rollstuhlfahrer?
geept es tsoo-gung fewr roll-shtool-fah-rer

Do you have wheelchair access?

4 🔊 USEFUL PHRASES

3 minutes

Learn these phrases, then test yourself, using the cover flap.

What time do you open/close?	**Wann öffnen/ schließen Sie?** *vunn erf-nen/shlee-sen zee*
Where are the toilets?	**Wo sind die Toiletten?** *voe zind dee twah-let-ten*
Is there wheelchair access?	**Gibt es Zugang für Rollstuhlfahrer?** *geept es tsoo-gung fewr roll-shtool-fah-rer*

5 🔊 PUT INTO PRACTICE

1 minutes

Complete this dialogue, then test yourself, using the cover flap.

Das Museum ist geschlossen.
duss moo-zay-oom isst ge-shlos-sen

The museum is closed.

Ask: Are you open on Mondays?

Sind Sie am Montag geöffnet?
zint zee um moen-tahk ge-erff-net

Ja, aber wir schließen früh.
yah, ah-ber veer shlee-sen frew

Yes, but we close early.

Ask: At what time?

Um wie viel Uhr?
oom vee-feel oor

3 minutes

Ja, da drüben ist ein Fahrstuhl.
yah, dar drew-ben isst ine fahr-shtool

Yes, there's an elevator over there.

Danke, ich hätte gern vier Eintrittskarten.
dun-ke, ikh het-te gairn feer ine-trits-kar-ten

Thank you, I'd like four entrance tickets.

Bitte sehr, und der Audioguide ist gratis.
bit-te zair, oont dair ow-dee-oh-guyde isst grah-tis

Here you are, and the audio guide is free.

1 WARM UP

1 minute

Say in German "**She is my stepmother**" (pp14–15).

What's the German for "**ticket**" (pp38–39)?

Say "**I am going to New York**" (pp40–41).

Am Flughafen
AT THE AIRPORT

Although the airport environment is largely international, it is sometimes useful to be able to ask your way around the terminal in German. It's a good idea to make sure you have a few one-euro coins when you arrive at the airport—you may need to pay for a luggage cart.

2 WORDS TO REMEMBER

4 minutes

der Check-in *dair tshek-in*	check-in
der Abflug *dair up-flook*	departures
die Ankunft *dee un-koonft*	arrivals
der Zoll *dair tsoll*	customs
die Passkontrolle *dee puss-kon-trol-le*	passport control
das Terminal *duss terr-mee-nahl*	terminal
der Flugsteig *dair flook-shtiek*	boarding gate
die Flugnummer *dee flook-noom-mer*	flight number
die Gepäckausgabe *dee ge-peck-ows-gah-be*	baggage reclaim

Familiarize yourself with these words, then test yourself, using the cover flap.

Flug 23 fliegt an Terminal 2 ab.
flook drie-oont-tsvun-tsik fleekt un terr-mee-nahl tswie up
Flight 23 leaves from Terminal 2.

3 USEFUL PHRASES

3 minutes

Learn these phrases, then test yourself, using the cover flap.

Geht der Flug nach Hannover pünktlich ab? *gayt dair flook nahkh hun-no-fer pewnkt-likh up*
Is the flight for Hanover on time?

Ich kann mein Gepäck nicht finden. *ikh kunn mine ge-peck nikht fin-den*
I can't find my baggage.

4 ◀))) PUT INTO PRACTICE

3 minutes

Complete this dialogue, then test yourself, using the cover flap.

Guten Abend. Kann ich Ihnen helfen?
goo-ten ah-bent. kunn ikh ee-nen hel-fen

Hello, can I help you?

Ask: Is the flight to Cologne on time?

Geht der Flug nach Köln pünktlich ab?
gayt dair flook nahkh kerln pewnkt-likh up

Ja.
yah

Yes.

Ask: Which gate does it leave from?

Von welchem Flugsteig geht er ab?
fon vel-khem flook-shtiek gayt air up

---

5 ◀))) MATCH AND REPEAT

4 minutes

Match the numbered items to the list, then test yourself, using the cover flap.

baggage check-in ❶

boarding pass ❷

ticket ❸

passport ❹

❺ suitcase   ❻ carry-on   ❼ cart

❶ **der Abfertigungs-schalter**
dair up-fer-ti-goongs-shull-ter

❷ **die Bordkarte**
dee bort-kar-te

❸ **das Flugticket**
duss flook-tik-ket

❹ **der Pass**
dair puss

❺ **der Koffer**
dair kof-fer

❻ **das Handgepäck**
duss hunt-ge-peck

❼ **der Gepäckwagen**
dair ge-peck-vah-gen

Wiederholung
REVIEW AND REPEAT

Places

❶ das Museum
duss moo-zay-oom

❷ das Rathaus
duss raht-hows

❸ die Brücke
dee brew-ke

❹ die Kunstgalerie
dee koonst-gal-le-ree

❺ der Dom
dair doem

❻ der Parkplatz
dair park-pluts

❼ der Platz
dair pluts

1 PLACES

4 minutes

Name these locations in German.

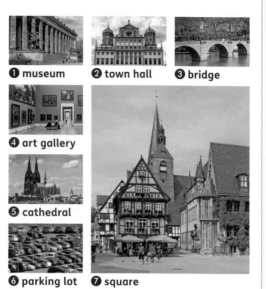

❶ museum ❷ town hall ❸ bridge

❹ art gallery

❺ cathedral

❻ parking lot ❼ square

Car parts

❶ die Windschutz-scheibe
dee vint-shoots-shie-be

❷ der Ladestecker
dair lah-de-shtek-ker

❸ die Ladesäule
dair lah-de-soy-le

❹ die Tür
dee tewr

❺ der Reifen
dair rie-fen

❻ das Ladekabel
dee lah-de-kah-bell

2 CAR PARTS

Name these car parts in German.

windshield ❶

charger ❷

door ❹ tire ❺ charging cable ❻

3 QUESTIONS

4 minutes

Ask the questions in German that match these answers.

❶ **Nein, es ist drei Minuten zu Fuß.**
nine, es isst drie mee-noo-ten tsoo fooss

❷ **Der Zug fährt von Bahnsteig fünf ab.**
dair tsook fairt fon bahn-shtiek fewnf up

❸ **Der Bus fährt um acht Uhr ab.**
dair booss fairt oom akht oor up

❹ **Kaffee, das macht zwei Euro fünfzig.**
kuf-fay, duss makht tsvie oy-roe fewnf-tsik

❺ **Nein, ich möchte keinen Wein.**
nine, ikh merkh-te kie-nen vine

❻ **Wir fahren nach Leipzig.**
veer fah-ren nahkh liep-tsik

Questions

❶ **Ist es weit?**
isst es viet

❷ **Von welchem Bahnsteig fährt der Zug ab?**
fon vel-khem bahn-shtiek fairt dair tsook up

❸ **Wann fährt der Bus ab?**
vunn fairt dair boos up

❹ **Was kostet der Kaffee?**
vuss kos-tet dair kuf-fay

❺ **Möchten Sie Wein?**
merkh-ten zee vine

❻ **Wo fahren Sie hin?**
voe fah-ren zee hin

---

3 minutes

❸ charging point/ station

4 VERBS

4 minutes

Fill in the blanks with the correct form of the missing verbs.

❶ Ich ___ Deutsche(r).

❷ Wir ___ mit dem Bus.

❸ Sie (she) ___ nach Dresden.

❹ Er ___ drei Töchter.

❺ ___ du Tee?

❻ Wie viele Kinder ___ Sie?

❼ Wo ___ die Toiletten?

Verbs

❶ **bin**
bin

❷ **fahren**
fah-ren

❸ **geht**
gayt

❹ **hat**
hut

❺ **möchtest**
merkh-test

❻ **haben**
hah-ben

❼ **sind**
zint

1 WARM UP
1 minute

Ask in German "**Do you accept credit cards?**" (pp38–39).

Ask "**How much is that?**" (pp18–19).

Ask "**Do you have children?**" (pp12–13).

Die Zimmer-reservierung
BOOKING A ROOM

There are different types of accommodations: **das Hotel**, rated one to five stars; **die Pension** or **der Gasthof**, which are traditional inns; and private accommodations, advertised as **Zimmer frei** or **Gästezimmer**. Airbnb, offering accommodations in private rooms and homes, is also a popular option.

2 ◀)) **USEFUL PHRASES**
3 minutes

Learn these phrases, then test yourself, using the cover flap.

Ist das Frühstück inbegriffen?
isst duss frew-shtewk in-be-grif-fen
Is breakfast included?

Sind Tiere zugelassen?
zint tee-re tsoo-ge-luss-sen
Are pets allowed?

Haben Sie Zimmer-service?
hah-ben zee tsim-mer-sair-vis
Do you have room service?

Wann muss ich das Zimmer freimachen?
vunn mooss ikh duss tsim-mer frie-ma-khen
What time do I have to vacate the room?

3 ◀)) **IN CONVERSATION**

Haben Sie noch Zimmer frei?
hah-ben zee nokh tsim-mer frie

Do you have any rooms available?

Ja, ein Doppelzimmer.
yah, ine dop-pel-tsim-mer

Yes, a double room.

Haben Sie ein Kinderbett?
hah-ben zee ine kin-der-bet

Do you have a cot?

4 WORDS TO REMEMBER

4 minutes

Familiarize yourself with these words, then test yourself, using the cover flap.

Hat das Zimmer Blick auf den Garten?
hut duss tsim-mer blick owf dayn gar-ten
Does the room have a view over the garden?

room	**das Zimmer** *duss tsim-mer*
single room	**das Einzelzimmer** *duss ine-tsel-tsim-mer*
double room	**das Doppelzimmer** *duss dop-pel-tsim-mer*
twin beds	**die zwei Einzelbetten** *dee tsvie ine-tsel-bet-ten*
bathroom	**das Badezimmer** *duss bah-de-tsim-mer*
shower	**die Dusche** *dee doo-she*
balcony	**der Balkon** *dair bull-kong*
key	**der Schlüssel** *dair shlews-sel*
air conditioning	**die Klimaanlage** *dee klee-mah-un-lah-ge*
breakfast	**das Frühstück** *duss frew-shtewk*

5 SAY IT

2 minutes

Do you have a single room, please?

Does the room have a balcony?

Cultural tip Some hotels and guesthouses will include breakfast in the price of a room; in others, you will be charged extra. Often, breakfast is in the style of a **Frühstücksbüffet** (*breakfast buffet*) and includes cereals, a selection of breads, cooked meats, cheeses, jams, fruit juices, and a choice of coffee or tea.

5 minutes

Ja, natürlich! Wie lange möchten Sie bleiben?
yah, na-tewr-likh! vee lun-ge merkh-ten zee blie-ben

Yes, of course! How long will you be staying?

Drei Nächte.
drie nekh-te

For three nights.

Sehr gut. Hier ist Ihr Schlüssel.
zair goot. heer isst eer shlews-sel

Very good. Here's your key.

1 WARM UP
1 minute

Ask "**Is there...?**" and reply "**There isn't...**" (pp48–49).

What does "**Kann ich Ihnen helfen?**" mean (pp48–49)?

Say "**They don't have any children**" (pp14–15).

Im Hotel
IN THE HOTEL

Although the larger hotels almost always have bathrooms en suite, there are still some **Pensionen** and guesthouses where you may have to share the facilities with other guests. Prices are generally quoted per room, not per person, so a family staying in one room can be an inexpensive option.

2 ◀))) MATCH AND REPEAT
6 minutes

Match the numbered items to the list, then test yourself, using the cover flap.

❶ **die Vorhänge**
dee foer-hen-ge

❷ **das Kissen**
duss kis-sen

❸ **die Couch**
dee kowtch

❹ **die Lampe**
dee lum-pe

❺ **das Kopfkissen**
duss kopf-kis-sen

❻ **die Minibar**
dee mini-bar

❼ **das Bett**
duss bet

❽ **die Decke**
dee dek-ke

❾ **die Tagesdecke**
dee tah-ges-dek-ke

❿ **der Nachttisch**
dair nukht-tish

❷ cushion

❶ curtains   ❸ sofa   ❹ lamp   ❺ pillow

❽ blanket   bedspread ❾

❻ minibar   ❼ bed   bedside table ❿

Cultural tip Hotel prices can vary widely. Rooms are more expensive during the busy season at summer or winter resorts, and in cities during trade fairs and festivals such as Munich's Oktoberfest (which actually starts in September), Frankfurt Book Fair, the Berlinale film festival, the Cologne Carnival, and the International Motor Show Germany in Munich and Hanover.

3 ◀))) USEFUL PHRASES

5 minutes

Learn these phrases, then test yourself, using the cover flap.

The room is too warm/cold. **Das Zimmer ist zu warm/kalt.**
duss tsim-mer isst tsoo varm/kullt

There are no towels. **Es gibt keine Handtücher.**
es geept kie-ne hunt-tew-kher

I need some soap. **Ich brauche Seife.**
ikh brow-khe zie-fe

The shower doesn't work. **Die Dusche funktioniert nicht.**
dee doo-she foonk-tsee-oe-neert nikht

The elevator is broken. **Der Fahrstuhl ist kaputt.**
dair fahr-shtool isst ka-poott

4 ◀))) PUT INTO PRACTICE

3 minutes

Complete this dialogue, then test yourself, using the cover flap.

Kann ich Ihnen helfen? *kunn ikh eenen hel-fen*

Can I help you?

Say: I need blankets.

Ich brauche Decken. *ikh brow-khe dek-ken*

Das Hotelpersonal wird sie bringen. *duss ho-tell-pair-soh-nal virt zee brin-gen*

Housekeeping will bring some.

Say: And the television is broken.

Und der Fernseher ist kaputt. *oont dair fairn-zay-er isst ka-poott*

Beim Camping
CAMPING

<table>
<tr><td>

1 WARM UP ⏱ 1 minute

Ask "**Can I?**" (pp34–35).

What is German for "**the shower**" (pp60–61)?

Say "**I need some towels**" (pp60–61).

</td><td>

Camping has long been popular in Germany. There are public and private campsites all over the country, including luxurious glamping sites. They all tend to be of a high standard, with a range of amenities that sometimes includes restaurants and pools. Tourist offices have information about sites in their area.

</td></tr>
</table>

2 🔊 USEFUL PHRASES

Learn these phrases, then test yourself, using the cover flap.

Kann ich ein Fahrrad ausleihen?
kunn ikh ine fahr-raht ows-lie-en
Can I rent a bicycle?

Ist das Wasser trinkbar?
isst duss vuss-ser trink-bahr
Is this drinking water?

Sind Lagerfeuer erlaubt?
zint lah-ger-foy-er er-lowpt
Are campfires allowed?

Laute Musik ist verboten.
lou-te moo-zeek isst fer-boe-ten
Loud music is forbidden.

Der Campingplatz ist ruhig.
dair kamping-pluts isst roo-hig
The campsite is quiet.

der Stromanschluss
dair shtrohm-un-shlooss
electrical hook-up

das Überzelt
duss ew-ber-tselt
fly sheet

die Zeltschnur
dee tselt-schnoor
guy rope

der Hering
dair hay-rin
tent peg

3 🔊 IN CONVERSATION

Ich brauche einen Platz für zwei Tage.
ikh brow-khe ie-nen pluts fewr tsvie tah-ge

I need a site for two days.

Es gibt einen beim Schwimmbad.
es geept ie-nen bime shvim-bad

There's one near the swimming pool.

Wie viel kostet es für einen Wohnwagen?
vee-feel kos-tet es fewr ie-nen vohn-vah-gen

How much is it for a caravan?

5 SAY IT
2 minutes

I need a site for
four days.

Can I rent a tent?

Where's the electrical
hook-up?

3 minutes

das Campingplatz-Büro
duss kamping-plutz-bew-roe
campsite office

die Toiletten
dee twah-let-ten
toilets

4 🔊 WORDS TO REMEMBER
4 minutes

Familiarize yourself with these words, then
test yourself, using the cover flap.

campsite	**der Campingplatz** *dair kam-ping-pluts*
site	**der Platz** *dair pluts*
tent	**das Zelt** *duss tselt*
ground sheet	**der Zeltboden** *dair tselt-bo-den*
sleeping bag	**der Schlafsack** *dair shlahf-zuck*
air mattress	**die Luftmatratze** *dee looft-mah-trat-se*
caravan	**der Wohnwagen** *dair voen-vah-gen*
camper van	**das Wohnmobil** *duss voen-moe-beel*
camping gas	**das Campinggas** *duss kam-ping-gahs*
campfire	**das Lagerfeuer** *duss lah-ger-foy-er*
drinking water	**das Trinkwasser** *duss trink-vuss-ser*
trash	**der Abfall** *dair up-full*
showers	**die Duschen** *dee doo-shen*

5 minutes

**Dreihundert Euro,
einen Tag im voraus.**
*drie-hoon-dairt oy-roe,
ie-nen tahk im for-ows*

Three hundred euros,
one day in advance.

**Kann ich einen Grill
mieten?**
*kunn ikh ie-nen grill
mee-ten*

Can I rent a grill?

**Ja, aber sie müssen eine
Kaution hinterlegen.**
*yah, ah-ber zee mews
sen ie-ne kow-tsee-oen
hin-ter-lay-gen*

Yes, but you must pay
a deposit.

1 WARM UP
1 minute

Say "**hot**" and "**cold**" (pp60–61).

What is the German for "**room**" (pp58–59), "**bed**," and "**pillow**" (pp60–61)?

Beschreibungen
DESCRIPTIONS

Adjectives are words used to describe people, things, and places, and can be used to easily make simple descriptive sentences: **das Zimmer ist kalt** (*the room is cold*). When adjectives come before a noun, they may take different endings, such as **-er**, **-e**, **-es**, or **-en** – for example, **ein kaltes Zimmer** (*a cold room*). Learn these in context as you encounter them.

2 🔊 WORDS TO REMEMBER
7 minutes

Familiarize yourself with these words, then test yourself, using the cover flap.

groß *groes*	big/tall
klein *kline*	small/short
heiß *hiess*	hot
kalt *kullt*	cold
gut *goot*	good
schlecht *shlekht*	bad
langsam *lung-zahm*	slow
schnell *shnell*	fast
laut *lowt*	noisy
ruhig *roo-hig*	quiet
hart *hart*	hard
weich *viekh*	soft
schön *shern*	beautiful
hässlich *hess-likh*	ugly
dunkel *doon-kel*	dark
hell *hell*	light

Der Hügel ist niedrig.
dair hew-gel isst nee-drikh
The hill is low.

Der Berg ist hoch.
dair bairg isst hoekh
The mountain is high.

Die Kirche ist alt.
dee kir-khe isst alt
The church is old.

Das Haus ist klein.
duss hows isst kline
The house is small.

Das Dorf ist sehr schön.
duss dorf isst zair shern
The village is very beautiful.

3 🔊 USEFUL PHRASES

4 minutes

To qualify a description, add **sehr** (*very*) or **zu** (*too*) in front of the adjective or surround it with **nicht… genug** (*not… enough*). Learn these phrases, then test yourself, using the cover flap.

This coffee is very hot. **Dieser Kaffee ist sehr heiß.**
dee-zer kuf-fay isst zair hiess

My room is very noisy. **Mein Zimmer ist sehr laut.**
mine tsim-mer isst zair lowt

My car is too small. **Mein Auto ist zu klein.**
mine ow-to isst tsoo kline

The bed is not soft enough. **Das Bett ist nicht weich genug.**
das bet isst nikht viekh ye-nookh

4 🔊 PUT INTO PRACTICE

3 minutes

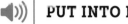

Complete this dialogue, then test yourself, using the cover flap.

Hier ist das Zimmer.
heer isst duss tsim-mer
Here is the room.

Say: The view is very beautiful.

Die Aussicht ist sehr schön.
dee ows-zikht isst zair shern

Dort ist das Badezimmer.
dort isst duss bah-de-tsim-mer
There is the bathroom.

Say: It is too small.

Es ist zu klein.
es isst tsoo kline

Wir haben kein anderes Zimmer.
veer hah-ben kine un-dair-es tsim-mer
We don't have any other rooms.

Say: Then we'll take the room.

Dann nehmen wir das Zimmer.
dan nay-men veer duss tsim-mer

Wiederholung
REVIEW AND REPEAT

Adjectives

❶ The room is too hot.

❷ My pillow is too small.

❸ The coffee is good.

❹ The bathroom is very cold.

❺ My car is not big enough.

---

1 ADJECTIVES

3 minutes

What do these sentences mean?

❶ Das Zimmer ist zu heiß.

❷ Mein Kopfkissen ist zu klein.

❸ Der Kaffee ist gut.

❹ Das Badezimmer ist sehr kalt.

❺ Mein Auto ist nicht groß genug.

Campsite

❶ das Zelt
duss tselt

❷ der Wohnwagen
dair voen-vah-gen

❸ die Zeltschnur
dee tselt-shnoor

❹ der Stromanschluss
dair shtrohm-un-shlooss

❺ die Toiletten
dee twah-let-ten

---

2 CAMPSITE

Name these campsite items in German.

❶ tent
camper van ❷
❸ guy rope
❹ electrical hook-up

3 AT THE HOTEL

4 minutes

You are booking a room in a hotel. Join in the conversation, replying in German, following the numbered English prompts.

Kann ich Ihnen helfen?
❶ Do you have any rooms free?

Ja, ein Doppelzimmer.
❷ Are pets allowed?

Ja, wie lange möchten Sie bleiben?
❸ Three nights.

Das macht zweihundertfünfzig Euro.
❹ Is breakfast included?

Selbstverständlich, hier ist der Schlüssel.
❺ Thank you very much.

At the hotel

❶ **Haben Sie noch Zimmer frei?**
hah-ben zee nokh tsim-mer frie

❷ **Sind Tiere zugelassen?**
zint tee-re tsoo-ge-luss-sen

❸ **Drei Nächte.**
drie nekh-te

❹ **Ist das Frühstück inbegriffen?**
isst duss frew-shtewk in-be-grif-fen

❺ **Vielen Dank.**
fee-len dunk

---

3 minutes

⑤ toilets

4 NEGATIVES

5 minutes

Make these sentences negative by using the correct form of the verb in brackets.

❶ Ich _____ Kinder. (haben)

❷ Sie _____ nach Hamburg. (fahren)

❸ Er _____ Wein. (möchten)

❹ Ich _____ Zucker in meinem Kaffee. (nehmen)

❺ Die Aussicht _____ sehr schön. (sein)

Negatives

❶ **habe keine**
hah-be kie-ne

❷ **fährt nicht**
fairt nikht

❸ **möchte keinen**
merkh-te kie-nen

❹ **nehme keinen**
nay-me kie-nen

❺ **ist nicht**
isst nikht

1 WARM UP
1 minute

Ask "**How do I get to the station?**" (pp50–51).

Say "**Turn left at the traffic lights**," "**Go straight**," and "**The station is across from the café**" (pp50–51).

Einkaufen
SHOPPING

Small, traditional, specialized shops can still be found in German town centers, although you will see some chains as well. You can also find big supermarkets and shopping centers on the outskirts of major towns. Markets selling fresh local produce can be found everywhere. You can find out the market day at the tourist office.

2 🔊 MATCH AND REPEAT

Match the numbered shops to the list, then test yourself, using the cover flap.

❶ **die Bäckerei**
  dee bek-ke-rie

❷ **die Konditorei**
  dee kon-dee-to-rie

❸ **der Zeitungskiosk**
  dair tsie-toongs-kee-osk

❹ **die Fleischerei**
  dee flie-she-rie

❺ **das Feinkostgeschäft**
  duss fine-kost-ge-sheft

❻ **die Buchhandlung**
  dee bookh-hund-loong

❼ **das Fischgeschäft**
  duss fish-ge-sheft

❽ **das Lebensmittelgeschäft**
  duss lay-bens-mit-tel-ge-sheft

❾ **die Bank**
  dee bunk

❶ baker

❷ cake shop

❹ butcher

❺ delicatessen

❼ fishmonger

❽ grocery

Cultural tip An **Apotheke** (*pharmacy*) dispenses prescription and over-the-counter medicine as well as a small range of high-end health and beauty products. Everyday toiletries, such as soap and shampoo, are usually bought at the **Drogerie**, often a self-service supermarket; it does not, however, sell any medicine. The **Zeitungskiosk** (*newsagent*) sells newspapers, magazines, postcards, candy, cell phone minutes, and small souvenirs.

Wo ist der Blumenladen?
voe isst dair bloo-men-lad-den
Where is the florist?

3 🔊 USEFUL PHRASES
4 minutes

Learn these phrases, then test yourself, using the cover flap.

Where can I find the hairdresser?	**Wo ist der Friseur?** *voe isst dair fri-zer*
Where do I pay?	**Wo kann ich zahlen?** *voe kunn ikh tsah-len*
Thank you, I'm just looking.	**Danke, ich schaue mich nur um.** *dun-ke, ikh show-e mikh noor oomm*
Do you sell SIM cards?	**Verkaufen Sie SIM-Karten?** *fer-kow-fen zee sim-kar-ten*
I'd like two of these.	**Ich hätte gern zwei von diesen.** *ikh het-te gairn tsvie fon dee-zen*
Can I place an order?	**Kann ich bitte bestellen?** *kunn ikh bit-te be-shtel-len*
Is there a department store in town?	**Gibt es in der Stadt ein Kaufhaus?** *geept es in dair shtutt ine kowf-hows*

❸ newsagent

❻ bookshop

❾ bank

4 🔊 WORDS TO REMEMBER
4 minutes

Familiarize yourself with these words, then test yourself, using the cover flap.

hardware shop	**der Baumarkt** *dair bow-markt*
antiques dealer	**der Antiquitätenladen** *dair an-ti-qvi-tay-ten-lah-den*
hairdresser	**der Friseur** *dair fri-zer*
jeweler	**der Juwelier** *dair yoo-ve-leer*
post office	**die Post** *dee posst*
shoe store	**das Schuhgeschäft** *duss shoo-ge-sheft*
dry cleaner	**die Reinigung** *dee rie-nee-goong*
pharmacy	**die Apotheke** *dee a-po-tay-ke*

5 SAY IT
2 minutes

Where can I find the bank?

Do you sell cheese?

I'd like three of these.

1 WARM UP

1 minute

What is German for "**40**," "**56**," "**77**," "**82**," and "**94**" (pp30–31)?

Say "**I'd like a big room**" (pp64–65).

Ask "**Do you have a small car?**" (pp64–65).

Auf dem Markt
AT THE MARKET

Germany uses the metric system of weights and measures. You need to ask for produce in kilograms and grams. You may find that the older generation still uses the term **ein Pfund** (*a pound*), meaning half a kilo. Some larger or more expensive items, such as melons or artichokes, may be sold **stückweise** or **am Stück** (*individually*).

2 🔊 MATCH AND REPEAT

Match the numbered items to the list, then test yourself, using the cover flap.

❶ die Kartoffeln
dee kar-toff-eln

❷ die Pilze
dee pill-tse

❸ der Rhabarber
dair ra-bar-ber

❹ die Radieschen
dee ra-dees-khen

❺ die Möhren
dee mer-ren

❻ der Brokkoli
dair broh-koe-lee

❼ der Kohlrabi
dair koel-rah-bee

❽ der Lauch
dair lowkh

❶ potatoes   ❷ mushrooms

radishes ❹   ❺ carrots   broccoli ❻

3 🔊 IN CONVERSATION

Ich hätte gern Tomaten.
ikh het-te gairn to-mah-ten

I'd like some tomatoes.

Die großen oder die kleinen?
dee groe-sen oe-der dee klie-nen

The large ones or the small ones?

Zwei Kilo kleine, bitte.
tsvie kee-lo klie-ne, bit-te

Two kilos of the small ones, please.

5 SAY IT
2 minutes

Three kilos of potatoes, please.

The mushrooms are too expensive.

How much is the rhubarb?

4 🔊 USEFUL PHRASES
5 minutes

In German, you don't need a word for *of* between the measurement unit (kilo) and the thing you are buying—for example, **ein Kilo Kirschen** (*a kilo of cherries*). Learn these phrases, then test yourself, using the cover flap.

Diese Würstchen sind zu teuer.
dee-ze vewrst-khen zint tsoo toy-er

These sausages are too expensive.

Was kostet ein Kilo Trauben?
vuss kos-tet ine kee-lo- trowben

How much is a kilo of grapes?

Das ist alles.
duss isst ull-les

That's all.

rhubarb ❸

4 minutes

❼ kohlrabi   ❽ leek

Cultural tip Germany uses the common European currency, the euro, divided into 100 cents. You will usually hear the price given as **zehn Euro zwanzig** (€10,20). Often, the word **Euro** is also omitted: **zwei dreißig** (€2,30)

3 minutes

Sonst noch etwas?
zonst nokh et-vuss

Anything else?

Das ist alles, danke. Was kostet das?
duss isst ull-les, dun-ke. vuss kos-tet duss

That's all, thank you. How much?

Sechs Euro fünfzig.
zeks oy-roe fewnf-tsik

Six euros, fifty.

1 WARM UP
1 minute

What are these items you could buy in a supermarket? (pp22–23).

das Fleisch
der Fisch
der Käse
der Fruchtsaft
der Wein
das Wasser

Im Supermarkt
AT THE SUPERMARKET

Supermarkets in Germany range from the very well stocked at the expensive end of the market to much cheaper budget chains. Some larger supermarkets, often located in the basement of department stores, have branches of independent bakeries alongside small restaurants where you can try the produce as you shop. Supermarket prices are usually lower than in smaller shops.

2 🔊 MATCH AND REPEAT
5 minutes

Match the numbered items to the list, then test yourself, using the cover flap.

❶ **die Haushaltswaren**
   dee hows-hults-vah-ren

❷ **die Kosmetika**
   dee kos-may-tee-ka

❸ **das Obst**
   duss opst

❹ **die Getränke**
   dee ge-tren-ke

❺ **die Fertiggerichte**
   dee fair-tikh-ge-rikh-te

❻ **das Gemüse**
   duss ge-mew-ze

❼ **die Tiefkühlkost**
   dee teef-kewl-kost

❽ **die Milchprodukte**
   dee milkh-pro-dook-te

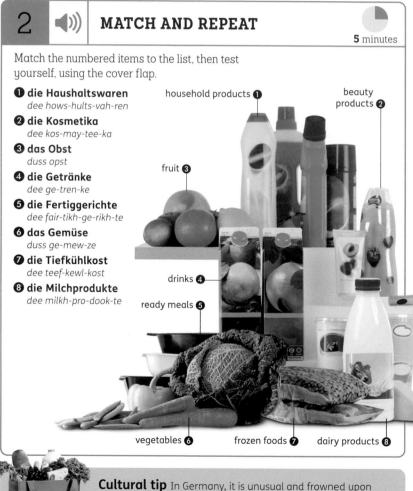

household products ❶
beauty products ❷
fruit ❸
drinks ❹
ready meals ❺
vegetables ❻
frozen foods ❼
dairy products ❽

Cultural tip In Germany, it is unusual and frowned upon to ask for a plastic bag for your purchases, and you will have to pay for them. Instead, people use their own baskets or reusable cotton bags that are sold at supermarkets.

3 🔊 USEFUL PHRASES
3 minutes

Learn these phrases, then test yourself, using the cover flap.

I would like a bag.	**Ich hätte gern eine Tragetasche.** *ikh het-te gairn ie-ne trah-ge-tush-e*
Where is the drinks aisle?	**Wo ist der Gang mit den Getränken?** *voe isst dair gung mit den ge-tren-ken*
Where is the checkout, please?	**Wo ist die Kasse, bitte?** *voe isst dee kuss-se, bit-te*
Please type in your PIN.	**Bitte geben Sie Ihre Geheimzahl ein** *bit-te gay-ben zee ee-re ge-hime-tsahl ine*

4 🔊 WORDS TO REMEMBER
4 minutes

Familiarize yourself with these words, then test yourself, using the cover flap.

milk	**die Milch** *dee milkh*
bread	**das Brot** *duss broet*
butter	**die Butter** *dee boott-ter*
ham	**der Schinken** *dair shin-ken*
salt	**das Salz** *duss zullts*
pepper	**der Pfeffer** *dair pfeff-fer*
laundry detergent	**das Waschpulver** *duss vush-pool-fer*
dishwashing liquid	**das Geschirrspülmittel** *duss ge-sheerr-shpewl-mit-tel*
toilet paper	**das Toilettenpapier** *duss twah-let-ten-pa-peer*
hand sanitizer	**das Handdesinfektionsmittel** *duss hund-des-in-fek-tsee-oens-mit-tel*

5 SAY IT
2 minutes

Where is the dairy products aisle?

May I have some ham, please?

Where are the frozen foods?

Kleidung und Schuhe
CLOTHES AND SHOES

Like in most of Europe, clothes and shoes in Germany are measured in metric sizes, although measurements may vary according to brand, cut, and style. Note that clothes size is **die Kleidergröße** and shoe size is **die Schuhgröße**.

| 1 | **WARM UP** 1 minute |

Say "**I'd like...**" (pp24–25).

Ask "**Do you have...?**" (pp14–15).

Say "**38**," "**42**," and "**46**" (pp30–31).

Say "**big**" and "**small**" (pp64–65).

2 ◀)) MATCH AND REPEAT

Match the numbered items to the list, then test yourself, using the cover flap.

❶ **das Hemd**
duss hemt

❷ **die Krawatte**
dee kra-vutt-te

❸ **die Jacke**
dee yuk-ke

❹ **der Ärmel**
dair airr-mel

❺ **die Tasche**
dee ta-she

❻ **die Hose**
dee hoe-ze

❼ **der Rock**
dair rok

❽ **die Strumpfhose**
dee shtroompf-hoe-ze

❾ **die Schuhe**
dee shoo-e

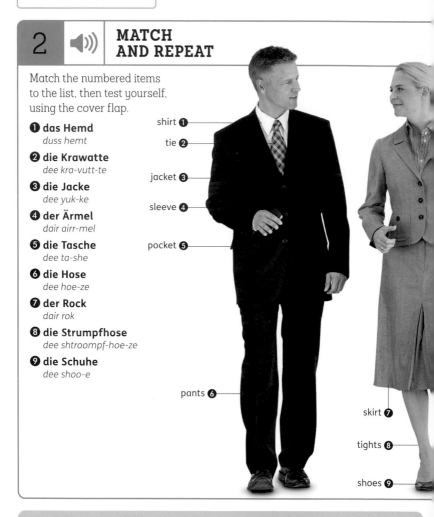

shirt ❶
tie ❷
jacket ❸
sleeve ❹
pocket ❺
pants ❻
skirt ❼
tights ❽
shoes ❾

Cultural tip Dress sizes usually range from 36 (US 4) through to 46 (US 16) and shoe sizes from 37 (US 6) to 45 (US 12). For men's shirts, a size 41 is a 16-inch collar, 43 is a 17-inch collar, and 45 is an 18-inch collar.

3 ◀)) USEFUL PHRASES

5 minutes

Learn these phrases, then test yourself, using the cover flap.

I'll take this in pink.	**Ich nehme das in Rosa.** *ikh nay-me duss in ro-sa*
Do you have this a size larger/smaller?	**Haben Sie das eine Nummer größer/kleiner?** *hah-ben zee duss ie-ne noom-mer grer-ser/klie-ner*
It's not what I'm looking for.	**Es ist nicht das, was ich suche.** *es isst nikht duss, vuss ikh zoo-khe*

4 ◀)) WORDS TO REMEMBER

4 minutes

3 minutes

In German, colors can be adjectives (pp64–65) or nouns; when nouns, they start with a capital: **der Rock ist rot** (*the skirt is red*) but **ich nehme diese in Rot** (*I'll take this in red*). Familiarize yourself with these words, then test yourself, using the cover flap.

red	**rot**	*roet*
white	**weiß**	*vies*
blue	**blau**	*blow*
yellow	**gelb**	*gelp*
green	**grün**	*grewn*
black	**schwarz**	*shvarts*

5 SAY IT

2 minutes

Do you have this jacket in black?

Do you have this in a 38?

Do you have a size smaller?

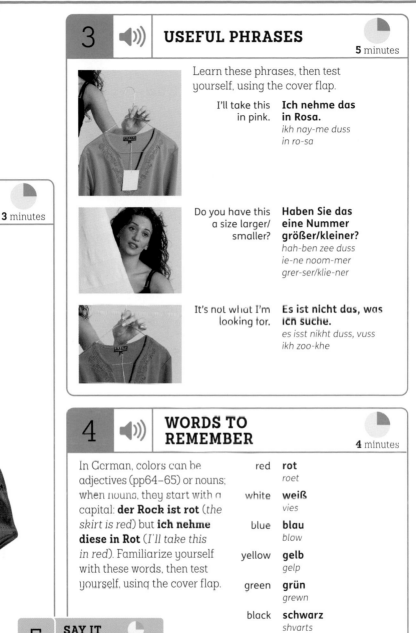

Wiederholung
REVIEW AND REPEAT

Antworten *Answers*
(Cover with flap)

Market

❶ **die Kartoffeln**
dee kar-toff-eln

❷ **die Radieschen**
dee ra-dees-khen

❸ **die Möhren**
dee mer-ren

❹ **der Brokkoli**
dair broh-koe-lee

❺ **der Kohlrabi**
dair koel-rah-bee

❻ **der Lauch**
dair lowkh

Description

❶ These shoes are too expensive.

❷ My room is very small.

❸ The bed is too hard.

Shops

❶ **die Bäckerei**
dee bek-ke-rie

❷ **das Lebensmittel-geschäft**
duss lay-bens-mit-tel-ge-sheft

❸ **die Buchhandlung**
dee bookh-hund-loong

❹ **das Fischgeschäft**
duss fish-ge-sheft

❺ **die Konditorei**
dee kon-dee-to-rie

❻ **die Fleischerei**
dee flie-she-rie

1 MARKET

3 minutes

Name these vegetables in German.

❶ potatoes ❸ carrots ❺ kohlrabi
❷ radish ❹ broccoli ❻ leeks

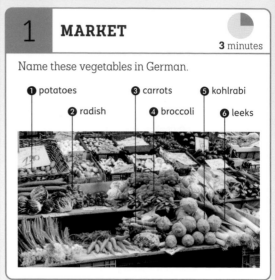

2 DESCRIPTION

2 minutes

What do these sentences mean?

❶ **Diese Schuhe sind zu teuer.**
❷ **Mein Zimmer ist sehr klein.**
❸ **Das Bett ist zu hart.**

3 SHOPS

3 minutes

Name these shops in German.

❶ baker ❷ grocery ❸ bookshop
❹ fishmonger ❺ cake shop ❻ butcher

4 SUPERMARKET

3 minutes

Name these products in German.

1 household products

2 beauty products

3 drinks

4 dairy products

5 frozen foods

Supermarket

1 die Haushalts-waren
dee hows-hults-vah-ren

2 die Kosmetika
dee kos-may-tee-ka

3 die Getränke
dee ge-tren-ke

4 die Milchprodukte
dee milkh-pro-dook-te

5 die Tiefkühlkost
dee teef-kewl-kost

5 MUSEUM

4 minutes

You are buying entrance tickets at a museum. Join in the conversation, replying in German, with the help of the numbered English prompts.

Guten Tag. Kann ich Ihnen helfen?
1 I'd like five tickets.

Das macht siebzig Euro.
2 That's very expensive!

Wir geben keine Ermäßigung für Kinder.
3 How much is an audio guide?

Fünf Euro.
4 Five tickets and five audio guides, please.

Fünfundneunzig Euro, bitte.
5 Here you are. Where are the toilets?

Dort drüben.
6 Thank you very much.

Museum

1 Ich hätte gern fünf Eintrittskarten.
ikh het-te gairn fewnf ine-trits-kar-ten

2 Das ist sehr teuer!
duss isst zair toy-er

3 Was kostet der Audioguide?
vuss kos-tet dair ow-dee-oh-guyde

4 Fünf Eintrittskarten und fünf Audioguides, bitte.
fewnf ine-trits-kar-ten oont fewnf ow-dee-oh-guydes, bit-te

5 Bitte sehr. Wo sind die Toiletten?
bit-te zair. voe zint dee twah-let-ten

6 Vielen Dank.
fee-len dunk

1 WARM UP
1 minute

Ask "**Which platform?**" (pp38–39).

What is the German for these family members: "**sister**", "**brother**", "**son**", "**daughter**", "**mother**", and "**father**"? (pp10–11).

Berufe
JOBS

Most job titles are masculine. They can be turned into the feminine equivalent by adding the suffix **-in**—for example, **der Elektriker/die Elektrikerin** (*male/female electrician*) or **der Klempner/die Klempnerin** (*male/female plumber*). When you state your occupation, you don't need to use **ein/eine** (*a/an*), as in: **ich bin Lektor(in)** (*I'm an editor*).

2 🔊 WORDS TO REMEMBER: JOBS
7 minutes

Familiarize yourself with these words, then test yourself, using the cover flap. The feminine form is also shown; for this, some jobs change the main vowel to an umlaut: **Arzt/Ärztin** (*male/female doctor*).

der/die Arzt/Ärztin *dair/dee artst/airts-tin*	doctor
der/die Zahnarzt/ Zahnärztin *dair/dee tsahn-artst/ tsahn-airts-tin*	dentist
der/die Krankenpfleger/ Krankenschwester *dair/dee krunk-en-pflay-ger/ krunk-en-shves-ter*	nurse
der/die Lehrer(in) *dair/dee lay-rer(in)*	teacher
der/die Buchhalter(in) *dair/dee bookh-hull-ter(in)*	accountant
der/die Rechtsanwalt/ Rechtsanwältin *dair/dee rekhts-un-vullt/ rekhts-un-vel-tin*	lawyer
der/die Grafiker(in) *dair/dee grah-fi-ker(in)*	designer
der/die Berater(in) *dair/dee be-rah-ter(in)*	consultant
der/die Sekretär(in) *dair/dee zek-re-tair(in)*	secretary
der/die Verkäufer(in) *dair/dee fer-koy-fer(in)*	shop assistant
der/die Koch/Köchin *dair/dee kokh/kerkhin*	cook/chef
der/die Ingenieur(in) *dair/dee in-jen-yewr(in)*	engineer
selbstständig *zelpst-shten-dikh*	self-employed

Ich bin Klempner.
ikh bin klemp-ner
I'm a plumber.

Sie ist Lehrerin.
zee isst lay-re-rin
She's a teacher.

3 PUT INTO PRACTICE

4 minutes

Complete this dialogue, then test yourself, using the cover flap.

Was machen Sie beruflich?
vuss ma-khen zee be-roof-likh

What do you do?

Say: I am a consultant.

Ich bin Berater.
ikh bin be-rah-ter

Bei welcher Firma arbeiten Sie?
bie vel-kher fir-ma ar-bie-ten zee

What company do you work for?

Say: I'm self-employed.

Ich bin selbstständig.
ikh bin zelpst-shten-dikh

Wie interessant!
vee in-tay-res-sunt

How interesting!

Ask: And what do you do?

Und was machen Sie beruflich?
oont vuss ma-khen zee be-roof-likh

Ich bin Zahnarzt.
ikh bin tsahn-artst

I'm a dentist.

Say: My sister is a dentist too.

Meine Schwester ist auch Zahnärztin.
mie-ne shves-ter isst owkh tsahn-airts-tin

4 WORDS TO REMEMBER: WORKPLACE

3 minutes

Die Zentrale ist in Bremen.
dee tsen-trah-le isst in bray-men
The head office is in Bremen.

Familiarize yourself with these words, then test yourself, using the cover flap.

head office	**die Zentrale** *dee tsen-trah-le*
branch	**die Zweigstelle** *dee tsviek-shtel-le*
department	**die Abteilung** *dee up-tie-loong*
reception	**der Empfang** *dair emp-fung*
supervisor	**der/die Vorgesetzte** *dair/dee for-ge-zets-te*
trainee	**der/die Auszubildende** *dair/dee ows-tsoo-bilden-de*

1 WARM UP
1 minute

Practice different ways of introducing yourself in different situations. Mention your name, your occupation, and any other information you'd like to give (pp8–9, pp14–15, and pp78–79).

Das Büro
THE OFFICE

An office environment or business situation has its own vocabulary in any language, but there are many items for which the terminology is virtually universal. Note that German computer keyboards have a different layout (QWERTZ) than the standard English QWERTY convention, and that cell phones are often called **das Handy**, although **das Smartphone** is common too.

2 🔊 WORDS TO REMEMBER
5 minutes

Familiarize yourself with these words, then test yourself, using the cover flap.

die Besprechung meeting
dee be-shpre-khoong

der Fotokopierer photocopier
dair fo-to-ko-pee-rer

der Computer computer
dair kom-pyoo-ter

der Monitor monitor
dair mo-nee-tor

die Maus mouse
dee mows

das Internet Internet
duss in-ter-net

die E-Mail email
dee ee-mayle

das Passwort password
duss puss-vort

das WLAN-Passwort Wi-Fi password
duss veh-lahn-puss-vort

die Konferenz conference
dee kon-fay-rents

die Tagesordnung agenda
dee tah-ges-ort-noong

der Terminkalender diary
dair terr-meen-ka-len-der

die Visitenkarte business card
dee vi-see-ten-kar-te

die Voicemail voicemail
dee voyse-mayle

3 🔊 MATC

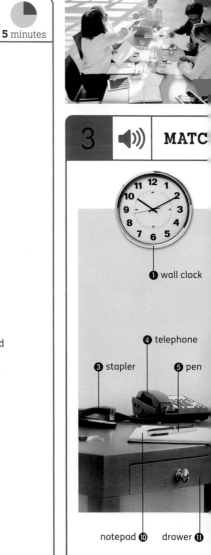

❶ wall clock

❹ telephone

❸ stapler ❺ pen

notepad ❿ drawer ⓫

4 🔊 USEFUL PHRASES

2 minutes

Learn these phrases, then test yourself, using the cover flap.

I want to send an email.
Ich möchte eine E-Mail schicken.
ikh merkh-te ie-ne ee-mayle shik-ken

I need to photocopy something.
Ich muss etwas kopieren.
ikh mooss et-vuss ko-pee-ren

I'd like to schedule an appointment.
Ich möchte einen Termin ausmachen.
ikh merkh-te ie-nen tair-meen ows-ma-khen

5 SAY IT

2 minutes

I'd like to arrange a conference.

Do you have a business card?

I have a laptop.

AND REPEAT

5 minutes

Match the numbered items to the list, then test yourself, using the cover flap.

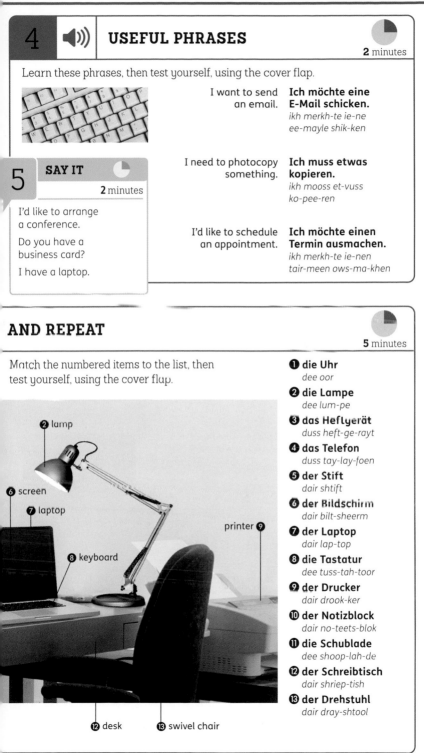

2 lamp
6 screen
7 laptop
printer **9**
8 keyboard
12 desk
13 swivel chair

1 die Uhr
dee oor

2 die Lampe
dee lum-pe

3 das Heftgerät
duss heft-ge-rayt

4 das Telefon
duss tay-lay-foen

5 der Stift
dair shtift

6 der Bildschirm
dair bilt-sheerm

7 der Laptop
dair lap-top

8 die Tastatur
dee tuss-tah-toor

9 der Drucker
dair drook-ker

10 der Notizblock
dair no-teets-blok

11 die Schublade
dee shoop-lah-de

12 der Schreibtisch
dair shriep-tish

13 der Drehstuhl
dair dray-shtool

Die akademische Welt
ACADEMIC WORLD

Say "**How interesting!**" (pp78–79), "**library**" (pp48–49), and "**appointment**" (pp32–33).

Ask "**What do you do?**" and answer "**I'm an accountant**" (pp78–79).

In Germany, as is now becoming standard across the EU, the first degree is **der Bachelor** (*bachelor's*), followed by **der Master** (*master's*), and then by **der Doktor** (*PhD*). Certain professional degrees require a qualifying **Staatsexamen** (*state exam*).

---

2 USEFUL PHRASES

3 minutes

Learn these phrases, then test yourself, using the cover flap.

Was ist Ihr Gebiet?
vuss isst eer ge-beet

What is your field?

Ich bin in der biochemischen Forschung tätig.
ikh bin in dair bee-oh-kay-mish-en for-shoong tay-tig

I am doing research in biochemistry.

Ich habe Jura studiert.
ikh hah-be yoo-ra shtoo-deert

I studied law.

Ich halte einen Vortrag über moderne Architektur.
ikh hul-te ie-nen vor-trahk ew-ber mo-dair-ne ar-khi-tek-toor

I am giving a presentation on modern architecture.

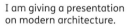

---

3 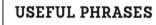 IN CONVERSATION

Guten Tag, ich bin Professor Stein.
goo-ten tahk, ikh bin pro-fes-sor shtien

Hello, I'm Professor Stein.

An welcher Universität arbeiten Sie?
un vel-kher oo-nee-vair-zee-tayt ar-bie-ten zee

Which university do you work at?

Ich bin Delegierte der Humboldt-Universität.
ikh bin day-lay-geer-te dair hoomm-bolt-oo-nee-vair-zee-tayt

I'm a delegate from Humboldt University.

4 WORDS TO REMEMBER

4 minutes

Familiarize yourself with these words, then test yourself, using the cover flap.

conference	**die Konferenz** *dee kon-fay-rents*
trade fair	**die Messe** *dee mes-se*
seminar	**das Seminar** *duss zay-mee-nahr*
lecture theatre	**der Vorlesungssaal** *dair for-lay-zoongs-zahl*
conference room	**das Konferenzzimmer** *duss kon-fay-rents-tsim-mer*
exhibition	**die Ausstellung** *dee ows-shtel-loong*
library	**die Bibliothek** *dee beeb-lee-o-tayk*
university lecturer	**der/die Dozent(in)** *dair/dee do-tsent(in)*
professor	**der/die Professor(in)** *dair/dee pro-fes-sor(in)*
medicine	**die Medizin** *dee may-dee-tseen*
science	**die Naturwissenschaften** *dee na-toor-vis-sen-shuft-ten*
literature	**die Literatur** *dee lit-er-a-toor*
engineering	**die Technik** *dee tekh-nik*

Wir haben einen Stand auf der Messe.
veer hah-ben ie-nen shtunt owf dair mes-se
We have a stand at the trade fair.

5 SAY IT

2 minutes

I'm doing research in medicine.

I studied literature.

She's the professor.

---

5 minutes

Was ist Ihr Gebiet?
vuss isst eer ge-beet

What's your field?

Ich bin in der technischen Forschung tätig.
ikh bin in dair tekh-nish-en for-shoong tay-tig

I'm doing research in engineering.

Wie interessant!
vee in-tay-res-sunt

How interesting!

Geschäftliches
IN BUSINESS

Say "**I'm a trainee**" (pp78–79).

Say "**I want to send an email**" (pp80–81).

Say "**I'd like to schedule an appointment**" (pp80–81).

While on business trips to Germany, you will make a good impression and receive a more friendly reception if you make the effort to begin meetings with a short introduction in German, even if your vocabulary is limited. After that, everyone will probably be happy to continue the meeting in English.

2 WORDS TO REMEMBER

Familiarize yourself with these words, then test yourself, using the cover flap.

der Manager
dair man-a-jer
executive

der Zeitplan *dair tsiet-plahn*	schedule
die Lieferung *dee lee-fe-roong*	delivery
die Bezahlung *dee be-tsah-loong*	payment
das Budget *duss bew-jay*	budget
der Preis *dair priez*	price
das Dokument *duss dock-oo-ment*	document
die Rechnung *dee rekh-noong*	invoice
der Kostenvoranschlag *dair kos-ten-for-un-shlahk*	estimate
der Gewinn *dair ge-vinn*	profits
der Absatz *dair up-zuts*	sales
die Zahlen *dee tsah-len*	figures

Sollen wir den Vertrag unterzeichnen?
zol-len veer dayn fer-trahk oon-ter-tsiekh-nen
Shall we sign the contract?

der Vertrag
dair fer-trahk
contract

Cultural tip Many German companies have **Gleitzeit** (*flexible working hours*). Generally, offices open at 9am or before, break for lunch at noon, and finish the day at about 5pm or earlier. In larger firms and offices, lunch is often eaten in a subsidized cafeteria together with colleagues.

3 🔊 USEFUL PHRASES

6 minutes

Learn these phrases, then test yourself, using the cover flap.

Bitte schicken Sie mir den Vertrag.
bit-te shik-ken zee meer dayn fer-trahk

Please send me the contract.

6 minutes

der Kunde
dair koonn-de
client

der Bericht
dair be-rikht
report

Haben wir uns auf einen Zeitplan geeinigt?
hah-ben veer oons owf ie-nen tsiet-plahn ge-ie-nikht

Have we agreed a schedule?

Wann können Sie liefern?
vunn kern-nen zee lee-fairn

When can you deliver?

Was ist das Budget?
vuss isst duss bew-jay

What's the budget?

Können Sie mir die Rechnung schicken?
kern-nen zee meer dee rekh-noong shik-ken

Can you send me the invoice?

4 SAY IT

2 minutes

Can you send me the estimate?

Have we agreed on a price?

What are the profits?

Wiederholung
REVIEW AND REPEAT

At the office

1 die Uhr
dee oor

2 der Laptop
dair lap-top

3 die Lampe
dee lum-pe

4 der Drucker
dair drook-ker

5 das Heftgerät
duss heft-ge-rayt

6 der Stift
dair shtift

7 der Notizblock
dair no-teets-blok

8 der Schreibtisch
dair shriep-tish

Jobs

1 der/die Arzt/Ärztin
dair/dee artst/airts-tin

2 der/die Klempner(in)
dair/dee klemp-ner(in)

3 der/die Verkäufer(in)
dair/dee fer-koy-fer(in)

4 der/die Buchhalter(in)
dair/dee bookh-hull-ter(in)

5 der/die Lehrer(in)
dair/dee lay-rer(in)

6 der/die Rechtsanwalt/Rechtsanwältin
dair/dee rekhts-un-vullt/rekhts-un-vel-tin

1 AT THE OFFICE

Name these items in German.

wall clock **1**   **2** laptop   **3** lamp

5 stapler   pen **6**   **7** notepad   **8** desk

2 JOBS

3 minutes

Name these jobs in German.

1 doctor
2 plumber
3 shop assistant
4 accountant
5 teacher
6 lawyer

4 minutes

4 printer

3 WORK

4 minutes

Answer these questions, following the numbered English prompts.

Bei welcher Firma arbeiten Sie?
❶ I work for myself.

Von welcher Universität sind Sie?
❷ I'm at the University of Köln.

Was ist Ihr Gebiet?
❸ I'm doing medical research.

Haben wir uns auf einen Zeitplan geeinigt?
❹ Yes, my secretary has the schedule.

Work

❶ **Ich bin selbstständig.**
ikh bin zelpst-shten-dikh

❷ **Ich bin von der Universität Köln.**
ikh bin fon dair oo-nee-vair-zee-tayt kewln

❸ **Ich bin in der medizinischen Forschung tätig.**
ikh bin in dair me-dee-tsee-nish-en for-shoong tay-tig

❹ **Ja, meine Sekretärin hat den Zeitplan.**
yah, mye-ne zek-re-tair-in hut dayn tsiet-plahn

4 HOW MUCH?

4 minutes

Answer these questions in German, using the amounts given in brackets.

❶ Was kostet der Kaffee? (€2.50)
❷ Was kostet das Zimmer? (€80)
❸ Was kostet das Kilo Tomaten? (€3.25)
❹ Was kostet der Parkplatz für drei Tage? (€150)

How much?

❶ **Das macht zwei Euro fünfzig.**
duss makht tsvie oy-roe fewnf-tsik

❷ **Es kostet achtzig Euro.**
es kos-tet akh-tsik oy-roe

❸ **Das macht drei Euro fünfund-zwanzig.**
duss makht drie oy-roe fewnf-oont-tsvun-tsik

❹ **Er kostet einhundertfünfzig Euro.**
air kos-tet ine-hoon-dairt-fewnf-tsik oy-roe

Der Körper
THE BODY

1 **WARM UP** 🍰

1 minute

Say "**I'm allergic to nuts**" (pp22–23).

Say the verb "**haben**" (*to have*) in all its forms (ich, du, er/sie/es, wir, ihr, sie/Sie) (pp14–15).

In German, many expressions to do with health are reflexive. In order to say *I am not feeling good* in German, you would say **ich fühle mich nicht wohl** (literally *I am not feeling myself well*). As in English, the reflexive pronoun (myself, yourself, etc.) changes depending on the context.

2 🔊 **MATCH AND REPEAT**: BODY

6 minutes

Match the numbered parts of the body to the list, then test yourself, using the cover flap.

❶ **die Hand**
dee hunt

❷ **der Ellbogen**
dair el-bo-gen

❸ **das Haar, die Haare**
duss hahr, dee hah-re

❹ **der Kopf**
dair kopf

❺ **der Arm**
dair arm

❻ **der Hals**
dair hulls

❼ **die Schulter**
dee shool-ter

❽ **die Brust**
dee broost

❾ **der Bauch**
dair bowkh

❿ **das Bein**
duss bine

⓫ **das Knie**
duss k-nee

⓬ **der Fuß**
dair fooss

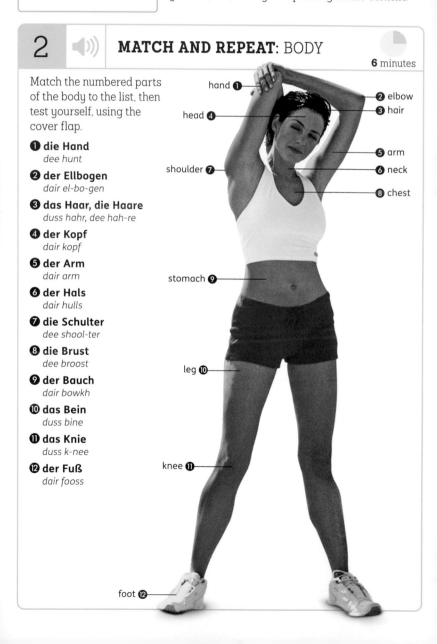

hand ❶
head ❹
shoulder ❼
stomach ❾
leg ❿
knee ⓫
foot ⓬

❷ elbow
❸ hair
❺ arm
❻ neck
❽ chest

3 🔊 MATCH AND REPEAT: FACE

3 minutes

Match the numbered facial features to the list, then test yourself, using the cover flap.

eyebrow ❶

❷ eye

ear ❸

❹ nose

mouth ❺

❶ **die Augenbraue**
dee ow-gen-brow-e

❷ **das Auge**
duss ow-ge

❸ **das Ohr**
duss ohr

❹ **die Nase**
dee nah-ze

❺ **der Mund**
dair moont

4 🔊 USEFUL PHRASES

3 minutes

Learn these phrases, then test yourself, using the cover flap.

I have a pain in my back. **Ich habe Schmerzen im Rücken.**
ikh hah-be shmair-sen im rewk-ken

I have a rash on my arm. **Ich habe einen Ausschlag am Arm.**
ikh hah-be ie-nen ows-shluk um arm

I don't feel good. **Ich fühle mich nicht wohl.**
ikh few-le mikh nikht voel

5 🔊 PUT INTO PRACTICE

2 minutes

Complete this dialogue, then test yourself, using the cover flap.

Was ist denn los?
vuss isst denn loes

What's the matter?

Say: I'm not feeling good.

Ich fühle mich nicht wohl.
ikh few-le mikh nikht voel

Wo tut es denn weh?
voe toot es den vayh

Where does it hurt?

Say: I have a pain in my shoulder.

Ich haben Schmerzen in der Schulter.
ikh hah-be shmair-sen in dair shool-ter

1 WARM UP
1 minute

Say "**I have a rash**" and "**I don't feel good**" (pp88–89).

Say the German for "**red**," "**green**," "**black**," and "**yellow**" (pp74–75).

In der Apotheke
AT THE PHARMACY

German pharmacies are indicated by a stylized red letter **A** for **Apotheke**. Pharmacists can give advice about minor health problems and are permitted to dispense a wide variety of medicine, even giving injections if necessary. There is an **Apotheken-Notdienst** (*24-hour pharmacy*) in most towns.

2 MATCH AND REPEAT
3 minutes

Match the numbered items to the list, then test yourself, using the cover flap.

❶ **der Verband**
dair fer-bunt

❷ **der Sirup**
dair zee-roop

❸ **die Tropfen**
dee trop-fen

❹ **die Salbe**
dee zull-be

❺ **das Pflaster**
duss pflus-ter

❻ **die Spritze**
dee shprit-se

❼ **das Zäpfchen**
duss tsepf-khen

❽ **die Tablette**
dee tub-let-te

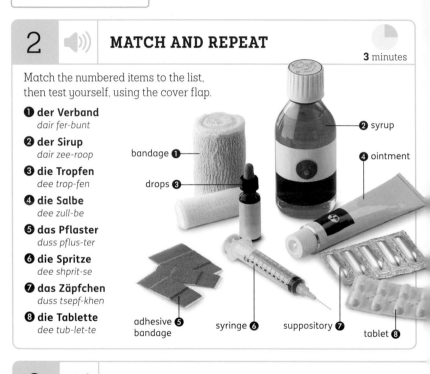

bandage ❶
drops ❸
syrup ❷
ointment ❹
adhesive bandage ❺
syringe ❻
suppository ❼
tablet ❽

3 IN CONVERSATION

Guten Tag, Sie wünschen?
goo-ten tahk, zee vewn-shen

Hello. What would you like?

Ich habe Bauchschmerzen.
ikh hah-be bowkh-shmairt-sen

I have a stomachache.

Haben Sie Durchfall?
hah-ben zee doorkh-full

Do you have diarrhea?

4 🔊 WORDS TO REMEMBER

2 minutes

Familiarize yourself with these words, then test yourself, using the cover flap. Note that in German you don't use the indefinite articles a/an to describe a pain.

Ich habe Kopfschmerzen.
ikh hah-be kopf-shmairt-sen
I have a headache.

headache	**Kopfschmerzen** *kopf-shmairt-sen*
stomachache	**Bauchschmerzen** *bowkh-shmairt-sen*
diarrhea	**Durchfall** *doorkh-full*
cold	**der Schnupfen** *dair shnoop-fen*
cough	**der Husten** *dair hoos-ten*
sunburn	**der Sonnenbrand** *dair zon-nen-brunt*
toothache	**Zahnschmerzen** *tsahn-shmairt-sen*

5 🔊 USEFUL PHRASES

4 minutes

Learn these phrases, then test yourself, using the cover flap.

Do you have face masks?	**Haben Sie Masken?** *hah-ben zee mas-ken*
Do you have that as a syrup?	**Haben Sie das auch als Sirup?** *hah-ben zee duss owkh ulls zee-roop*
I'm allergic to penicillin.	**Ich bin allergisch gegen Penizillin.** *ikh bin ull-lair-gish gay-gen pay-nee-tsee-leen*

6 SAY IT

2 minutes

I have a cold.

Do you have that as an ointment?

Do you have a cough?

3 minutes

Nein, aber ich habe auch Kopfschmerzen.
nine, ah-ber ikh hah-be owkh kopf-shmairt-sen

No, but I also have a headache.

Nehmen Sie dies.
nay-men zee dees

Take this.

Haben Sie das auch als Sirup?
hah-ben zee duss owkh ulls zee-roop

Do you have that as a syrup?

Beim Arzt
AT THE DOCTOR

1 WARM UP
1 minute

Say "**I need some tablets**" and "**He needs some ointment**" (pp60–61 and pp90–91).

What is the German for "**I don't have a son**" (pp14–15)?

In an emergency, dial 112 for an ambulance. If it isn't urgent, book an appointment with the doctor and pay when you leave. You can usually be reimbursed if you have comprehensive travel and medical insurance. German doctors are titled according to their specialist qualifications, such as **Internist** (*internal medicine*), **Kardiologe** (*heart specialist*), or **Allgemeinarzt** (*general practitioner*).

2 USEFUL PHRASES YOU MAY HEAR
3 minutes

Learn these phrases, then test yourself, using the cover flap.

Es ist nichts Ernsthaftes.
es isst nikhts airnst-huff-tes
It's not serious.

Nehmen Sie irgendwelche Medikamente?
nay-men zee ir-gent-vel-khe may-dee-ka-men-te
Are you taking any medications?

Sie haben eine Niereninfektion.
zee hah-ben ie-ne nee-ren-infek-tsee-oen
You have a kidney infection.

Sie müssen ins Krankenhaus gehen.
zee mews-sen ins krunk-en-hows gay-en
You need to go to the hospital.

Bitte öffnen Sie Ihren Mund.
bit-te erf-nen zee ee-ren moont
Please open your mouth.

Wir müssen ein paar Tests machen.
veer mews-sen ine pahr tests ma-khen
We need to do a few tests.

3 IN CONVERSATION

Was ist denn los?
vuss isst den loes

What's the matter?

Ich habe Schmerzen in der Brust.
ikh hah-be shmairt-sen in dair broost

I have a pain in my chest.

Ich werde Sie untersuchen.
ikh vair-de zee oon-ter-zoo-khen

I'll examine you.

4 🔊 USEFUL PHRASES YOU MAY NEED TO SAY

4 minutes

Learn these phrases, then test yourself, using the cover flap.

Ich bin schwanger.
ikh bin shvun-ger
I'm pregnant.

I'm diabetic.	**Ich bin Diabetiker(in).** *ikh bin dee-ar-bay-ti-kair(in)*
I'm epileptic.	**Ich bin Epileptiker(in).** *ikh bin ay-pee-lep-ti-kair(in)*
I have asthma.	**Ich habe Asthma.** *ikh hah-be ast-ma*
I have a heart condition.	**Ich bin herzkrank.** *ikh bin hairts-krunk*
I feel faint.	**Ich fühle mich schwach.** *ikh few-le mikh shvakh*
I have a fever.	**Ich habe Fieber.** *ikh hah-be fee-ber*
It's urgent.	**Es ist dringend.** *es isst dring-ent*
I'm here for my vaccination.	**Ich habe einen Impftermin.** *ikh hah-be ie-nen impf-terr-meen*

Cultural tip EU nationals can get free emergency medical treatment in Germany with a European Health Insurance Card (EHIC) or E111 form. For UK nationals, the Global Health Insurance Card (GHIC) has replaced the EHIC. Travelers from all other countries should make sure they have comprehensive travel and medical insurance.

5 SAY IT

2 minutes

Do I need tests?

My son needs to go to the hospital.

It's not urgent.

5 minutes

Ist es etwas Ernsthaftes?
isst es et-vuss airnst-huff-tes

Is it serious?

Nein, nur Verdauungs-beschwerden.
nine, noor fer-dow-oongs-be-shvair-den

No, only indigestion.

Ein Glück!
ine glewkk

What a relief!

1 WARM UP
1 minute

Ask "**How long is the journey?**" (pp42–43).

Ask "**Do I need tests?**" (pp92–93).

What is the German for "**mouth**" and "**head**" (pp88–89)?

Im Krankenhaus
AT THE HOSPITAL

Many big hospitals in Germany are attached to universities and are known as **Universitäts-klinikum**. A ward is called **die Station**, and the outpatient department is **die Ambulanz**. It is useful to know a few basic phrases relating to hospitals for use in an emergency or in case you need to visit a friend or colleague in the hospital.

2 🔊 USEFUL PHRASES
5 minutes

Learn these phrases, then test yourself, using the cover flap.

Wann ist Besuchszeit?
vunn isst be-zookhs-tsiet
What are the visiting hours?

Gibt es hier eine induktive Höranlage?
geept es heer ie-ne in-dook-tee-ve her-un-lah-ge
Is a hearing loop available?

Wie lange wird das dauern?
vee lun-ge virt duss dow-ern
How long will it take?

Wo ist das Wartezimmer?
voe isst duss var-te-tsim-mer
Where is the waiting room?

Tut das weh?
toot duss vayh
Will it hurt?

Bitte legen Sie sich hier hin.
bit-te lay-gen zee zikh heer hin
Please lie down here.

Sie dürfen nichts essen.
zee dewr-fen nikhts es-sen
You must not eat.

die Infusion
dee in-foo-zee-oen
intravenous drip

Bewegen Sie nicht den Kopf.
be-vay-gen zee nikht dayn kopf
Don't move your head.

Wir müssen eine Blutprobe machen.
veer mews-sen ie-ne bloot-proe-be ma-khen
We'll have to do a blood test.

Geht es Ihnen besser?
gayt es ee-nen bes-ser
Are you feeling better?

3 🔊 WORDS TO REMEMBER

4 minutes

Familiarize yourself with these words, then test yourself, using the cover flap.

Ihre Röntgenaufnahme ist normal.
ee-re rernt-gen-owf-nah-me isst nor-mal
Your x-ray is normal.

emergency department	**die Unfallstation** *dee oon-full-shtah-tsee-oen*
x-ray department	**die Röntgenabteilung** *dee rernt-gen-up-tie-loong*
children's ward	**die Kinderstation** *dee kin-der-shtah-tsee-oen*
operating room	**der Operationssaal (der OP)** *dair o-pay-rah-tsee-oens-zahl (dair oe-pay)*
waiting room	**das Wartezimmer** *duss var-te-tsim-mer*
elevator	**der Aufzug** *dair owf-tsoog*
stairs	**die Treppe** *dee trep-pe*

4 🔊 PUT INTO PRACTICE

3 minutes

Complete this dialogue, then test yourself, using the cover flap.

Sie haben eine Entzündung.
zee hah-ben ie-ne ent-tsewn-doong

You have an infection.

Ask: Will you need to do tests?

Müssen Sie Untersuchungen machen?
mews-sen zee oon-ter-zoo-khoong-en ma-khen

Zuerst machen wir eine Blutprobe.
tsoo-airst ma-khen veer ie-ne bloot-proe-be

First we will do a blood test.

Ask: Will it hurt?

Tut das weh?
toot duss vayh

5 SAY IT

2 minutes

Does he need a blood test?

Where is the children's ward?

Do I need an x-ray?

Nein, keine Angst.
nine, kie-ne unkst

No, don't worry.

Ask: How long will it take?

Wie lange wird das dauern?
vee lun-ge virt duss dow-ern

Wiederholung
REVIEW AND REPEAT

Antworten *Answers*
(Cover with flap)

The body

❶ **der Kopf**
dair kopf

❷ **der Arm**
dair arm

❸ **die Brust**
dee broost

❹ **der Bauch**
dair bowkh

❺ **das Bein**
duss bine

❻ **das Knie**
duss k-nee

❼ **der Fuß**
dair fooss

---

1 THE BODY

4 minutes

Name these body parts in German.

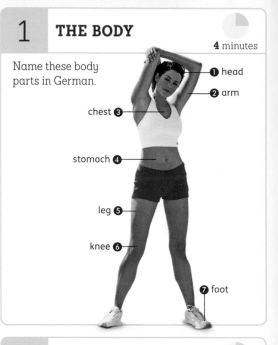

❶ head
❷ arm
chest ❸
stomach ❹
leg ❺
knee ❻
❼ foot

On the phone

❶ **Ich möchte bitte
Susanne Hahn
sprechen.**
*ikh merkh-te bit-te
zu-zan-ne haahn
shpre-khen*

❷ **Jochen Schegel von
der Druckerei Gohl.**
*yo-khen shle-gel fon
dair drook-er-ie goel*

❸ **Kann ich eine
Nachricht
hinterlassen?**
*kunn ikh ie-ne
nahkh-rikht
hin-ter-luss-sen*

❹ **Der Termin für
Montag elf Uhr
ist in Ordnung.**
*dair terr-meen fewr
mohn-tahk elf oor
isst in ord-noong*

---

2 ON THE PHONE

4 minutes

You are scheduling an appointment. Join in the conversation, replying in German, following the numbered English prompts.

Hallo, Firma Apex.
❶ I'd like to speak to Susanne Hahn.

Ja, mit wem spreche ich?
❷ Jochen Schlegel of Gohl Printers.

Es tut mir leid, da ist besetzt.
❸ Can I leave a message?

Aber selbstverständlich.
❹ The appointment on Monday at 11 am is fine.

3 CLOTHING

3 minutes

Name these items of clothing in German.

tie ❶
❷ jacket
❸ skirt
pants ❹
❺ tights
shoes ❻

Clothing

❶ **die Krawatte**
dee kra-vutt-te

❷ **die Jacke**
dee yuk-ke

❸ **der Rock**
dair rok

❹ **die Hose**
dee hoe-ze

❺ **die Strumpfhose**
dee shtroompf-hoe-ze

❻ **die Schuhe**
dee shoo-e

4 AT THE DOCTOR'S

4 minutes

Say these sentences in German.

❶ I don't feel good.

❷ Will you need to do tests?

❸ I have a heart condition.

❹ Do I need to go to the hospital?

❺ I'm pregnant.

❻ I'm here for my vaccination.

At the doctor's

❶ **Ich fühle mich nicht wohl.**
ikh fewh-le mikh nikht voel

❷ **Müssen Sie Untersuchungen machen?**
mews-sen zee oon-ter-zoo-khoong-en ma-khen

❸ **Ich bin herzkrank.**
ikh bin hairts-krunk

❹ **Muss ich ins Krankenhaus gehen?**
mooss ikh ins krunk-en-hows gay-en

❺ **Ich bin schwanger.**
ikh bin shvun-ger

❻ **Ich habe einen Impftermin.**
ikh hah-be ie-nen impf-terr-meen

1 WARM UP
1 minute

Say the months of the year in German (pp28–29).

Ask "**Is there an art gallery?**" (pp48–49) and "**How many brothers do you have?**" (pp14–15).

Zu Hause
AT HOME

Most Germans live in rented apartments (**die Wohnungen**); relatively few own their homes (**die Eigenheime**). The size of a dwelling is given in square meters and described in terms of the number of main rooms in addition to kitchen and bathroom: **2 ZKB** means **2 Zimmer, Küche, Badezimmer**, where the two rooms could be one bedroom and one living room

2 ◀◎)) MATCH AND REPEAT

Match the numbered items to the list, then test yourself, using the cover flap.

❶ **die Dachrinne**
dee dukh-rin-ne

❷ **das Fenster**
duss fens-ter

❸ **das Dach**
duss dukh

❹ **der Schornstein**
dair shorn-shtine

❺ **die Straße**
dee shtrah-se

❻ **die Tür**
dee tewr

❼ **der Blumenkasten**
dair bloo-men-kass-ten

❽ **die Mauer**
dee mow-er

gutter ❶   ❷ window   ❸ roof

❺ roadway   ❻ door   ❼ window box

Cultural tip A detached house is known as an **Einfamilienhaus** (*one-family house*), while a semi-detached house is called a **Zweifamilienhaus** (*two-family house*). A terraced house is a **Reihenhaus** (literally *house in a row*), while a high-rise block is a **Hochhaus**. The center of town is the **Innenstadt**, and a suburb is a **Vorstadt** or **Vorort**.

Wie hoch ist die monatliche Miete?
vee hoekh isst dee mo-naht-li-khe mee-te
What is the monthly rent?

5 minutes

4 chimney

wall **8**

Learn these phrases, then test yourself, using the cover flap.

Gibt es eine Garage?
geept es ie-ne ga-ra-je
Is there a garage?

Ab wann ist es frei?
up vunn isst es frie
When is it available?

Ist es möbliert?
isst es mer-bleert
Is it furnished?

Familiarize yourself with these words, then test yourself, using the cover flap.

room	**das Zimmer** *duss tsim-mer*
floor	**der Fußboden** *dair foos-bo-den*
ceiling	**die Decke** *dee dek-ke*
cellar	**der Keller** *dair kel-lerr*
attic	**der Dachboden** *dair dukh-boe-den*
bedroom	**das Schlafzimmer** *duss shlahf-tsim-mer*
bathroom	**das Badezimmer** *duss bah-de-tsim-mer*
living room	**das Wohnzimmer** *duss vohn-tsim-mer*
dining room	**das Esszimmer** *duss ess-tsim-mer*
kitchen	**die Küche** *dee kew-khe*

5 **SAY IT** **2** minutes

Is there a dining room?

Is it large?

Is it available in July?

Im Haus
IN THE HOUSE

1 WARM UP
1 minute

What is the German for "**room**" (pp58–59), "**desk**" (pp80–81), "**bed**" (pp60–61), and "**window**" (pp98–99)?

How do you say "**soft**," "**beautiful**," and "**big**" (pp64–65)?

If you're renting an apartment or a house in Germany, the rent is often described as **kalt** (*cold*). This means that utilities such as electricity and heating have to be paid for separately in addition to the rent. You will need to check this in advance with the landlord or agent. Furnished apartments in holiday resorts are known as **Ferienwohnung**, and rents for these tend to be all-inclusive.

2 ◀))) MATCH AND REPEAT
3 minutes

Match the numbered items to the list, then test yourself, using the cover flap.

❶ **der Kühlschrank**
dair kewl-shrunk

❷ **der Herd**
dair hairt

❸ **das Spülbecken**
duss shpewl-bek-ken

❹ **die Arbeitsfläche**
dee ar-biets-flay-khe

❺ **die Mikrowelle**
dee mee-kro-vel-le

❻ **der Backofen**
dair bak-oe-fen

❼ **der Tisch**
dair tish

❽ **der Stuhl**
dair shtool

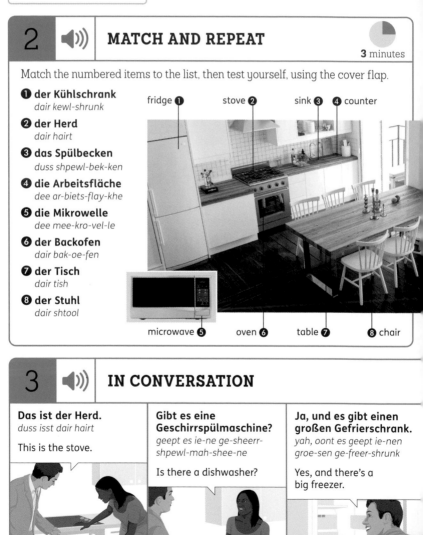

fridge ❶　　stove ❷　　sink ❸　　❹ counter

microwave ❺　　oven ❻　　table ❼　　❽ chair

3 ◀))) IN CONVERSATION

Das ist der Herd.
duss isst dair hairt

This is the stove.

Gibt es eine Geschirrspülmaschine?
geept es ie-ne ge-sheerr-shpewl-mah-shee-ne

Is there a dishwasher?

Ja, und es gibt einen großen Gefrierschrank.
yah, oont es geept ie-nen groe-sen ge-freer-shrunk

Yes, and there's a big freezer.

4 🔊 WORDS TO REMEMBER

2 minutes

Familiarize yourself with these words, then test yourself, using the cover flap.

Die Couch ist neu.
dee kowtch isst noy
The sofa is new.

wardrobe	**der Schrank** *dair shrunk*
armchair	**der Sessel** *dair zes-sel*
carpet	**der Teppich** *dair tep-pikh*
bathtub	**die Badewanne** *dee bah-de-vunn-ne*
toilet	**die Toilette (das WC)** *dee twah-let-te (duss vay-tsay)*
sink	**das Waschbecken** *duss vush-bek-ken*
curtains	**die Gardine** *dee gar-dee-ne*

5 🔊 USEFUL PHRASES

4 minutes

Learn these phrases, then test yourself, using the cover flap.

Is electricity included?	**Ist der Strom inbegriffen?** *isst dair shtroem in-be-grif-fen*
I don't like the curtains.	**Die Gardinen gefallen mir nicht.** *dee gar-dee-nen ge-fall-en meer nikht*
The stove doesn't work.	**Der Herd funktioniert nicht.** *dair hairt foonk-tsee-oe-neert nikht*

6 SAY IT

2 minutes

Is there a microwave?

I don't like the carpet.

What a soft sofa!

3 minutes

Ist das Spülbecken neu?
isst duss shpewl-bek-ken noy

Is the sink new?

Ja, natürlich. Und hier ist die Waschmaschine.
yah, na-tewr-likh. oont heer isst dee vush-mah-shee-ne

Yes, of course. And here's the washing machine.

Was für schöne Fliesen!
vuss fewr shern-ne flee-sen

What beautiful tiles!

Der Garten
THE GARDEN

Many Germans who live in apartments rent **Kleingärten** (allotments). Rather than just growing fruits and vegetables, they often turn them into attractive gardens, with flowerbeds, ponds, terraces, decks, and barbecues for entertaining. The yard of a block of apartments may be communal, while houses usually have private gardens. Check with the agent.

2 ◀)) WORDS TO REMEMBER
3 minutes

Familiarize yourself with these words, then test yourself, using the cover flap.

der Rasenmäher *dair rah-zen-may-er*	lawn mower
die Gabel *dee gah-bel*	fork
der Spaten *dair shpah-ten*	spade
der Rechen *dair re-khen*	rake
das Gartencenter *duss gar-ten-tsen-ter*	garden center

3 ◀)) MATCH AND REPEAT

Match the numbered items to the list, then test yourself, using the cover flap.

tree ❶

lawn ❷

path ❸   weeds ❹   terrace ❺

4 USEFUL PHRASES

4 minutes

Learn these phrases, then test yourself, using the cover flap.

Is the garden private?	**Ist der Garten privat?** *isst dair gar-ten pree-vaht*
The gardener comes once a week.	**Der Gärtner kommt einmal in der Woche.** *dair gairt-ner komt ine-mahl in dair vo-khe*
Can you please mow the lawn?	**Können Sie bitte den Rasen mähen?** *kern-nen zee bit-te dayn rah-zen may-en*
The garden needs watering.	**Der Garten muss gegossen werden.** *dair gar-ten mooss ge-gos-sen vair-den*

5 SAY IT

2 minutes

The lawn needs watering.
Are there any flowers?
The gardener comes on Fridays.

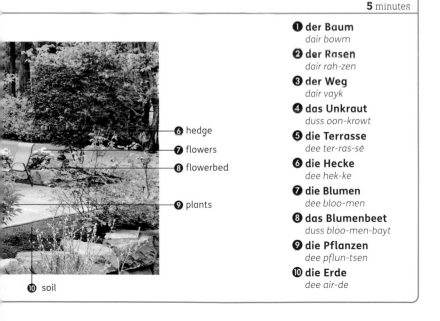

5 minutes

① **der Baum** *dair bowm*
② **der Rasen** *dair rah-zen*
③ **der Weg** *dair vayk*
④ **das Unkraut** *duss oon-krowt*
⑤ **die Terrasse** *dee ter-ras-se*
⑥ **die Hecke** *dee hek-ke*
⑦ **die Blumen** *dee bloo-men*
⑧ **das Blumenbeet** *duss bloo-men-bayt*
⑨ **die Pflanzen** *dee pflun-tsen*
⑩ **die Erde** *dee air-de*

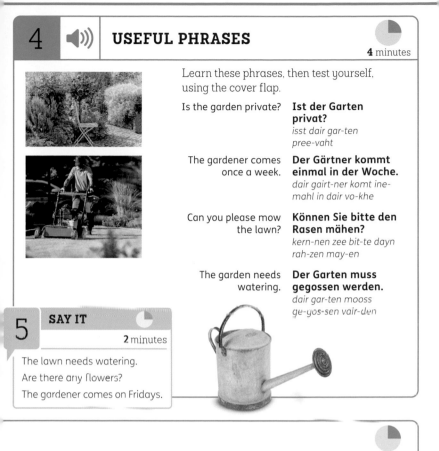

⑥ hedge
⑦ flowers
⑧ flowerbed
⑨ plants
⑩ soil

1 WARM UP
1 minute

Say "**My name is John**" (pp8–9).

How do you say "**Don't worry**" (pp94–95)?

What is "**your**" in German? (pp12–13).

Haustiere
PETS

Nearly half of all German households include at least one pet, which is often treated like a member of the family. Pet passports may be available to allow travelers to take their pets with them to Germany. Consult your vet for details of how to obtain the necessary vaccinations and paperwork.

2 MATCH AND REPEAT

Match the numbered animals to the list, then test yourself, using the cover flap.

❶ **das Kaninchen**
duss kah-neen-khen

❷ **der Fisch**
dair fish

❸ **der Vogel**
dair foe-gel

❹ **die Katze**
dee kut-se

❺ **der Hund**
dair hoont

❻ **der Hamster**
dair hums-ter

❷ fish

❶ rabbit

dog ❺

❹ cat

3 USEFUL PHRASES

4 minutes

Learn these phrases, then test yourself, using the cover flap.

Ist dieser Hund freundlich?
isst dee-zer hoont froynd-likh
Is this dog friendly?

Kann ich meinen Blindenhund mitbringen?
kunn ikh mie-nen blin-den-hoont mit-bring-en
Can I bring my guide dog?

Ich habe Angst vor Katzen.
ikh hah-be unkst foer kut-tsen
I'm frightened of cats.

Mein Hund beißt nicht.
mine hoont biesst nikht
My dog doesn't bite.

Diese Katze hat Flöhe.
dee-ze kut-se hut fler-we
This cat has fleas.

Cultural tip Many dogs in Germany are working or guard dogs, and you may encounter them tethered or roaming free. Approach farms and rural houses with care and keep away from the dog's territory. Look out for warning notices, such as **Warnung vor dem Hunde** (*beware of the dog*).

WARNUNG VOR DEM HUNDE

4 WORDS TO REMEMBER

4 minutes

Familiarize yourself with these words, then test yourself, using the cover flap.

3 minutes

bird **3**

hamster **6**

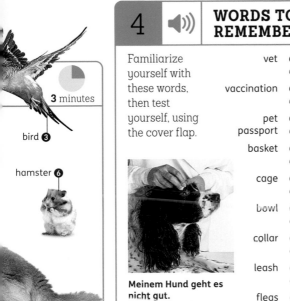

vet	**der Tierarzt**
	dair teer-artst
vaccination	**die Impfung**
	dee imp-foong
pet passport	**der Tierpass**
	dair teer-puss
basket	**der Korb**
	dair korp
cage	**der Käfig**
	dair kay-fik
bowl	**die Schüssel**
	dee shews-sel
collar	**das Halsband**
	duss hulls-bunt
leash	**die Leine**
	dee lie-ne
fleas	**die Flöhe**
	die fler-we

Meinem Hund geht es nicht gut.
mie-nem hoont gayt es nikht goot
My dog is not well.

5 PUT INTO PRACTICE

3 minutes

Complete this dialogue, then test yourself, using the cover flap.

Ist das Ihr Hund?
isst duss eer hoont

Is this your dog?

Say: Yes, he's named Hasso.

Ja, er heißt Hasso.
yah, er hiesst hus-so

Ich habe Angst vor Hunden.
ikh hah-be unkst foer hoon-den

I'm frightened of dogs.

Say: Don't worry, he's well behaved.

Keine Angst, er ist brav.
kie-ne unkst, er isst brahv

Antworten Answers
(Cover with flap)

Wiederholung
REVIEW AND REPEAT

Colors

❶ Schwarz
shvarts

❷ Weiß
vies

❸ Rot
roet

❹ Grün
grewn

❺ Gelb
gelp

1 COLORS

4 minutes

Fill in the blanks with the correct German masculine or feminine form of the color given in brackets.

❶ Haben Sie diese Jacke in _____ ? (black)

❷ Ich nehme den Rock in _____ . (white)

❸ Haben Sie die Hose in _____ ? (red)

❹ Nein, aber ich habe eine in _____ . (green)

❺ Ich möchte diese Schuhe in _____ . (yellow)

Kitchen

❶ der Kühlschrank
dair kewl-shrunk

❷ der Herd
dair hairt

❸ der Backofen
dair bak-oe-fen

❹ das Spülbecken
duss shpewl-bek-ken

❺ die Mikrowelle
dee mee-kro-vel-le

❻ der Tisch
dair tish

❼ der Stuhl
dair shtool

2 KITCHEN

Name these items in German.

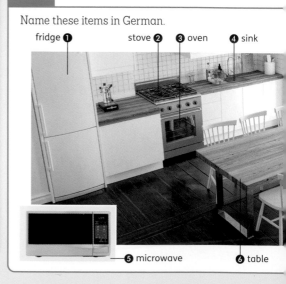

fridge ❶   stove ❷   ❸ oven   ❹ sink

❺ microwave   ❻ table

3 HOUSE

4 minutes

You are visiting a house in Germany. Join in the conversation, replying in German, following the numbered English prompts.

Hier ist das Wohnzimmer.
❶ What a lovely sofa.

Ja, und da ist auch eine große Küche.
❷ How many rooms?

Es gibt drei Zimmer.
❸ Do you have a garage?

Nein, aber da ist ein großer Garten.
❹ When is the house available?

Ab Juli.
❺ What is the monthly rent?

House

❶ **Was für eine schöne Couch!**
vuss fewr ie-ne shern-ne kowtch

❷ **Wie viele Zimmer gibt es?**
vee fee-le tsim-mer geept es

❸ **Haben Sie eine Garage?**
hah-ben zee ie-ne ga-ra-je

❹ **Ab wann ist das Haus frei?**
up vunn isst duss hows frie

❺ **Wie hoch ist die monatliche Miete?**
vee hoekh isst dee mo-naht-li-khe mee-te

---

4 minutes

4 AT HOME

3 minutes

Name these things in German.

❶ washing machine ❹ dining room
❷ sofa   ❺ tree
❸ attic   ❻ garden

❼ chair

At home

❶ **die Waschmaschine**
dee vush-mah-shee-ne

❷ **die Couch**
dee kowtch

❸ **der Dachboden**
dair dukh-boe-den

❹ **das Esszimmer**
duss es-tsim-mer

❺ **der Baum**
dair bowm

❻ **der Garten**
dair gar-ten

1 **WARM UP**

1 minute

Ask "**How do I get to the bank?**" and "**How do I get to the post office?**" (pp50–51, pp68–69).

What's the German for "**passport**" (pp54–55)?

Ask "**What time is the meeting?**" (pp30–31).

Wechselstube, Bank und Post
BUREAU DE CHANGE, BANK, AND MAIL

You can exchange one currency for another at a bureau de change. You can also get cash at a bank ATM but may be charged a fee. The post office also serves as a bank (with ATMs at some branches), in addition to printing stamps on demand. Stamps may also be available at **der Zeitungskiosk** (p68).

2 ◀)) **WORDS TO REMEMBER**: MAIL

3 minutes

Familiarize yourself with these words, then test yourself, using the cover flap.

der Briefkasten mailbox
dair breef-kuss-ten

die Briefmarken stamps
dee breef-mar-ken

der Umschlag envelope
dair oom-shlahk

per Luftpost air mail
pair looft-posst

per Einschreiben registered
pair ine-shrie-ben mail

die Postleitzahl postcode
dee posst-lite-tsahl

der/die Briefträger(in) mailman/
dair/dee breef-tray-ger(in) mailwoman

die Postkarte postcard
dee posst-kar-te

das Paket package
duss pa-kayt

Wie hoch ist das Porto nach England?
vee hoekh isst duss por-toe nahkh eng-lant
What is the postage for England?

3 ◀)) **IN CONVERSATION**: BUREAU DE CHANGE

Ich möchte Geld wechseln.
ikh merkh-te gelt vek-zeln

I would like to change some money.

Was möchten Sie wechseln?
vuss merkh-ten zee vek-zeln

What would you like to exchange?

Ich möchte für fünfhunder Dollar Euro kaufen.
ikh merkh-te fewr fewnf-hoon-dairt doll-lar oy-roe kow-fen

I would like to buy euros for five hundred dollars.

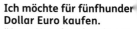

4 🔊 **WORDS TO REMEMBER**: BANK

2 minutes

Familiarize yourself with these words, then test yourself, using the cover flap.

die Debit-Karte
dee de-bit-kar-te
debit card

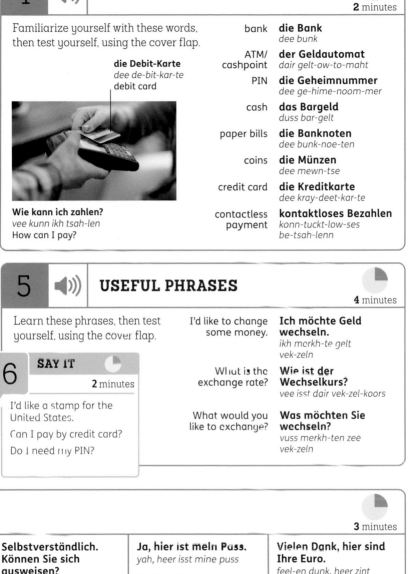

Wie kann ich zahlen?
vee kunn ikh tsah-len
How can I pay?

bank	**die Bank** *dee bunk*
ATM/ cashpoint	**der Geldautomat** *dair gelt-ow-to-maht*
PIN	**die Geheimnummer** *dee ge-hime-noom-mer*
cash	**das Bargeld** *duss bar-gelt*
paper bills	**die Banknoten** *dee bunk-noe-ten*
coins	**die Münzen** *dee mewn-tse*
credit card	**die Kreditkarte** *dee kray-deet-kar-te*
contactless payment	**kontaktloses Bezahlen** *konn-tuckt-low-ses be-tsah-lenn*

5 🔊 **USEFUL PHRASES**

4 minutes

Learn these phrases, then test yourself, using the cover flap.

6 **SAY IT**

2 minutes

I'd like a stamp for the United States.

Can I pay by credit card?

Do I need my PIN?

I'd like to change some money. **Ich möchte Geld wechseln.** *ikh merkh-te gelt vek-zeln*

What is the exchange rate? **Wie ist der Wechselkurs?** *vee isst dair vek-zel-koors*

What would you like to exchange? **Was möchten Sie wechseln?** *vuss merkh-ten zee vek-zeln*

3 minutes

Selbstverständlich. Können Sie sich ausweisen?
zelpst-fer-shtend-likh. kern-nen zee zikh ows-vie-zen

Of course. Do you have any identification?

Ja, hier ist mein Pass.
yah, heer isst mine puss

Yes, here is my passport.

Vielen Dank, hier sind Ihre Euro.
feel-en dunk, heer zint ee-re oy-roe

Thank you, here are your euros.

1 WARM UP
1 minute

What's the German for "**It doesn't work**" (pp60–61)?

Say "**today**" and "**tomorrow**" in German (pp28–29).

Dienstleistungen
SERVICES

You can combine the German words on these pages with the vocabulary you learned in week 10 to help you explain basic problems and arrange most repairs. When organizing building work or a repair, it's a good idea to agree on the price and method of payment in advance.

2 🔊 WORDS TO REMEMBER:
SERVICES

4 minutes

Familiarize yourself with these words, then test yourself, using the cover flap. The feminine form is given in brackets.

der/die Klempner(in) *dair/dee klemp-ner(in)*	plumber
der/die Elektriker(in) *dair/dee ay-lek-tree-ker(in)*	electrician
der/die Mechaniker(in) *dair/dee me-khah-nee-ker(in)*	mechanic
der/die Bauarbeiter(in) *dair/dee bow-ar-bie-ter(in)*	builder
der/die Maler(in) *dair/dee mah-ler(in)*	painter/ decorator
der/die Schreiner(in) *dair/dee shrie-ner(in)*	carpenter
der/die Maurer(in) *dair/dee mow-rer(in)*	bricklayer
die Haushaltshilfe *dee hous-hahlts-hil-feh*	cleaning staff

Ich brauche keinen Mechaniker.
ikh brow-khe kie-nen me-khah-nee-ker
I don't need a mechanic.

3 🔊 IN CONVERSATION

Die Waschmaschine funktioniert nicht.
dee vush-mah-shee-ne foonk-tsee-oen-eert nikht

The washing machine is not working.

Ja, die Pumpe ist kaputt.
yah, dee poom-pe isst ka-poott

Yes, the pump is broken.

Können Sie die reparieren?
kern-nen zee dee re-pah-ree-ren

Can you repair it?

4 USEFUL PHRASES

3 minutes

Learn these phrases, then test yourself, using the cover flap.

Please clean the bathroom.	**Bitte putzen Sie das Badezimmer.**	*bit-te poot-tsen zee duss bah-de-tsim-mer*
Can you repair the boiler?	**Können Sie den Boiler reparieren?**	*kern-nen zee dayn boi-ler re-pah-ree-ren*
Do you know a good electrician?	**Kennen Sie einen guten Elektriker?**	*ken-nen zee ie-nen goo-ten ay-lek-tree-ker*

Wo kann ich das reparieren lassen?
voe kunn ikh duss re-pah-ree-ren luss-sen
Where can I get this repaired?

5 PUT INTO PRACTICE

4 minutes

Complete this dialogue, then test yourself, using the cover flap.

Ihr Tor ist kaputt.
eer tohr isst ka-poott
Your gate is broken.

Ask: Do you know a good carpenter?

Kennen Sie einen guten Schreiner?
ken-nen zee ie-nen goo-ten shrie-ner

Ja, es gibt einen im Ort.
yah, es geept ie-nen im ort
Yes, there is one in the village.

Ask: Do you have the telephone number?

Haben Sie die Telefonnummer?
hah ben zee dee tay-lay-foen-noom-mer

---

3 minutes

Nein, Sie brauchen eine neue.	**Können Sie das heute machen?**	**Nein, ich komme morgen wieder.**
nine, zee brow-khen ie-ne noy-e	*kern-nen zee duss hoy-te ma-khen*	*nine, ikh kom-me mor-gen vee-der*
No, you'll need a new one.	Can you do it today?	No, I'll come back tomorrow.

Kommen
TO COME

The verb **kommen** (*to come*) is another important verb. Apart from its literal meaning, it can mean *happen*, as in *how come?* In addition, it can be combined with adverbs, such as **her** (*here*) or **herein** (*in*). It also occurs in many frequently used expressions, such as **das kommt davon, dass…** (*that's because…*).

1 WARM UP
1 minute

Ask "**How do I get to the library?**" (pp48–49).

How do you say "**cleaning staff**" (pp110–11)?

Say "**It's 9:30**," "**10:45**," and "**12:00**" (pp10–11 and pp30–31).

2 🔊 **KOMMEN**: TO COME
6 minutes

Practice **kommen** (*to come*) and the sample sentences, then test yourself, using the cover flap.

ich komme
ikh kom-me
I come

du kommst
doo komst
you come (informal singular)

er/sie/es kommt
air/zee/es komt
he/she/it comes

wir kommen
veer kom-men
we come

ihr kommt
eer komt
you come (informal plural)

Sie/sie kommen
zee kom-men
you come (formal singular or plural)/ they come

Ich komme aus London.
ikh kom-me ows london
I come from London.

Wir kommen jeden Dienstag.
veer kom-men yay-den deens-tahk
We come every Tuesday.

Er kommt aus China.
air komt ows khee-nah
He comes from China.

Sie kommen mit dem Zug.
zee kom-men mit daym tsook
They come by train.

Conversational tip Kommen is used in many (usually friendly) commands, such as **kommen Sie herein** (*come in*) or **komm her** (*come here*). Often, it can also appear together with a second verb, when in English we might link two verbs with *and*—for example, **komm setz dich** (*come and sit down*) or **kommt essen** (*come and eat*).

3 USEFUL PHRASES

4 minutes

Learn these phrases, then test yourself, using the cover flap.

Die Haushaltshilfe kommt jeden Montag.
dee hous-hahlts-hil-feh komt yay-den moen-tahk
The cleaning staff come every Monday.

When can I come?	**Wann kann ich kommen?** *vunn kunn ikh kom-men*
Where does she come from?	**Woher kommt sie?** *vo-hair komt zee*
Why don't you come in? (informal/formal)	**Komm doch herein/ Kommen Sie doch herein.** *kom dokh hair-rien/ kom-men zee dokh hair-rien*
Come with me. (informal/formal)	**Komm mit/ Kommen Sie mit.** *kom mit/ kom-men zee mit*

4 PUT INTO PRACTICE

4 minutes

Complete this dialogue, then test yourself, using the cover flap.

Guten Tag, Friseursalon Hannelore.
goo-ten tahk, fri-zer-zah-long hun-ne-loe-re

Hello, this is Hannelore's hair salon.

Say: I'd like an appointment.

Ich hätte gern einen Termin.
ikh het-te gairn ie-nen ter-meen

Wann möchten Sie kommen?
vunn merkh-ten zee kom-men

When would you like to come?

Ask: Can I come today?

Kann ich heute kommen?
kunn ikh hoy-te kom-men

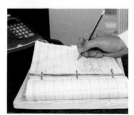

Natürlich. Um wie viel Uhr?
na-tewr-likh. oomm vee-feel oor

Yes, of course. What time?

Say: At 10:30am.

Um halb elf.
oomm hulp elf

Polizei und Verbrechen
POLICE AND CRIME

If you are the victim of a crime or are in a traffic accident in Germany, report it to the nearest police station or call 110. Be aware that the **Verkehrspolizei** (*traffic police*) carry out checks and impose fines for traffic regulation violations.

1 WARM UP
1 minute

What's the German for "**big/tall**" and "**small/short**" (pp64–65)?

Say "**The room is big**" and "**The bed is small**" (pp64–65).

2 ◀))) WORDS TO REMEMBER: CRIME
4 minutes

Familiarize yourself with these words, then test yourself, using the cover flap.

der Diebstahl *dair deep-shtahl*	burglary
der Polizeibericht *dair po-lee-tsie-be-rikht*	police report
der/die Dieb(in) *dair/dee deep(in)*	thief
die Polizei *dee po-lee-tsie*	police
die Aussage *dee ows-zah-ge*	statement
der/die Zeuge/Zeugin *dair/dee tsoy-ge/tsoy-ginn*	witness
der/die Rechtsanwalt/ Rechtsanwältin *dair/dee rekhts-un-vullt/ rekhts-un-vel-tin*	lawyer

Ich brauche einen Rechtsanwalt.
ikh brow-khe ie-nen rekhts-un-vullt
I need a lawyer.

3 ◀))) USEFUL PHRASES
3 minutes

Learn these phrases, then test yourself, using the cover flap.

Ich bin bestohlen worden. *ikh bin be-shtoe-len vor-den*	I've been robbed.
Was ist gestohlen worden? *vuss isst ge-shtoe-len vor-den*	What was stolen?
Haben Sie den Täter gesehen? *hah-ben zee den tay-ter ge-zay-en*	Did you see who did it?
Wann ist es passiert? *vunn isst es puss-seert*	When did it happen?

die Kamera
dee kamera
camera

der Geldbeutel
dair gelt-boy-tel
purse

4 🔊 WORDS TO REMEMBER: APPEARANCE

5 minutes

Familiarize yourself with these words, then test yourself, using the cover flap. Remember that adjectives may have different endings if placed before a noun (p64).

Sie hat lange, schwarze Haare.
zee hut lun-ge, shvar-tse hah-re
She has long black hair.

Er hat eine Glatze und einen Bart.
air hut ie-ne glut-se oont ie-nen bart
He is bald and has a beard.

man	**der Mann** *dair munn*
woman	**die Frau** *dee frow*
tall	**groß** *groes*
short	**klein** *kline*
young	**jung** *yoong*
old	**alt** *ullt*
fat	**dick** *dick*
thin	**dünn** *dewnn*
long/short hair	**lange/kurze Haare** *lun-ge/koor-tse hah-re*
glasses	**die Brille** *dee bril-le*
beard	**der Bart** *dair bart*

5 🔊 PUT INTO PRACTICE

2 minutes

Complete this dialogue, then test yourself, using the cover flap.

Wie sah er aus? **Klein und dick.**
vee zah air ows *kline oont dick*
What did he look like?
Say: Short and fat.

Und die Haare? **Lang, mit Bart.**
oont dee hah-re *lung, mit bart*
And the hair?
Say: Long, with a beard.

Cultural tip If you have a car accident or serious breakdown on a highway, use one of the special telephones that you can find at regular intervals. Elsewhere, phone 110 for the police or 112 for the ambulance or fire service. Both emergency numbers are free calls from landlines, pay phones, and cell phone. Operators can usually speak English as well as German.

Antworten *Answers*
(Cover with flap)

Wiederholung
REVIEW AND REPEAT

To come

❶ komme
kom-me

❷ kommt
komt

❸ kommen
kom-men

❹ kommt
komt

❺ kommen
kom-men

1 TO COME

3 minutes

Fill in the blanks with the correct form of **kommen** (*to come*).

❶ Ich _____ um vier Uhr.

❷ Der Gärtner _____ einmal in der Woche.

❸ Wir _____ Dienstag zum Essen.

❹ _____ ihr mit?

❺ Meine Eltern _____ mit dem Zug.

Bank and post

❶ die Postkarten
dee posst-kar-ten

❷ das Paket
duss pa-kayt

❸ die Briefmarken
dee breef-mar-ken

❹ die Debit-Karte
dee de-bit-kar-te

2 BANK AND POST

4 minutes

Name these items in German.

postcards **❶**   **❷** package

stamps **❸**

debit card **❹**

3 APPEARANCE

4 minutes

What do these sentences mean?

❶ Der Mann ist groß und dünn.

❷ Sie hat kurze Haare und eine Brille.

❸ Ich bin klein und habe lange Haare.

❹ Sie ist alt und dick.

❺ Er hat eine Glatze und einen Bart.

Appearance

❶ The man is tall and thin.

❷ She has short hair and glasses.

❸ I'm short, and I have long hair.

❹ She is old and fat.

❺ He is bald and has a beard.

4 THE PHARMACY

4 minutes

You are asking a pharmacist for advice. Join in the conversation, replying in German, following the numbered English prompts.

Guten Tag, kann ich Ihnen helfen?
❶ I have a cough.
Und haben Sie auch Schnupfen?
❷ No, but I have a headache.
Nehmen Sie diese Tabletten.
❸ Do you have that as a syrup?
Selbstverständlich. Bitte sehr.
❹ Thank you. How much is that?
Sechs Euro.
❺ Here you are. Goodbye.

The pharmacy

❶ **Ich habe Husten.**
ikh hah-be hoos-ten

❷ **Nein, aber ich habe Kopfschmerzen.**
nine, ah-ber ikh hah-be kopf-shmairt-sen

❸ **Haben Sie das auch als Sirup?**
hah-ben zee duss owkh ulls zee-roop

❹ **Danke. Was macht das?**
dun-ke. vuss mukht duss

❺ **Bitte sehr. Auf Wiedersehen.**
bit-te zair. owf vee-der-zay-en

Die Freizeit
LEISURE TIME

What is the German for "**museum**" and "**art gallery**" (pp48–49)?

Say "**I don't like the curtains**" (pp100–101).

Ask "**Do you want…?**" informally (pp24–25).

In Germany, the arts—from opera and avant-garde music to drama and performance art—are avidly followed and receive great public support. Be prepared for any of these topics to be the subject of conversation in social situations. **Lust haben**, meaning to *like the idea of doing something*, is a useful expression for discussing leisure activities.

2 ◀))) WORDS TO REMEMBER

Familiarize yourself with these words, then test yourself, using the cover flap.

das Theater *duss tay-ah-ter*	theater
die Musik *dee moo-zeek*	music
die Kunst *dee koonst*	art
das Kino *duss kee-no*	cinema
die Videospiele *dee vee-dee-oh-shpee-le*	video games
der Nachtclub *dair nakht-kloob*	nightclub
der Sport *dair shport*	sport
die Besichtigungen *dee be-zikh-tee-goong-en*	sightseeing

der Rang
dair rung
balcony

das Publikum
duss poo-blee-koomm
audience

das Parkett
duss par-ket
orchestra

Ich liebe Opern.
ikh lee-be oh-pairn
I love opera.

3 ◀))) IN CONVERSATION

Hi Antonia, hast du Lust, heute Morgen Tennis zu spielen?
hi un-toh-nee-ya, husst doo loost, hoy-te mor-gen ten-nis tsoo shpee-len

Hi Antonia, do you want to play tennis this morning?

Nein danke, ich habe andere Pläne.
nine dun-ke, ikh hah-be un-dair-e plae-ne

No thank you, I have other plans.

Oh, was hast du denn vor?
oh, vuss husst doo denn for

Oh, what are you going to do?

5 SAY IT
2 minutes

I'm interested in music.
I prefer sports.
I like the theater.
Shopping bores me!

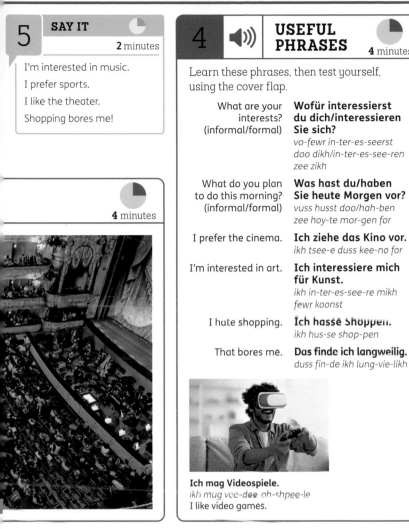

4 🔊 USEFUL PHRASES
4 minutes

Learn these phrases, then test yourself, using the cover flap.

What are your interests? (informal/formal) — **Wofür interessierst du dich/interessieren Sie sich?**
vo-fewr in-ter-es-seerst doo dikh/in-ter-es-see-ren zee zikh

What do you plan to do this morning? (informal/formal) — **Was hast du/haben Sie heute Morgen vor?**
vuss husst doo/hah-ben zee hoy-te mor-gen for

I prefer the cinema. — **Ich ziehe das Kino vor.**
ikh tsee-e duss kee-no for

I'm interested in art. — **Ich interessiere mich für Kunst.**
ikh in-ter-es-see-re mikh fewr koonst

I hate shopping. — **Ich hasse Shoppen.**
ikh hus-se shop-pen

That bores me. — **Das finde ich langweilig.**
duss fin-de ikh lung-vie-likh

Ich mag Videospiele.
ikh mug vee-dee-oh-shpee-le
I like video games.

4 minutes

Ich gehe auf Besichtigungstour! Möchtest du mitkommen?
ikh gay-he owf be-zikh-tee-goongs-toor. merkh-test doo mit-kom-men

I am going sightseeing! Do you want to join me?

Das klingt schön, aber ich möchte Tennis spielen.
duss klingt shern, ah-ber ikh merkh-te ten-nis shpee-len

That sounds nice, but I want to play tennis.

Kein Problem, viel Spaß!
kine pro-blaym, feel shpahss

No problem, enjoy your game!

Sport und Hobbys
SPORT AND HOBBIES

1 **WARM UP**
1 minute

Ask "**Do you** (formal) **want to play tennis?**" (pp118–119).

Say "**I like the cinema,**" "**I prefer sightseeing,**" and "**That doesn't interest me**" (pp118–119).

Germany is a nation of sports enthusiasts. Many people cycle, jog, swim, or work out at the gym, and many follow sports as spectators. Hiking is very popular, as are basketball, skiing, and ice hockey. The verb **spielen** (*to play*) is mainly used for ball games, while **gehen** (*to go*) is often used for activities like hiking, swimming, or skiing.

2 ◀))) **WORDS TO REMEMBER:** SPORTS
5 minutes

Familiarize yourself with these words, then test yourself, using the cover flap.

das T-Shirt
duss tee-shirt
T-shirt

die kurze Hose
dee koor-tse hoe-se
shorts

der Fußball *dair foos-bull*	soccer
das Tennis *duss ten-nis*	tennis
das Schwimmen *duss shvim-men*	swimming
das Segeln *duss zay-geln*	sailing
das Angeln *duss ung-eln*	fishing
das Radfahren *duss raht-fah-ren*	cycling
das Wandern *duss vunn-dairn*	hiking
das Skifahren *duss shee-fah-ren*	skiing
das Golf *duss golf*	golf

die Fußballschuhe
dee foos-bull-shoo-e
soccer shoes

Ich spiele jeden Tag Fußball.
ikh shpee-le yay-den tahk foos-bull
I play soccer every day.

3 ◀))) **USEFUL PHRASES**
2 minutes

Learn these phrases, then test yourself, using the cover flap.

Ich spiele Basketball.
ikh shpee-le basket-bull.
I play basketball.

Wir spielen gern Tennis.
veer shpee-len gairn ten-nis.
We like playing tennis.

Sie malt.
zee mahlt.
She paints.

4 WORDS TO REMEMBER: HOBBIES

4 minutes

Familiarize yourself with these words and phrases, then test yourself, using the cover flap.

do-it-yourself	**das Basteln** *duss bass-teln*
pottery	**die Töpferei** *dee ter-pfe-rie*
flower arranging	**das Blumenstecken** *duss bloo-men-shtek-en*
gardening	**die Gartenarbeit** *dee gar-ten-ar-biet*
singing	**das Singen** *duss zing-en*

Can I join a club?	**Kann ich einem Klub beitreten?** *kunn ikh ien-em kloop bie-tray-ten*
Do I have to be a member?	**Muss man Mitglied sein?** *moos munn mit-gleet zine*
Can I rent the equipment?	**Kann ich die Ausrüstung mieten?** *kumm ikh dee ows-rews-toong mee-ten*

Heute ist schönes Wetter zum Wandern.
hoy-te isst shern-nes vetter tsoom vunn-dairn
It's nice weather for hiking today.

5 PUT INTO PRACTICE

3 minutes

Complete this dialogue, then test yourself, using the cover flap.

Was machst du gern?
vuss mukhst doo gairn
What do you like doing?
Say: I like playing tennis.

Ich spiele gern Tennis.
ikh shpee-le gairn ten-nis

Spielst du auch Golf?
shpeelst doo owkh golf
Do you also play golf?
Say: No, I play soccer.

Nein, ich spiele Fußball.
nine, ikh shpee-le foos-bull

Spielst du oft?
shpeelst doo oft
Do you play often?
Say: Yes, I play every week.

Ja, ich spiele jede Woche.
yah, ikh shpee-le yay-de vokh-e

1 WARM UP
1 minute

Say "**my husband**" and "**my wife**" (pp10–11).

How do you say "**lunch**" and "**dinner**" in German (pp20–21)?

Say "**Sorry, I'm busy**" (pp32–33).

Leute treffen
SOCIALIZING

In Germany, a lot of socializing takes place outside the home. People meet up to go to a play, a film, or a sports event, or they go out for a meal or a drink. Friends and family also invite each other for meals, especially for special occasions. It is best to use the more polite **Sie** form to talk to people until they call you **du**, at which point you can reciprocate.

2 ◀)) USEFUL PHRASES

Learn these phrases, then test yourself, using the cover flap.

Ich möchte Sie zum Abendessen einladen.
ikh merkh-te zee tsoom ah-bent-ess-sen ine-lah-den
I'd like to invite you to dinner.

Sind Sie nächsten Mittwoch frei?
zint zee nayks-ten mit-vokh frie
Are you free next Wednesday?

Vielleicht ein andermal.
feel-liekht ine un-der-mahl
Perhaps another time.

Danke für die Einladung.
dun-ke fewr dee ine-lah-doong.
Thank you for inviting us.

die Gastgeberin
dee gust-gay-be-rin
hostess

3 ◀)) IN CONVERSATION

Möchten Sie zum Mittagessen kommen?
merkh-ten zee tsoom mit-tahk-ess-sen kom-men

Would you like to come to lunch?

Mit Vergnügen. Wann?
mit fer-g-new-gen. vunn

I'd be delighted. When?

Wie wär's mit Donnerstag?
vee vairs mit don-ners-tahk

What about Thursday?

Cultural tip When you visit someone for the first time, it is usual to take flowers or wine. Having seen their house, you can take a slightly more personal gift if invited again.

3 minutes

der Gast
dair gust
guest

---

4 🔊 WORDS TO REMEMBER
3 minutes

Familiarize yourself with these words, then test yourself, using the cover flap.

party	**die Party** *dee par-tee*
dinner party	**das Abendessen** *duss ah-bent-ess-sen*
cocktail party	**die Cocktailparty** *dee kock-tayl-par-tee*
reception	**der Empfang** *dair emp-fung*
invitation	**die Einladung** *dee ine-lah-doong*

---

5 🔊 PUT INTO PRACTICE
5 minutes

Complete this dialogue, then test yourself, using the cover flap.

Können Sie heute Abend zu einem Empfang kommen?
ker-nen zee hoy-te ah-bent tsoo ie-nem emp-fung kom-men

Can you come to a reception tonight?

Say: Yes, I'd love to.

Ja, gerne.
yah, gair-ne

Er beginnt um zwanzig Uhr.
er be-ginnt oom tsvun tsik oor

It starts at eight o'clock.

Ask: What should I wear?

Was trägt man?
vuss traygt munn

---

3 minutes

Das passt mir gut.
duss pusst meer goot

That's good for me.

Bringen Sie Ihren Mann mit.
brin-gen zee ee-ren munn mit

Bring your husband.

Danke. Um wie viel Uhr?
dun-ke. oom vee-feel oor

Thank you. At what time?

Wiederholung
REVIEW AND REPEAT

Animals

❶ die Katze
dee kut-se

❷ der Hamster
dair hums-ter

❸ der Fisch
dair fish

❹ der Vogel
dair foh-gel

❺ das Kaninchen
duss kah-neen-khen

❻ der Hund
dair hoont

1 ANIMALS

Name these animals in German.

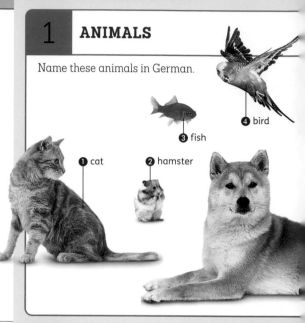

❸ fish

❹ bird

❶ cat

❷ hamster

I like...

❶ Ich spiele Basketball.
ikh shpee-le basket-bull

❷ Ich spiele gern Tennis.
ikh shpee-le gairn ten-nis

❸ Ich mag kein Fußball.
ikh mug kine foos-bull

❹ Ich male gern.
ikh mah-le gairn

2 I LIKE...

4 minutes

Say these sentences in German.

❶ I play basketball.
❷ I like playing tennis.
❸ I don't like soccer.
❹ I like painting.

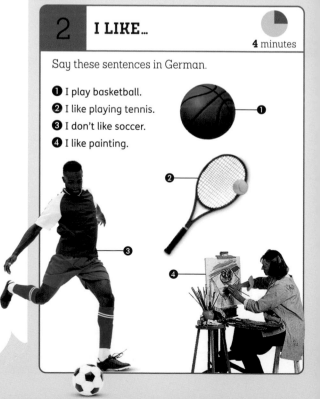

3 minutes

❺ rabbit

❻ dog

3 LEISURE
4 minutes

Name these sports and leisure activities in German.

❶ sailing
❷ art
❸ sightseeing
❹ cinema
❺ hiking
❻ swimming

Leisure
❶ **das Segeln**
duss zay-geln
❷ **die Kunst**
dee koonst
❸ **die Besichtigungen**
dee be-zikh-tee-goong-en
❹ **das Kino**
duss kee-no
❺ **das Wandern**
duss vunn-dairn
❻ **das Schwimmen**
duss shvim-men

4 AN INVITATION
4 minutes

You are invited for dinner. Join in the conversation, replying in German, following the numbered English prompts.

Möchten Sie am Freitag zum Essen kommen?
❶ I'm sorry, I'm busy.
Wie wär's mit Samstag?
❷ I'd be delighted.
Bringen Sie Ihre Kinder mit.
❸ Thank you. At what time?
Um halb eins.
❹ That's good for me.

An invitation
❶ **Es tut mir leid, ich habe schon etwas vor.**
es toot meer liet, ikh hah-be shoen et-vuss for
❷ **Mit Vergnügen.**
mit fer-g-new-gen
❸ **Danke. Um wieviel Uhr?**
dun-ke. oom vee-feel oor
❹ **Ja, das passt mir.**
yah, duss pusst meer

Reinforce and progress

Regular practice is the key to maintaining and advancing your language skills. In this section, you will find a variety of suggestions for reinforcing and extending your knowledge of German. Many involve returning to exercises in the book and extending their scope by using the dictionaries. Go back through the lessons in a different order, mix and match activities to make up your own daily 15-minute program, or focus on topics that are of particular relevance to your current needs.

1   WARM UP

1 minute

Say "**He is**" and "**They are**" (pp14–15).

Say "**He is not**" and "**They are not**" (pp14–15).

What is German for "**the children**" (pp10–11)?

Match, repeat, and extend
Remind yourself of words related to specific topics by returning to the Match and Repeat and Words to Remember exercises. Test yourself, using the cover flap. Discover new words in that area by referring to the dictionary and menu guide.

Keep warmed up
Revisit the Warm Up boxes to remind yourself of key words and phrases. Make sure you work your way through all of them on a regular basis.

2   🔊   MATCH AND REPEAT

5 minutes

Match the numbered items to the list, then test yourself, using the cover flap.

❶ **die Dachrinne**
dee dukh-rin-ne

❷ **das Fenster**
duss fens-ter

❸ **das Dach**
duss dukh

❹ **der Schornstein**
dair shorn-shtine

❺ **die Straße**
dee shtrah-se

❻ **die Tür**
dee tewr

❼ **der Blumenkasten**
dair bloo-men-kass-ten

❽ **die Mauer**
dee mow-er

gutter ❶   ❷ window   ❸ roof   ❹ chimney

❺ roadway   ❻ door   ❼ window box   wall ❽

3   🔊   IN CONVERSATION

Carry on conversing
Reread the In Conversation panels. Say both parts of the conversation, paying attention to the pronunciation. Where possible, try incorporating new words from the dictionary.

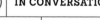

Guten Tag, ich bin Professor Stein.
goo-ten tahk, ikh bin pro-fes-sor shtien

Hello, I'm Professor Stein.

An welcher Universität arbeiten Sie?
un vel-kher oo-nee-vair-zee-tayt ar-bie-ten zee

Which university do you work at?

Ich bin Delegierte der Humboldt-Universität.
ikh bin day-lay-geer-te dair hoomm-bolt-oo-nee-vair-zee-tayt

I'm a delegate from Humboldt University.

Practice words and phrases
Return to the Words to Remember, Useful Phrases, and Put into Practice exercises. Test yourself, using the cover flap. When you are confident, devise your own versions of the phrases, using new words from the dictionary.

4 🔊 USEFUL PHRASES: MONTHS

2 minutes

Learn these phrases, then test yourself, using the cover flap.

| My children are on vacation in August. | **Meine Kinder haben im August Ferien.** *mye-ne kin-der hah-ben im August fay-ree-en* |
| My birthday is in June. | **Mein Geburtstag ist im Juni.** *mine ge-boorts-tahk isst im yoo-nee* |

5 SAY IT

2 minutes

I'm doing research in medicine.
I studied literature.
She's the professor.

Say it again
The Say It exercises are a useful instant reminder for each lesson. Practice these, using your own vocabulary variations from the dictionary or elsewhere in the lesson.

6 BE OR HAVE

5 minutes

Fill in the blanks with the correct form of **haben** (*to have*) or **sein** (*to be*).

❶ Das _____ mein Mann.
❷ Sie (she) _____ müde.
❸ Wir _____ Deutsche.
❹ _____ Sie eine Besprechung?
❺ Sie (she) _____ eine Schwägerin.
❻ Ich _____ kein Handy.
❼ _____ du glücklich?
❽ Ich _____ verheiratet.

Review and repeat again
Work through a Review and Repeat lesson as a way of reinforcing words and phrases presented in the course. Return to the main lesson for any topic about which you are no longer confident.

Using other resources

As well as working with this book, try the following language extension ideas:

Visit a German-speaking country and try out your new skills with native speakers. Find out whether there is a German community near you. There may be shops, cafés, restaurants, and clubs. Try to visit some of these and use your German to order food and drink and strike up conversations. Most native speakers will be happy to speak German to you.

Join a language class or club. There are usually evening and day classes available at a variety of different levels. Or you could start a club yourself if you have friends who are also interested in keeping up their German.

Look at German magazines and newspapers. The pictures will help you understand the text. Advertisements are also a useful way of expanding your vocabulary.

Use the Internet, where you can find all kinds of websites for learning languages, some of which offer free online help and activities. You can also find German websites for everything from renting a house to shampooing your pet. You can even access German radio and TV stations online. Start by going to a search engine and typing in a subject that interests you, or give yourself a challenge, such as finding a two-bedroom house for rent by the river in Hamburg.

Menu guide

This guide lists the most common terms you may encounter on German menus or when shopping for food. If you can't find an exact phrase, try looking up its component parts.

A

Aal *eel*
am Spieß *on the spit*
Ananas *pineapples*
Apfel *apple*
Apfel im Schlafrock *baked apple in puff pastry*
Apfelsaft *apple juice*
Apfelsinen *oranges*
Apfelstrudel *apple strudel*
Apfeltasche *apple turnover*
Apfelwein *cider*
Aprikosen *apricots*
Arme Ritter *bread soaked in milk and egg, then fried*
Artischocken *artichokes*
Auberginen *eggplants*
Auflauf *baked pudding or casserole*
Aufschnitt *cold meats*
Austern *oysters*

B

Backobst *dried fruit*
Backpflaume *prune*
Baiser *meringue*
Balkansalat *cabbage and pepper salad*
Bananen *bananas*
Bandnudeln *ribbon noodles*
Basilikum *basil*
Bauernauflauf *bacon and potato casserole*
Bauernfrühstück *fried potato, bacon, and egg*
Bauernomelett *bacon and potato omelet*
Bechamelkartoffeln *potatoes in creamy sauce*
Bedienung *service*
Beilagen *side dishes*
Berliner *jelly doughnut*
Bier *beer*
Birnen *pears*
Biskuit *sponge cake*
Bismarckhering *filleted pickled herring*
Blätterteig *puff pastry*
blau *cooked in vinegar; virtually raw (steak)*
Blumenkohl *cauliflower*
blutig *rare*
Blutwurst *black pudding*
Bockwurst *large frankfurter*
Bohnen *beans*

Bouillon *clear soup*
Braten *roast meat*
Brathering *pickled and fried herring, served cold*
Bratkartoffeln *fried potatoes*
Bratwurst *grilled pork sausage*
Brot *bread*
Brötchen *roll*
Brühwurst *parboiled sausage*
Brust *breast*
Bückling *smoked red herring*
Buletten *burgers; meat or fish pastry*
Bunte Platte *mixed platter*
Burgundersoße *Burgundy wine sauce*
Buttercremetorte *buttercream cake*
Buttermilch *buttermilk*

C, D

Champignons *mushrooms*
Cordon bleu *cordon bleu*
Currywurst mit Pommes frites *curried pork sausage with chips*
Dampfnudeln *sweet yeast dumpling*
Deutsches Beefsteak *minced meat patty*
Dicke Bohnen *fava beans*
Dillsoße *dill sauce*
durchgebraten *well-done*
durchwachsen *with fat*
durchwachsener Speck *side bacon*

E

Eier *eggs*
Eierauflauf *omelet*
Eierkuchen *pancake*
Eierpfannkuchen *egg pancake*
Eierspeise *egg dish*
eingelegt *pickled*
Eintopf *stew*
Eintopfgericht *stew*
Eis *ice, ice cream*
Eisbecher *sundae*
Eisbein *knuckles of pork*
Eisschokolade *iced chocolate with ice cream and whipped cream*
Eissplittertorte *ice cream cake*
Endiviensalat *endive salad*
englisch *rare*

Entenbraten *roast duck*
entgrätet *deboned (fish)*
Erbsen *peas*
Erdbeertorte *strawberry cake*
Essig *vinegar*

F

Falscher Hase *meatloaf*
Fasan *pheasant*
Fenchel *fennel*
Fett *fat*
Filet *filet (steak)*
Fisch *fish*
Fischfrikadellen *fishcakes*
Fischstäbchen *fishsticks*
Flädlesuppe *consommé with pancake strips*
flambiert *flambéed*
Fleischbrühe *bouillon*
Fleischkäse *meatloaf*
Fleischklößchen *meatball(s)*
Fleischpastete *meat pie*
Fleischsalat *diced meat salad with mayonnaise*
Fleischwurst *pork sausage*
Fond *stock*
Forelle *trout*
Forelle Müllerin (Art) *breaded trout with butter and lemon*
Frikadelle *meat or fish pastry*
Frikassee *fricassee*
fritiert *(deep-) fried*
Fruchtsaft *fruit juice*
Frühlingsrolle *spring roll*

G

Gans *goose*
Gänseleberpastete *goose-liver pâté*
garniert *garnished*
Gebäck *pastries, cakes*
gebacken *baked*
gebraten *roast*
gedünstet *steamed*
Geflügel *poultry*
Geflügelleberragout *chicken liver ragoût*
gefüllt *stuffed*
gefüllte Kalbsbrust *veal roll*
gekocht *boiled*
Gelee *jelly*
gemischter Salat *mixed salad*
Gemüse *vegetable(s)*
Gemüseplatte *assorted vegetables*

gepökelt salted, pickled
geräuchert smoked
Gericht dish
geschmort braised, stewed
Geschnetzeltes strips of fried meat in cream sauce
gespickt larded
Getränke beverages
Gewürze spices
Gewürzgurken gherkins
Goldbarsch type of perch
Götterspeise jelly
gratiniert au gratin
Grieß semolina
Grießklößchen semolina dumplings
grüne Bohnen French beans
grüne Nudeln green pasta
grüner Aal fresh eel
Grünkohl (curly) kale
Gulasch goulash
Gulaschsuppe goulash soup
Gurkensalat cucumber salad

H

Hackfleisch mince
Hähnchen chicken
Hähnchenkeule chicken leg
Haifischflossensuppe shark-fin soup
Hammelbraten roast mutton
Hammelfleisch mutton
Hammelkeule leg of mutton
Hammelrücken saddle of mutton
Hartkäse hard cheese
Haschee hash
Hasenkeule haunch of hare
Hasenpfeffer hare casserole
Hauptspeisen main courses
Hecht pike
Heidelbeeren bilberries, blueberries
Heilbutt halibut
Heringsstipp herring salad
Heringstopf pickled herring in sauce
Herz heart
Herzragout heart ragoût
Himbeeren raspberries
Himmel und Erde potato and apple purée with black pudding or liver sausage
Hirn brains
Hirschbraten roast venison
Honig honey
Honigmelone honeydew
Hoppelpoppel bacon and potato omelet
Hüfte haunch
Huhn chicken
Hühnerbrühe chicken broth
Hühnerfrikassee chicken fricassee
Hülsenfrüchte peas and beans, pulses
Hummer lobster

J, K

Jägerschnitzel cutlet with mushrooms
Kabeljau cod
Kaffee coffee
Kaiserschmarren sugared pancake with raisins
Kakao cocoa
Kalbfleisch veal
Kalbsbries sweetbread
Kalbsfrikassee veal fricasse
Kalbshaxe leg of veal
Kalbsnierenbraten roast veal with kidney
Kalbsschnitzel veal cutlet
kalte Platte cold platter
kaltes Büfett cold buffet
Kaltschale cold sweet fruit soup, cold savory soup
Kaninchen rabbit
Kapern capers
Karamellpudding caramel blancmange
Karotten carrots
Karpfen carp
Kartoffelbrei mashed potato
Kartoffeln potatoes
Kartoffelpuffer potato fritters
Kartoffelpüree mashed potato
Käse cheese
Käsegebäck cheese crackers
Käsekuchen cheesecake
Käseplatte selection of cheeses
Käse-Sahne-Torte cream cheesecake
Käsespätzle homemade noodles with cheese
Kasseler Rippenspeer smoked pork loin
Kasserolle casserole
Kassler smoked pork loin
Kastanien chestnuts
Katenrauchwurst smoked sausage
Keule leg, haunch
Kieler Sprotten smoked herring
Kirschen cherries
klare Brühe consommé
Klöße dumplings
Knäckebrot crispbread
Knacker spicy fried sausage
Knackwurst spicy fried sausage
Knoblauch garlic
Knochen bone
Knochenschinken ham on the bone
Knödel dumplings
Kognak brandy
Kohl cabbage
Kohlrouladen stuffed cabbage leaves
Kohl und Pinkel cabbage, potatoes, sausage, and smoked meat
Kompott stewed fruit

Konfitüre jam
Königinpastete vol-au-vent
Königsberger Klopse meatballs in caper sauce
Königskuchen type of fruit cake
Kopfsalat lettuce
Kotelett chop
Krabben shrimp
Krabbencocktail shrimp cocktail
Kraftbrühe beef consommé
Krapfen jelly doughnut
Kräuter herbs
Krautsalat coleslaw
Krautwickel stuffed cabbage leaves
Krebs crayfish
Kresse cress
Kroketten croquettes
Kruste crust
Kuchen cake
Kürbis pumpkin

L

Labskaus meat, fish, and potato stew
Lachs salmon
Lachsforelle sea trout
Lachsschinken smoked rolled fillet of ham
Lamm lamb
Lammrücken lamb roast
Langusten crayfish
Lauch leek
Leber liver
Leberkäse baked pork and beef loaf
Leberpastete liver pâté
Leberwurst liver pâté
Lebkuchen gingerbread
Leipziger Allerlei mixed vegetables
Linsen lentils

M

mager lean
Majoran marjoram
Makrele mackerel
Makronen macaroons
Mandeln almonds
mariniert marinaded, pickled
Markklößchen marrow dumplings
Marmelade jam
Maronen sweet chestnuts
Matjes(hering) young herring
Medaillons small fillets
Meeresfische seafish
Meeresfrüchte seafood
Meerrettich horseradish
Miesmuscheln mussels
Milch milk
Milchshake milk shake
Milchreis rice pudding
Mineralwasser (sparkling) mineral water

Mohnkuchen *poppyseed cake*
Möhren *carrots*
Mohrrüben *carrots*
Most *fruit wine*
Mus *purée*
Muscheln *mussels*
Muskat(nuss) *nutmeg*
MwSt (Mehrwertsteuer) *VAT*

N, O

nach Art des Hauses *of the house*
nach Hausfrauenart *home-style cooking*
Nachspeisen *desserts*
Nachtisch *dessert*
Napfkuchen *ring-shaped poundcake*
natürlich *natural*
Nieren *kidneys*
Nudeln *pasta, noodles*
Nüsse *nuts*
Obstsalat *fruit salad*
Ochsenschwanzsuppe *oxtail soup*
Öl *oil*
Oliven *olives*
Orangen *oranges*
Orangensaft *orange juice*

P

Palatschinken *stuffed pancakes*
paniert *with breadcrumbs*
Paprika *peppers*
Paprikaschoten *peppers*
Pastete *pie, vol-au-vent*
Pellkartoffeln *potatoes boiled in their skins*
Petersilie *parsley*
Pfannkuchen *pancake(s)*
Pfeffer *pepper*
Pfifferlinge *chanterelles*
Pfirsiche *peaches*
Pflaumen *plums*
Pflaumenkuchen *plum tart*
Pflaumenmus *plum jam*
Pichelsteiner Eintopf *vegetable stew with beef*
pikant *spicy*
Pilze *mushrooms*
Platte *selection*
pochiert *poached*
Pökelfleisch *salt meat*
Pommes (frites) *French fries*
Porree *leek*
Potthast *braised beef with sauce*
Poularde *young chicken*
Preiselbeeren *cranberries*
Presskopf *headcheese*
Pumpernickel *black rye bread*
Püree *mashed potato*
püriert *puréed*
Putenschenkel *turkey leg*
Puter *turkey*

Q, R

Quark *curd cheese*
Radieschen *radishes*
Rahm *(sour) cream*
Räucheraal *smoked eel*
Räucherhering *kipper, smoked herring*
Räucherlachs *smoked salmon*
Räucherspeck *smoked bacon*
Rauchfleisch *smoked meat*
Rehbraten *roast venison*
Rehgulasch *venison goulash*
Rehkeule *haunch of venison*
Rehrücken *venison roast*
Reibekuchen *potato waffles*
Reis *rice*
Reisbrei *creamed rice*
Reisrand *with rice*
Remoulade *mayonnaise flavored with herbs, mustard, and capers*
Renke *whitefish*
Rettich *radish*
Rhabarber *rhubarb*
Rheinischer Sauerbraten *roast pickled beef*
Rinderbraten *pot roast*
Rinderfilet *filet steak*
Rinderrouladen *beef olives*
Rinderzunge *ox tongue*
Rindfleisch *beef*
Rippchen *spareribs*
Risi-Pisi *rice and peas*
roh *raw*
Rohkostplatte *selection of raw vegetables (and fruit)*
Rollmops *rolled-up pickled herring*
rosa *rare to medium*
Rosenkohl *Brussels sprouts*
Rosinen *raisins*
Rostbraten *roast*
Rostbratwurst *barbecued sausage*
Rösti *fried potatoes and onions*
Röstkartoffeln *fried potatoes*
Rotbarsch *type of perch*
Rote Bete *beet*
rote Grütze *red fruit jelly*
Rotkohl *red cabbage*
Rotkraut *red cabbage*
Rotwein *red wine*
Rührei er *scrambled eggs*
Russische Eier *stuffed eggs, deviled eggs, eggs mimosa*

S

Sahne *cream*
Salate *salads*
Salatplatte *selection of salads*
Salatsoße *salad dressing*
Salz *salt*
Salzburger Nockerln *sweet soufflés*
Salzheringe *salted herrings*

Salzkartoffeln *boiled potatoes*
Salzkruste *salty crusted skin*
Sandkuchen *type of Madeira cake*
sauer *sour*
Sauerbraten *roast pickled beef*
Sauerkraut *pickled white cabbage*
Sauerrahm *sour cream*
Schaschlik *(shish-)kebab*
Schattenmorellen *morello cherries*
Schellfisch *haddock*
Schildkrötensuppe *turtle soup*
Schinken *ham*
Schinkenröllchen *rolled ham*
Schlachtplatte *selection of fresh sausages*
Schlagsahne *whipped cream*
Schlei *tench*
Schmorbraten *pot roast*
Schnecken *snails*
Schnittlauch *chives*
Schnitzel *breaded scallopini*
Schnitzel Balkan-Art *veal with peppers and relishes*
Schokolade *chocolate*
Scholle *plaice*
Schulterstück *slice of shoulder*
Schwarzbrot *brown rye bread*
Schwarzwälder Kirschtorte *Black Forest cherry cake*
Schwarzwurzeln *salsify*
Schwein *pork*
Schweinebauch *belly of pork*
Schweinefleisch *pork*
Schweinerippe *cured pork chop*
Schweinerollbraten *rolled roast of pork*
Schweineschmorbraten *roast pork*
Schweineschnitzel *breaded pork cutlet*
Schweinshaxe *knuckle of pork*
Seelachs *pollack (fish)*
Seezunge *sole*
Sekt *sparkling wine*
Sellerie *celeriac*
Semmel *bread roll*
Senf *mustard*
Senfsahnesoße *mustard and cream sauce*
Senfsoße *mustard sauce*
Serbisches Reisfleisch *diced pork, onions, tomatoes, and rice*
Soleier *pickled eggs*
Soße *sauce, gravy*
Soufflé *soufflé*
Spanferkel *suckling pig*
Spargel *asparagus*
Spätzle *homemade noodles*
Speck *fatty bacon*
Speisekarte *menu*
Spezialität des Hauses *house speciality*

Spiegeleier *fried eggs*
Spießbraten *joint roasted on a spit*
Spinat *spinach*
Spitzkohl *white cabbage*
Sprotten *herring*
Sprudel(wasser) *mineral water*
Stachelbeeren *gooseberries*
Stangen(weiß)brot *French bread*
Steinbutt *turbot*
Steinpilze *cep mushrooms*
Stollen *Christmas fruit loaf*
Strammer Max *ham and fried egg on bread*
Streuselkuchen *cake with crumble topping*
Sülze *headcheese*
Suppen *soups*
Suppengrün *mixed herbs and vegetables (used in soup)*
süß *sweet*
süß-sauer *sweet-and-sour*
Süßspeisen *sweet dishes*
Süßwasserfische *freshwater fish*
Szegediner Gulasch *goulash with pickled cabbage*

T

Tafelwasser (still) *table water*
Tafelwein *table wine*
Tagesgericht *dish of the day*
Tageskarte *menu of the day*
Tagessuppe *soup of the day*
Tatar *steak tartare*
Taube *pigeon*
Tee *tea*
Teigmantel *pastry case*
Thunfisch *tuna*
Tintenfisch *squid*

Tomaten *tomatoes*
Törtchen *tart(s)*
Torte *gâteau*
Truthahn *turkey*

U, V

überbacken *au gratin*
Ungarisches Gulasch *Hungarian goulash*
ungebraten *not fried*
Vanille *vanilla*
Vanillesoße *vanilla sauce*
verlorene Eier *poached eggs*
Vollkornbrot *dark whole-grain bread*
vom Grill *grilled*
vom Kalb *veal*
vom Rind *beef*
vom Rost *grilled*
vom Schwein *pork*
Vorspeisen *hors d'oeuvres, appetizers*

W

Waffeln *waffles*
Waldorfsalat *salad with celery, apples, and walnuts*
Wasser *water*
Wassermelone *watermelon*
Weichkäse *soft cheese*
Weinbergschnecken *snails*
Weinbrand *brandy*
Weincreme *pudding with wine*
Weinschaumcreme *creamed pudding with wine*
Weinsoße *wine sauce*
Weintrauben *grapes*
Weißbier *wheat beer*
Weißbrot *white bread*
Weißkohl *white cabbage*
Weißkraut *white cabbage*
Weißwein *white wine*

Weißwurst *veal sausage*
Weizenbier *fizzy, light-colored beer made with wheat*
Wiener Schnitzel *veal in breadcrumbs*
Wild *game*
Wildschweinkeule *haunch of wild boar*
Wildschweinsteak *wild boar steak*
Windbeutel *cream puff*
Wirsing *savoy cabbage*
Wurst *sausage*
Würstchen *frankfurter(s)*
Wurstplatte *selection of sausages*
Wurstsalat *sausage salad*
Wurstsülze *sausage brawn*
würzig *spicy*

Z

Zander *pike-perch*
Zitrone *lemon*
Zitronencreme *lemon cream*
Zucchini *zucchini*
Zucker *sugar*
Zuckererbsen *peapod*
Zunge *tongue*
Zungenragout *tongue ragoût*
Zutaten *ingredients*
Zwiebeln *onions*
Zwiebelringe *onion rings*
Zwiebelsuppe *onion soup*
Zwiebeltorte *onion tart*
Zwischengerichte *entrées*

Dictionary
ENGLISH TO GERMAN

In German, the gender of a noun is indicated by the word for *the*: **der** for a masculine noun, **die** for feminine, and **das** for neuter. **Die** is also used with plural nouns, and the abbreviations *m pl*, *f pl*, and *nt pl* are used to indicate their gender here. The feminine form of most occupations and personal attributes is made by adding **-in** to the masculine form: *accountant* **Buchhalter(in)**, for example. Exceptions to this rule are listed separately. Adjectives and verbs are denoted by *adj* and *verb*.

A

about: about 16 **etwa 16**
accelerator **das Gaspedal**
accident **der Unfall**
accommodations **die Unterkunft**
accountant **der/die Buchhalter(in)**
across from: across from the hotel **gegenüber dem Hotel**
ache **der Schmerz**
adaptor **der Adapter**
address **die Adresse**
adhesive bandage **das Pflaster**
admission charge **der Eintrittspreis**
after **nach**
aftershave **das Rasierwasser**
again **nochmal**
against **gegen**
agenda **die Tagesordnung**
agent **der Vertreter**
air **die Luft**
air-conditioning **die Klimaanlage**
aircraft **das Flugzeug**
airline **die Fluglinie**
airmail **die Luftpost**
air mattress **die Luftmatratze**
airport **der Flughafen**
airport bus **der Flughafenbus**
aisle **der Gang**
alarm clock **der Wecker**
alcohol **der Alkohol**
all **alle(s)**; *all the streets* **alle Straßen**; *that's all* **das ist alles**
allergic (adj) **allergisch**
allotment **der Kleingarten, der Schrebergarten**
almost **fast**
alone (adj) **allein**
already **schon**
always **immer**
am: I am **ich bin**
ambulance **der Krankenwagen**
America **Amerika**

American **der/die Amerikaner(in)**; (adj) **amerikanisch**
and **und**
ankle **der Knöchel**
another (different) **ein anderer**; (one more) **noch ein**; *another time* **ein andermal**; *another room* **ein anderes Zimmer**; *another coffee, please* **noch einen Kaffee, bitte**
answering machine **der Anrufbeantworter**
antique dealer **der Antiquitätenladen**
antiques shop **das Antiquitätengeschäft**
antiseptic **das Antiseptikum**
apartment **die Wohnung**
aperitif **der Aperitif**
appetite **der Appetit**
apple **der Apfel**
application form **das Antragsformular**
appointment **der Termin**
apricot **die Aprikose**
April **April**
are: you are (singular informal) **du bist**; (singular formal; plural formal) **Sie sind**; (plural informal) **ihr seid**; *we are* **wir sind**; *they are* **sie sind**
arm **der Arm**
armchair **der Sessel**
arrivals **die Ankunft**
art **die Kunst**
art gallery **die Kunstgalerie**
artist **der/die Künstler(in)**
as: as soon as possible **so bald wie möglich**
ashtray **der Aschenbecher**
asthma **das Asthma**
at: at the post office **auf der Post**; *at the station* **am Bahnhof**; *at night* **in der Nacht**; *at 3 o'clock* **um 3 Uhr**
ATM **der Geldautomat**
attic **der Dachboden**

attractive (adj) **attraktiv**
August **August**
aunt **die Tante**
Australia **Australien**
Australian **der/die Australier(in)**; (adj) **australisch**
Austria **Österreich**
Austrian **der/die Österreicher(in)**; (adj) **österreichisch**
automatic (adj) **automatisch**
away: is it far away? **ist es weit von hier?**; *go away!* **gehen Sie weg!**
awful (adj) **furchtbar**

B

baby **das Baby**
back (not front) **die Rückseite**; (part of body) **der Rücken**
backpack **der Rucksack**
bacon **der Speck**; *bacon and eggs* **Eier mit Speck**
bad (adj) **schlecht**
bag **die Tasche**
baggage **das Gepäck**; *baggage claim* **die Gepäckausgabe**
bait **der Köder**
bake (verb) **backen**
baker **der/die Bäcker(in)**
bakery **die Bäckerei**
balcony **der Balkon**
ball **der Ball**
ballet **das Ballett**
Baltic **die Ostsee**
banana **die Banane**
band (musicians) **die Band**
bandage **der Verband**
bank **die Bank**
banknote **der (Geld)schein**
bar (drinks) **die Bar**
barbecue **der Grill**
barber's **der Herrenfriseur**
bargain **das Sonderangebot**
basement **das Untergeschoss**
basin (sink) **das Spülbecken**
basket **der Korb**

bath **das Bad**; (tub) **die Badewanne**; *to have a bath* (verb) **ein Bad nehmen**
bathroom **das Badezimmer**
bathtub **die Badewanne**
battery **die Batterie**
Bavaria **Bayern**
beach **der Strand**
beans **die Bohnen** (f pl)
beard **der Bart**
beautiful (adj) **schön**
because **weil**
bed **das Bett**; *bed linen* **die Bettwäsche**
bedroom **das Schlafzimmer**
bedside table **der Nachttisch**
bedspread **die Tagesdecke**
beef **das Rindfleisch**
beer **das Bier**
before... **vor...**
beginner **der Anfänger**
behind... **hinter...**
beige (adj) **beige**
Belgian **der/die Belgier(in)**; (adj) **belgisch**
Belgium **Belgien**
bell (church) **die Glocke**; (door) **die Klingel**
below... **unter...**
belt **der Gürtel**
beside **neben**
best (adj) **bester**
better (adj) **besser**
between... **zwischen...**
bicycle **das Fahrrad**
big (adj) **groß**
bikini **der Bikini**
bill **die Rechnung**
biochemistry **die Biochemie**
bird **der Vogel**
birthday **der Geburtstag**; *happy birthday!* **Herzlichen Glückwunsch!**
birthday card **die Geburtstagskarte**
birthday present **das Geburtstagsgeschenk**
biscuit **der Keks**
bite (by dog) **der Biss**; (by insect) **der Stich**; (verb: by dog) **beißen**; (verb: by insect) **stechen**
bitter (adj) **bitter**
black (adj) **schwarz**
blackberry **die Brombeere**
black currant **die schwarze Johannisbeere**
Black Forest **der Schwarzwald**
blanket **die Decke**
bleach **das Bleichmittel**; (verb: hair) **bleichen**
blind (unsighted) **blind**
blinds **die Jalousie**
blister **die Blase**
blond (adj) **blond**
blood **das Blut**; *blood test* **die Blutprobe**

blouse **die Bluse**
blue (adj) **blau**
boarding pass **die Bordkarte**
boat **das Schiff**; (small) **das Boot**
body **der Körper**; (corpse) **die Leiche**
boil (verb) **kochen**
boiled (adj) **gekocht**
boiler **der Boiler**
bolt (on door) **der Riegel**; (verb) **verriegeln**
bone **der Knochen**
book **das Buch**; (verb) **buchen**
bookshop **die Buchhandlung**
boot (footwear) **der Stiefel**
border **die Grenze**
boring (adj) **langweilig**
born: *I was born in...* **ich bin in... geboren**
both **beide**; *both of us* **wir beide**; *both... and...* **sowohl... als auch...**
bottle **die Flasche**
bottle opener **der Flaschenöffner**
bottom **der Boden**; (sea) **der Grund**
bowl **die Schüssel**
box **die Schachtel**
boxing **das Boxen**
box office **die Kasse**
boy **der Junge**
boyfriend **der Freund**
bra **der Büstenhalter, der BH**
bracelet **das Armband**
braces **die Hosenträger** (m pl)
brake **die Bremse**; (verb) **bremsen**
branch **die Zweigstelle**
brandy **der Weinbrand**
bread **das Brot**
breakdown (car) **die Panne**
breakfast **das Frühstück**
breathe (verb) **atmen**
bricklayer **der/die Maurer(in)**
bridge **die Brücke**; (game) **das Bridge**
briefcase **die Aktentasche**
Britain **Großbritannien**
British **britisch**
broccoli **der Brokkoli**
brochure **die Broschüre**
broken (adj: arm, etc.) **gebrochen**; (vase, etc.) **zerbrochen**; (machine, etc.) **kaputt**; *broken leg* **der Beinbruch**
brooch **die Brosche**
brother **der Bruder**
brother-in-law **der Schwager**
brown (adj) **braun**
bruise **der blaue Fleck**
brush **die Bürste**; (paint) **der Pinsel**; (verb: hair) **bürsten**; (floor) **kehren**

Brussels **Brüssel**
bucket **der Eimer**
budget **das Budget**
builder **der/die Bauarbeiter(in)**
building **das Gebäude**
bumper **die Stoßstange**
bureau de change **die Wechselstube**
burglar **der Einbrecher**
burn **die Verbrennung**; (verb) **brennen**
bus **der Bus**; *bus station* **der Busbahnhof**
business **das Geschäft**; *it's none of your business* **das geht Sie nichts an**
business card **die Visitenkarte**
busy (occupied) (adj) **beschäftigt**; (bar, etc.) **voll**
but **aber**
butcher's **die Metzgerei**
butter **die Butter**
button **der Knopf**
buy (verb) **kaufen**
by: *by the window* **am Fenster**; *by Friday* **bis Freitag**

C

cabbage **der Kohl**
cable car **die Drahtseilbahn**
café **das Café**
cage **der Käfig**
cake **der Kuchen**
cake shop **die Konditorei**
calculator **der Rechner**
call *what's it called?* **wie heißt das?**
camera **die Kamera**
camper van **das Wohnmobil**
campfire **das Lagerfeuer**
camping gas **das Campinggas**
campsite **der Campingplatz**; *campsite office* **die Campingplatzverwaltung**
camshaft **die Nockenwelle**
can (container) **die Dose**; (verb: to be able) *can I have...?* **kann ich...haben?**; *can you...?* **können Sie...?**
Canada **Kanada**
Canadian **der/die Kanadier(in)**; (adj) **kanadisch**
canal **der Kanal**
candle **die Kerze**
candy **die Süßigkeit, der Bonbon**
canoe **das Kanu**
can opener **der Dosenöffner**
cap (bottle) **der Verschluss**; (hat) **die Mütze**
car **das Auto**
caravan **der Wohnwagen**
carburetor **der Vergaser**
card **die Karte**

careful (adj) **sorgfältig**; *be careful!* **passen Sie auf!**

caretaker **der/die Hausmeister(in)**

carpenter **der/die Schreiner(in)**

car repairs **die Werkstatt**

carriage (train) **der Wagen**

carrot **die Möhre, die Karotte**

carry-on bag **das Handgepäck**

car seat (for baby) **der Kindersitz**

case (suitcase) **der Koffer**

cash **das Bargeld**; (verb) **einlösen**; *to pay cash* (verb) **bar bezahlen**

cashier **der/die Kassierer(in)**

cassette **die Kassette**; cassette player **der Kassettenrekorder**

castle **das Schloss, die Burg**

cat **die Katze**

cathedral **der Dom**

cauliflower **der Blumenkohl**

cave **die Höhle**

ceiling **die Decke**

cellar **der Keller**

cell phone **das Handy, das Mobiltelefon**

cemetery **der Friedhof**

center (middle) **die Mitte**

central heating **die Zentralheizung**

certificate **die Bescheinigung**

chair **der Stuhl**

change (money) **das Kleingeld**; (verb: money) **wechseln**; (verb: clothes) **sich umziehen**

charger **das Ladegerät** (for mobiles); **der Ladestecker** (for electric vehicles)

charging cable **das Ladekabel**

charging station **die Ladesäule**

cheap (adj) **billig**

check **der Scheck**; checkbook **das Scheckheft**

check in (desk) **der Abfertigungsschalter, die Abfertigung**; (verb) **einchecken**

checkout **die Kasse**

cheers! **prost!**

cheese **der Käse**

cherry **die Kirsche**

chess **Schach**

chest (part of body) **die Brust**; (furniture) **die Truhe**

chest of drawers **die Kommode**

chewing gum **der Kaugummi**

chicken **das Huhn**; (cooked) **das Hähnchen**

child **das Kind**

children **die Kinder** (nt pl)

children's ward **die Kinderstation**

chimney **der Schornstein**

china **das Porzellan**

chips **die Chips** (m pl)

chocolate **die Schokolade**; box of chocolates **die Schachtel Pralinen**

chop (food) **das Kotelett**; (verb: to cut) **kleinschneiden**

Christmas **Weihnachten**

church **die Kirche**

cigar **die Zigarre**; (thin) **das Zigarillo**

cigarette **die Zigarette**

circle **der Rang**

city **die (Groß)stadt**; city centre **das Stadtzentrum**

class **die Klasse**

classical music **die klassische Musik**

clean (adj) **sauber**

cleaner **die Haushaltshilfe**

clear **klar**

clever **klug**

client **der Kunde**

clock **die Uhr**

close (near) **nah**; (stuffy) **stickig**; (verb) **schließen**

closed **geschlossen**

clothes **die Kleidung**

clothespin **die Wäscheklammer**

clothes size **die Kleidergröße**

club **der Klub**

clubs (cards) **Kreuz**

clutch **die Kupplung**

coach **der Überlandbus, der Reisebus**; (verb: train) **trainieren**; coach station **der Busbahnhof**

coat **der Mantel**

coat hanger **der (Kleider)bügel**

coffee **der Kaffee**; black coffee **der Kaffee ohne Milch**

coin **die Münze**

cold (illness) **der Schnupfen, die Erkältung**; (adj) **kalt**; *I have a cold* **ich habe Schnupfen, ich bin erkältet**; *I am cold* **mir ist kalt**

collar **das Halsband, der Kragen**

collection (stamps, etc.) **die Sammlung**; (postal) **die Leerung**

Cologne **Köln**

color **die Farbe**; color film **der Farbfilm**

comb **der Kamm**

come (verb) **kommen**; *I come from…* **ich komme aus…**; *come here!* **kommen Sie her!** *come back* **zurückkommen**

compact disc **die Compact-Disc, die CD**

compartment **das Abteil**

complicated (adj) **kompliziert**

computer **der Computer**

concert **das Konzert**

conditioner (hair) **die Haarspülung**

condom **das Kondom**

conductor (bus) **der Schaffner**; (orchestra) **der Dirigent**

conference **die Konferenz**; conference room **das Konferenzzimmer**

congratulations! **herzlichen Glückwunsch!**

consulate **das Konsulat**

consultant **der/die Berater(in)**

contact lenses **die Kontaktlinsen** (f pl)

contactless payment **kontaktloses Bezahlen**

contraceptive **das Verhütungsmittel**

contract **der Vertrag**

cook **der/die Koch/Köchin**; (verb) **kochen**

cooker **der Herd**

cool (adj) **kühl**

cork **der Korken**

corkscrew **der Korkenzieher**

corner **die Ecke**

corridor **der Korridor**

cosmetics **die Kosmetika**

cost (verb) **kosten**; *what does it cost?* **was kostet das?**

cot **das Kinderbett**

cotton **die Baumwolle**

cotton ball **die Watte**

cough **der Husten**; (verb) **husten**

countertop **die Arbeitsfläche**

country **das Land**

cousin **der/die Vetter/Kusine**

crab **die Krabbe**

cramp **der Krampf**

crayfish **der Krebs**

cream (for cake, etc.) **die Sahne**; (lotion) **die Creme**

credit card **die Kreditkarte**

crowded **überfüllt**

cruise **die Kreuzfahrt**

crutches **die Krücken** (f pl)

cry (verb: weep) **weinen**; (verb: shout) **rufen**

cucumber **die Gurke**

cuff links **die Manschettenknöpfe** (m pl)

cup **die Tasse**

cupboard **der Schrank**

curls **die Locken** (f pl)

curry **das Curry**

curtain **der Vorhang**

cushion **das Kissen**

Customs **der Zoll**
cut **der Schnitt;**
(verb) **schneiden**
cycling **das Radfahren**

D

dad **der Papa**
dairy products **die
Milchprodukte** (nt pl)
damp (adj) **feucht**
dance **der Tanz;** (verb)
tanzen
Dane **der/die Däne/Dänin**
dangerous (adj) **gefährlich**
Danish (adj) **dänisch**
Danish pastry **das Teilchen**
Danube **die Donau**
dark (adj) **dunkel**
daughter **die Tochter**
day **der Tag**
dead (adj) **tot**
deaf (adj) **taub**
dear (adj) (person) **lieb;**
(expensive) **teuer**
debit card **die Debit-Karte**
debit card **die Scheckkarte**
December **Dezember**
deck chair **der Liegestuhl**
decorator **der/die Maler(in)**
deep (adj) **tief**
delayed (adj) **verspätet**
delegate **der/die
Delegierte(r)**
deliberately **absichtlich**
delicatessen **das
Feinkostgeschäft**
delivery **die Lieferung**
Denmark **Dänemark**
dentist **der Zahnarzt**
dentures **die Prothese,
das Gebiss**
deny (verb) **bestreiten**
deodorant **das Deodorant**
department **die Abteilung**
department store **das
Kaufhaus**
departure **die Abfahrt**
departure lounge **die
Abflughalle**
departures **der Abflug**
deposit **die Kaution**
designer **der/die Grafiker(in)**
desserts **der Nachtisch**
develop (film) (verb)
entwickeln
diabetic **der/die Diabetiker(in)**
diamond (gem) **der Diamant**
diamonds (cards) **Karo**
diaper **die Windel**
diarrhea **der Durchfall**
diary **der Terminkalender**
(appointments); **das
Tagebuch** (personal)
dictionary **das
Wörterbuch**
die (verb) **sterben**
diesel **der Diesel**

different (adj) **verschieden;**
that's different! **das ist
etwas anderes!;** *I'd like a
different kind* **ich möchte
gern eine andere Sorte**
difficult (adj) **schwierig**
dining room **das Esszimmer**
dinner **das Abendessen**
directory (telephone)
das Telefonbuch
dirty (adj) **schmutzig**
disabled (adj) **behindert**
discounts **die Ermäßigungen**
dishwasher **die
Geschirrspülmaschine**
dishwashing liquid **das
Geschirrspülmittel**
disposable diapers **die
Einwegwindeln**
dive **der Sprung;**
(verb) **tauchen**
diving board **das Sprungbrett**
divorced (adj) **geschieden**
DIY **das Basteln**
do (verb) **tun;** *how do you
do?* **guten Tag;** (on being
introduced) **freut mich**
doctor **der Arzt**
document **das Dokument**
dog **der Hund**
doll **die Puppe**
dollar **der Dollar**
door **die Tür**
double room **das
Doppelzimmer**
doughnut **der Berliner**
down **herunter;** (position)
unten; *down here* **hier
unten**
drawer **die Schublade**
drawing pin **die Heftzwecke,
der Reißnagel**
dress **das Kleid**
drink **das Getränk;** (verb)
trinken; *would you like
a drink?* **möchten Sie
etwas trinken?**
drinking water **das
Trinkwasser**
drive (verb) **fahren**
driver **der/die Fahrer(in)**
driveway **die Einfahrt**
driving license **der
Führerschein**
drops **die Tropfen** (m pl)
drunk (adj) **betrunken**
dry (adj) **trocken**
dry cleaner **die Reinigung**
dummy (for baby) **der
Schnuller**
during **während**
dustbin **die Mülltonne**
duster **das Staubtuch**
Dutch (adj) **niederländisch**
Dutchman/Dutchwoman **der
die Niederländer(in)**
duty-free **zollfrei**
duvet **die Steppdecke**

E

each (every) **jeder, alle;** *five
euros each* **fünf Euro das
Stück**
ear **das Ohr;** *ears* **die
Ohren** (nt pl)
early (adj) **früh**
earphones **die Ohrhörer**
earrings **die Ohrringe** (m pl)
east **der Osten**
easy (adj) **leicht**
eat (verb) **essen**
editor **der/die Lektor(in)**
egg **das Ei**
eight **acht**
eighteen **achtzehn**
eighty **achtzig**
either: either of them **einer
von beiden;** *either... or...*
entweder... oder...
elastic (adj) **elastisch;** *elastic
band* **das Gummiband**
elbow **der Ellbogen**
electric (adj) **elektrisch**
electrical hook-up **der
Stromanschluss**
electrician **der/die
Elektriker(in)**
electricity **der Strom**
elevator (in building) **der
Aufzug**
eleven **elf**
else: something else **etwas
anderes;** *someone else*
jemand anders;
somewhere else **woanders**
email **die E-Mail**
email address **die E-Mail-
Adresse**
embarrassing (adj) **peinlich**
embassy **die Botschaft**
emerald **der Smaragd**
emergency **der Notfall**
emergency brake
die Notbremse
emergency department
die Unfallstation
emergency exit **der
Notausgang**
empty (adj) **leer**
end **das Ende**
engaged (adj) (couple)
verlobt; (occupied)
besetzt
engine (motor) **der Motor**
engineer **der/die Ingenieur(in)**
engineering **die Technik**
England **England**
English (adj) **englisch;**
(language) **Englisch**
English Channel **der
Ärmelkanal;** *Channel
Tunnel* **der Eurotunnel**
Englishman/Englishwoman
der/die Engländer(in)
enlargement **die
Vergrößerung**

enough (adj) **genug**

entertainment **die Unterhaltung**

entrance **der Eingang**;

entrance ticket **die Eintrittskarte**

envelope **der Umschlag**

epileptic **der/die Epileptiker(in)**

eraser **der Radiergummi**

escalator **die Rolltreppe**

especially **besonders**

estimate **der Kostenvoranschlag**

evening **der Abend**

every **jeder**

everyone **jeder**

everything **alles**

everywhere **überall**

example **das Beispiel**; *for example* **zum Beispiel**

excellent (adj) **ausgezeichnet**

excess baggage **das Mehrgepäck**

exchange (verb) **(um)tauschen**

exchange rate **der Wechselkurs**

excursion **der Ausflug**

excuse me! **Entschuldigung!**

executive **der/die Manager(in)**

exhaust **der Auspuff**

exhibition **die Ausstellung**

exit **der Ausgang**

expensive (adj) **teuer**

extension lead **die Verlängerungsschnur**

eye **das Auge**;

eyes **die Augen**

eyebrow **die Augenbraue**

eyeglasses **die Brille**

F

face **das Gesicht**

face mask **die Maske**

faint (adj) (unclear) **undeutlich**; (verb) **ohnmächtig werden**

fair (funfair) **der Jahrmarkt, die Kirmes**; (adj) (just) **gerecht, fair**

false teeth **die Prothese, das Gebiss**

family **die Familie**

fan (ventilator) **der Ventilator**; (enthusiast) **der Fan**

fan belt **der Keilriemen**

fantastic (adj) **fantastisch**

far (adj) **weit**; *how far is it?* **wie weit ist es?**

fare **der Fahrpreis**

farm **der Bauernhof**

farmer **der Bauer**

fashion **die Mode**

fast (adj) **schnell**

fat **das Fett**; (adj: person) **dick**

father **der Vater**

February **Februar**

feel (touch) **fühlen**; *I feel hot* **mir ist heiß**; *I feel like... ich möchte gern...*; *I don't feel well* **mir ist nicht gut**

feet **die Füße** (m pl)

fence **der Zaun**

ferry **die Fähre**

fever **das Fieber**

fiancé **der Verlobte**

fiancée **die Verlobte**

field **das Feld**; (of work) **das Gebiet**

fifteen **fünfzehn**

fifty **fünfzig**

fig **die Feige**

figures **die Zahlen** (f pl)

filling (in tooth, cake) **die Füllung**; (in sandwich) **der Belag**

film **der Film**

filter **der Filter**

filter papers **das Filterpapier**

finger **der Finger**

fire **das Feuer**

fire department **die Feuerwehr**

fire extinguisher **der Feuerlöscher**

fireworks **das Feuerwerk**

first **erster**; *first class* **erster Klasse**

first aid **die Erste Hilfe**

first floor **der erste Stock**

first name **der Vorname**

fish **der Fisch**

fishing **das Angeln**; *to go fishing* **Angeln gehen**

fishmonger's **das Fischgeschäft**

five **fünf**

fizzy (adj) **sprudelnd**

fizzy water **das Wasser mit Kohlensäure, das Sprudelwasser**

flag **die Fahne**

flash (camera) **der Blitz**

flat (adj) (level) **flach**; (apartment) **die Wohnung**

flat tire **die Reifenpanne, der platte Reifen**; *have a flat tyre* **einen Platten haben**

flavor **der Geschmack**

flea **der Floh**

flea spray **das Flohspray**

flier **das Überzelt**

flight **der Flug**; *flight number* **die Flugnummer**; *flight ticket* **das Flugticket**

flippers **die (Schwimm)flossen** (f pl)

floor (ground) **der Fußboden, der Boden**; (story) **der Stock**

florist **der Blumenladen**

flour **das Mehl**

flower **die Blume**; *flower arranging* **das Blumenstecken**; *flowerbed* **das Blumenbeet**

flute **die Flöte**

fly (insect) **die Fliege**; (verb) **fliegen**

flyover **die Überführung**

fog **der Nebel**

folk music **die Volksmusik**

food **das Essen**

food poisoning **die Lebensmittelvergiftung**

foot **der Fuß**

football **der Fußball**

for **für**; *for me* **für mich**; *what for?* **wofür?**; *for a week* **für eine Woche**

foreigner **der/die Ausländer(in)**

forest **der Wald**

forget (verb) **vergessen**

fork **die Gabel**

fortnight **zwei Wochen**

forty **vierzig**

fountain **der Brunnen**

four **vier**

fourteen **vierzehn**

fourth **vierter**

France **Frankreich**

free **frei**; (no charge) **kostenlos, gratis**

freezer **der Gefrierschrank**

French (adj) **französisch**

French fries **die Fritten, die Pommes**

Frenchman **der Franzose**

Frenchwoman **die Französin**

Friday **Freitag**

fridge **der Kühlschrank**

fried (adj) **gebraten**

friend **der/die Freund(in)**

friendly (adj) **freundlich**

*front: in front of... **vor...**

frost **der Frost**

frozen foods **die Tiefkühlkost**

fruit **das Obst, die Frucht**

fruit juice **der Fruchtsaft**

fry (verb) **braten**

frying pan **die (Brat)pfanne**

full **voll**; *I'm full (up)* **ich bin satt**

full board **die Vollpension**

funny (adj) **komisch**

furniture **die Möbel**

G

garage **die Garage**; (for repairs) **die Werkstatt**

garden **der Garten**

garden center **das Gartencenter**

gardener **der/die Gärtner(in)**

gardening **die Gartenarbeit**

garlic **der Knoblauch**

gas **das Benzin**

gas station **die Tankstelle**

gate **das Tor**; (garden gate) **die Pforte**; (at airport) **der Flugsteig**

gay (adj) (homosexual **schwul**

gear **der Gang**
gear stick **der Schaltknüppel**
gel (hair) **das Gel**
general practitioner
Allgemeinarzt
German **der/die Deutsche;**
(adj) **deutsch;**
(language) **Deutsch**
Germany **Deutschland**
get (verb: fetch) **holen;** have
you got...? **haben Sie...?;** to
get the train (verb) **den Zug
nehmen**
get back: we get back
tomorrow **wir kommen
morgen zurück;** to get
something back (verb)
etwas zurückbekommen
get in **hereinkommen;**
(verb: arrive) **ankommen**
get off (bus, etc.) **aussteigen**
get on (bus, etc.) **einsteigen**
get out **herauskommen;**
(verb: bring out)
herausholen
get up (verb: rise) **aufstehen**
gift **das Geschenk**
gin **der Gin**
ginger (spice) **der Ingwer**
girl **das Mädchen**
girlfriend **die Freundin**
give (verb) **geben**
glad (adj) **froh**
glass **das Glas**
glasses **die Brille**
gloves **die Handschuhe**
(m pl)
glue **der Leim, der Klebstoff**
go (verb) **gehen;** (travel)
fahren; (by plane) **fliegen**
gold **das Gold**
golf **das Golf**
good (adj) **gut**
goodbye **Auf Wiedersehen**
good night **Guten Abend**
government **die Regierung**
granddaughter **die Enkelin**
grandfather **der Großvater**
grandmother **die Großmutter**
grandparents **die Großeltern**
grandson **der Enkel**
grapes **die Trauben** (f pl)
grass **das Gras**
gray (adj) **grau**
Great Britain **Großbritannien**
great: great! (adj) **prima!**
green (adj) **grün**
grill **der Grill**
grilled (adj) **gegrillt**
grocery **das
Lebensmittelgeschäft**
ground floor **das Erdgeschoss**
groundsheet **der Zeltboden,
die Bodenplane**
guarantee **die Garantie;**
(verb) **garantieren**
guard **der Wächter**
guest **der Gast**

guide **der Reiseführer**
guide book **der (Reise)führer**
guide dog **der Blindenhund**
guided tour **die Führung**
guitar **die Gitarre**
gun (rifle) **das Gewehr;**
(pistol) **die Pistole**
gutter **die Dachrinne**

H

hair **das Haar**
haircut **der Haarschnitt**
hairdresser's **der Friseur;**
(ladies') **der Friseursalon**
hair dryer **der Fön**
hair spray **das Haarspray**
half **halb;** half an hour
eine halbe Stunde
half board **die Halbpension**
half-brother **der Halbbruder**
half-sister **die Halbschwester**
ham **der Schinken**
hamburger **der Hamburger**
hammer **der Hammer**
hamster **der Hamster**
hand **die Hand**
handbag **die Handtasche**
handbrake **die Handbremse**
handle (door) **die Klinke**
handshake **der Händedruck**
handsome (adj) **gut
aussehend**
hangover **der Kater**
happy (adj) **glücklich**
harbor **der Hafen**
hard (adj) **hart,** (difficult)
schwer
hardware shop **der Baumarkt**
hat **der Hut**
have (verb) **haben:** I have
Ich habe; you have
(singular informal) **du
hast;** (plural informal) **ihr
habt;** (singular formal)
plural formal) **Sie haben;**
we have **wir haben;** they
have **sie haben;** do you
have ...? **haben Sie ...?;** I
have to go **ich muss gehen**
hay fever **der
Heuschnupfen**
he **er**
head **der Kopf**
headache **die
Kopfschmerzen;**
headache pill **die
Kopfschmerztablette**
headlights **die Scheinwerfer**
(m pl)
head office **die Zentrale**
headphones **der
Kopfhörer**
hear (verb) **hören**
hearing aid **das Hörgerät**
hearing loop **die induktive
Höranlage**
heart **das Herz**

heart condition: I have a
heart condition **Ich bin
herzkrank**
hearts (cards) **Herz**
heater **das Heizgerät**
heating **die Heizung**
heavy (adj) **schwer**
hedge **die Hecke**
heel (shoe) **der Absatz;**
(foot) **die Ferse**
hello **guten Tag;**
(on phone) **hallo**
help **die Hilfe;** (verb) **helfen**
her: it's her **sie ist es;**
it's for her **es ist für sie;**
give it to her **geben Sie es
ihr;** her book **ihr Buch;**
her shoes **ihre Schuhe;**
it's hers **es gehört ihr**
hi **hallo**
high (adj) **hoch**
hiking **das Wandern**
hill **der Berg**
him: it's him **er ist es;** it's for
him **es ist für ihn;** give it
to him **geben Sie es ihm**
hire **leihen, mieten**
his: his book **sein Buch;**
his shoes **seine Schuhe;**
it's his **es gehört ihm**
history **die Geschichte**
hitchhike (verb) **trampen**
HIV-positive (adj) **HIV-positiv**
hobby **das Hobby**
holiday **die Ferien,
der Urlaub**
Holland **Holland**
home: at home **zu Hause**
homeopathy **die
Homöopathie**
honest (adj) **ehrlich**
honey **der Honig**
honeymoon **die
Hochzeitsreise**
hood (car) **die Motorhaube**
horn (car) **die Hupe;**
(animal) **das Horn**
horrible (adj) **schrecklich**
hospital **das Krankenhaus;**
(attached to university) **das
Universitätsklinikum**
host **der/die Gastgeber(in)**
hour **die Stunde**
house **das Haus**
household products **die
Haushaltswaren** (f pl)
housekeeping **das
Hotelpersonal**
how? **wie?**
humanities **die
Geisteswissenschaften**
(f pl)
hundred **hundert**
hungry: I'm hungry
ich habe Hunger
hurry: I'm in a hurry
ich bin in Eile
husband **der (Ehe)mann**

I

I **ich**
ice **das Eis**
ice cream **die Eiscreme**
ice skates **die Schlittschuhe**
ice-skating: to go ice-skating (verb) **Schlittschuh laufen gehen**
if **wenn**
ignition **die Zündung**
ill (adj) **krank**
immediately **sofort**
impossible (adj) **unmöglich**
in **in**; in English **auf Englisch**; in the hotel **im Hotel**
indicator **der Blinker**
indigestion **die Magenverstimmung**
infection **die Infektion, die Entzündung**
information **die Information**
injection **die Spritze**
injury **die Verletzung**
ink **die Tinte**
inn **das Gasthaus**
inner tube **der Schlauch**
insect **das Insekt**
insect repellent **das Insektenmittel**
insomnia **die Schlaflosigkeit**
instant coffee **der Pulverkaffee**
insurance **die Versicherung**
interesting (adj) **interessant**
Internet **das Internet**
interpret **dolmetschen**
interpreter **der/die Dolmetscher(in)**
intravenous drip **die Infusion**
invitation **die Einladung**
invoice **die Rechnung**
Ireland **Irland**
Irish (adj) **irisch**
Irishman **der Ire**
Irishwoman **die Irin**
iron (material) **das Eisen**; (for clothes) **das Bügeleisen**; (verb) **bügeln**
is: he/she/it is... **er/sie/es ist...**
island **die Insel**
it **es**
Italian **der/die Italiener(in)**; (adj) **italienisch**
Italy **Italien**

J

jacket **die Jacke**
jam **die Marmelade, die Konfitüre**
January **Januar**
jazz **der Jazz**
jeans **die Jeans**
jellyfish **die Qualle**
jeweler **der Juwelier**
jeweler's **das Juweliergeschäft**
jewelry **der Schmuck**
job **die Arbeit**
jog (verb) **joggen**; to go for a jog (verb) **joggen gehen**
joke **der Witz**
journey **die Fahrt, die Reise**
July **Juli**
jumper **der Pullover**
June **Juni**
just (only) **nur**; it's just arrived **es ist gerade angekommen**

K

kettle **der Wasserkessel**
key **der Schlüssel**
keyboard **die Tastatur**
kidney **die Niere**
kilo **das Kilo**
kilometer **der Kilometer**
kitchen **die Küche**
knee **das Knie**
knife **das Messer**
knit **stricken**
knitwear **die Strickwaren** (f pl)
know **wissen**; (be acquainted with) **kennen**; I don't know **ich weiß nicht**
kohlrabi **der Kohlrabi**

L

label **das Etikett**
lace **die Spitze**
laces (shoe) **die Schnürsenkel** (m pl)
lady **die Dame**
lake **der See**
lamb (animal) **das Lamm**; (meat) **das Lammfleisch**
lamp **die Lampe**
lampshade **der Lampenschirm**
land **das Land**; (verb) **landen**
language **die Sprache**
laptop **der Laptop**
large (adj) **groß**
last (adj: final) **letzter**; last week **letzte Woche**; at last! **endlich!**
late (adj) **spät**; the bus is late **der Bus hat Verspätung**
later (adj) **später**
laugh (verb) **lachen**
laundry (place) **die Wäscherei**; (dirty clothes) **die Wäsche**
lawn **der Rasen**
lawnmower **der Rasenmäher**
lawyer **der Rechtsanwalt/ die Rechtsanwältin**
laxative **das Abführmittel**
lazy (adj) **faul**

lead **die Leine**
lead-free (adj) **bleifrei**
leaf **das Blatt**
leaflet **die Broschüre, der Flyer**
learn (verb) **lernen**
leather **das Leder**
lecture hall **der Vorlesungssaal**
leek **der Lauch, der Porree**
left (adj: not right) **links**; there's nothing left **es ist nichts mehr übrig**
left luggage locker **das Gepäckschließfach**
left side **die linke Seite**
leg **das Bein**
lemon **die Zitrone**
lemonade **die Limonade**
length **die Länge**
lens **die Linse**
less (adj) **weniger**
lesson **die Stunde**
letter (mail) **der Brief**; (alphabet) **der Buchstabe**
lettuce **der Kopfsalat**
library **die Bibliothek, die Bücherei**
license **die Genehmigung**; (driving) **der Führerschein**
life **das Leben**
lift: could you give me a lift? **können Sie mich mitnehmen?**
light **das Licht**; (adj) **leicht**; (not dark) **hell**
light bulb **die (Glüh)birne**
lighter **das Feuerzeug**; lighter fuel **das Feuerzeugbenzin**
light meter **der Belichtungsmesser**
like: I like you **ich mag Sie**; I like swimming **ich schwimme gern**; it's like... **es ist wie...**; like this **so**
lime (fruit) **die Limette**
lip balm **der Lippen-Fettstift**
lipstick **der Lippenstift**
liqueur **der Likör**
list **die Liste**
liter **der Liter**
literature **die Literatur**
litter **der Abfall**
little (adj: small) **klein**; it's a little big **es ist ein bisschen zu groß**; just a little **nur ein bisschen**
liver **die Leber**
lobster **der Hummer**
lollipop **der Lutscher**
long (adj) **lang**
lost property **das Fundbüro**
lot: a lot **viel**
loud (adj) **laut**; (color) **grell**
lounge **das Wohnzimmer**; (in hotel) **die Lounge**

love **die Liebe**; (verb) **lieben**
low (adj) **niedrig**; (voice) **tief**
luck **das Glück**; *good luck!*
　　viel Glück!
luggage **der Koffer, das**
　　Gepäck; *luggage cart* **der**
　　Gepäckwagen; *luggage*
　　rack **die Gepäckablage**
lunch **das Mittagessen**
Luxembourg
　　Luxemburg

M

mad (adj) **verrückt**
magazine **die Zeitschrift**
mail **die Post**
mailbox **der Briefkasten**
main courses **die**
　　Hauptgerichte (nt pl)
main road **die Hauptstraße**
make **machen**
makeup **das Make-up**
man **der Mann**
manager **der/die**
　　Geschäftsführer(in)
many: not many (adj) **nicht**
　　viele
map (of country)
　　die Landkarte;
　　(of town) **der Stadtplan**
marble **der Marmor**
March **März**
margarine **die Margarine**
market **der Markt**
marmalade **die**
　　Orangenmarmelade
married (adj) **verheiratet**
mascara **die Mascara,**
　　die Wimperntusche
Mass (church) **die Messe**
match (light) **das**
　　Streichholz; (sport)
　　das Spiel
material (fabric) **der Stoff**
matter: it doesn't matter
　　das macht nichts
mattress **die Matratze**
May **Mai**
maybe **vielleicht**
me: it's me **ich bin's**; *it's for*
　　me **es ist für mich**; *give it*
　　to me **geben Sie es mir**
meal **das Essen**
mean: what does this mean?
　　was bedeutet das?
meat **das Fleisch**
mechanic **der/die**
　　Mechaniker(in)
medication **die Medikamente**
　　(nt pl)
medicine **die Medizin**
meeting **die Besprechung,**
　　das Treffen
melon **die Melone**
men **die Männer**
men's toilets **die**
　　Herrentoilette

menu **die Speisekarte**
message **die Nachricht**
metro station **die**
　　U-Bahnstation
microwave **die**
　　Mikrowelle
middle: in the middle
　　in der Mitte
midnight **die Mitternacht**
milk **die Milch**
mine: it's mine **es gehört mir**
mineral water **das**
　　Mineralwasser
minute **die Minute**
mirror **der Spiegel**
mistake **der Fehler**
modem **das Modem**
modern architecture **die**
　　moderne Architektur
Monday **Montag**
money **das Geld**
monitor **der Monitor,**
　　der Bildschirm
month **der Monat**
monument **das Denkmal**
moon **der Mond**
moped **das Moped**
more **mehr**
morning **der Morgen**; *in the*
　　morning **am Morgen**
mother **die Mutter**
motorbike **das Motorrad**
motorboat **das Motorboot**
motorway **die Autobahn**
mountain **der Berg**
mountain bike
　　das Mountainbike
mouse **die Maus**
mousse (for hair)
　　der Schaumfestiger
moustache **der Schnurrbart**
mouth **der Mund**
move (verb) **bewegen**;
　　(house) **umziehen**;
　　don't move! **stillhalten!**
movie **der Film**
movie theater **das Kino**
Mr. **Herr**
Mrs. **Frau**
Ms. **Frau**
much (adj) **viel**
mum **die Mama**
Munich **München**
museum **das Museum**
mushroom **der Pilz**
music **die Musik**
musical instrument **das**
　　Musikinstrument
musician **der/die**
　　Musiker(in)
music system **die**
　　Musikanlange
mussels **die Muscheln** (f pl)
must: I must... **ich muss...**
mustard **der Senf**
my: my book **mein Buch**;
　　my keys **meine**
　　Schlüssel

N

nail (metal, finger) **der Nagel**
nail clippers **der Nagelzwicker**
nail file **die Nagelfeile**
nail polish **der Nagellack**
name **der Name**; *last name*
　　der Nachname; *what's*
　　your name? **wie heißen Sie?**
napkin **die Serviette**
narrow (adj) **eng**
near (adj) **nah**; *near the door*
　　nahe der Tür; *near London*
　　in der Nähe von London
necessary (adj) **notwendig**
neck **der Hals**
necklace **die Halskette**
need (verb) **brauchen**; *I*
　　need... **ich brauche...**;
　　there's no need **das ist**
　　nicht nötig
needle **die Nadel**
negative (photo) **das Negativ**
nephew **der Neffe**
Netherlands **die Niederlande**
never **nie**
new (adj) **neu**
news **die Nachrichten**
newsagent's (shop) **der**
　　Zeitungskiosk
newspaper **die Zeitung**
New Zealand **Neuseeland**
New Zealander **der/die**
　　Neuseeländer(in)
next **nächster**;
　　next week **nächste Woche**
nice (adj: attractive) **hübsch**;
　　(pleasant) **angenehm**;
　　(to eat) **lecker**
niece **die Nichte**
night **die Nacht**
nightclub **der Nachtclub**
nightgown **das Nachthemd**
night porter **der Nachtportier**
nine **neun**
nineteen **neunzehn**
ninety **neunzig**
no (response) **nein**;
　　I have no money
　　ich habe kein Geld
noisy (adj) **laut**
noon (midday) **der Mittag**
north **der Norden**
Northern Ireland **Nordirland**
North Sea **die Nordsee**
nose **die Nase**
not **nicht**
notebook **das Notizbuch**
notepad **der Notizblock**
notes **die Banknoten** (f pl)
nothing **nichts**
novel **der Roman**
November **November**
now **jetzt**
nowhere **nirgendwo**
number **die Zahl**; (telephone)
　　die Nummer *number plate*
　　das Nummernschild

nurse **der/die Krankenpfleger/ Krankenschwester**
nut (fruit or seed) **die Nuss**; (for bolt) **die Mutter**

O

occasionally **gelegentlich**
October **Oktober**
of **von**; the name of the hotel **der Name des Hotels**
office **das Büro**
often **oft**
oil **das Öl**
ointment **die Salbe**
OK **okay**
old (adj) **alt**; how old are you? **wie alt sind Sie?**
olive **die Olive**
omelet **das Omelette**
on... **auf...**
one (number) **eins**; one beer/sausage **ein Bier/eine Wurst**
one million **eine Million**
onion **die Zwiebel**
online maps **die Online-Karten**
only **nur**
open (verb) **öffnen**; (adj) **offen**
opening times **die Öffnungszeiten**
opera **die Oper**
operating room **der Operationssaal**
operation **die Operation**
operator **die Vermittlung**
optician **der/die Augenarzt/ Augenärztin**
or **oder**
orange (adj) (color) **orange**; (fruit) **die Orange**
orange juice **der Orangensaft**
orchestra **das Orchester**
ordinary (adj) **gewöhnlich**
other: the other... **der/die/das andere...**
our **unser/e**; it's ours **es gehört uns**
out **aus**; he's out **er ist nicht da**
outside **außerhalb**
oven **der Backofen**
over (more than) **über**; (finished) **vorbei**; (across) **über**;
over there **dort drüben**
overtake (verb) **überholen**
oyster **die Auster**

P

package (parcel) **das Paket**
packet **das Paket**; (cigarettes) **die Schachtel**
pack of cards **das Kartenspiel**

padlock **das Vorhängeschloss**
page **die Seite**
pain **der Schmerz**
painkiller (medicine) **die Schmerztablette**
paint **die Farbe**
pair **das Paar**
pajamas **der Schlafanzug**
palace **der Palast**
pale (adj) **blass**
pancake **der Pfannkuchen**
paper **das Papier**; (newspaper) **die Zeitung**
paraffin **das Paraffin**
pardon? **wie bitte?**
parents **die Eltern**
park **der Park**; (verb) **parken**; no parking **Parken verboten**
parking lot **der Parkplatz**
parsley **die Petersilie**
parting (hair) **der Scheitel**
party (celebration) **die Party**; (group) **die Gruppe**; (political) **die Partei**
passenger **der Fahrgast, der Passagier**
passport **der Pass, der Ausweis**; passport control **die Passkontrolle**
password **das Passwort**
pasta **die Nudeln** (f pl)
pastry **das Gebäck**
path **der Weg**
pavement **der Bürgersteig**
pay (verb) **bezahlen**
payment **die Bezahlung**
peach **der Pfirsich**
peanuts **die Erdnüsse** (f pl)
pear **die Birne**
pearl **die Perle**
peas **die Erbsen** (f pl)
pedestrian **der Fußgänger**
pedestrian zone **die Fußgängerzone**
pen **der Stift**
pencil **der Bleistift**;
pencil sharpener **der Bleistiftspitzer**
penicillin **das Penizillin**
penknife **das Taschenmesser**
pen pal **der/die Brieffreund(in)**
people **die Leute**
pepper **der Pfeffer**; (red/ green) **der Paprika**
peppermints **die Pfefferminzbonbons**
per: per night **pro Nacht**
perfect (adj) **perfekt**
perfume **das Parfüm**
perhaps **vielleicht**
perm **die Dauerwelle**
pet passport **der Tierpass**
pets **die Haustiere** (nt pl)
pharmacy **die Apotheke**; 24-hour duty pharmacy **der Apotheken-Notdienst**
phone booth **die Telefonzelle**

phonecard **die Telefonkarte**
photocopier **der Fotokopierer**
photograph **das Foto**; (verb) **fotografieren**
photographer **der Fotograf**
phrase book **der Sprachführer**
piano **das Klavier**
pickpocket **der Taschendieb**
picnic **das Picknick**
piece **das Stück**
pill **die Tablette**
pillow **das Kopfkissen**
pilot **der/die Pilot(in)**
pin **die Stecknadel**
PIN (number) **die Geheimnummer**
pineapple **die Ananas**
pink (adj) **rosa**
pipe (for smoking) **die Pfeife**; (for water) **das Rohr**
piston **der Kolben**
place **der Platz**; (town, etc.) **der Ort**; at your place **bei Ihnen**
plant **die Pflanze**
plastic **das Plastik**
plastic bag **die Tragetasche, die Plastiktüte**
plate **der Teller**
platform **das Gleis, der Bahnsteig**
play (theater) **das Stück**; (verb) **spielen**
please **bitte**
plug (electrical) **der Stecker**; (sink) **der Stöpsel**
plumber **der/die Klempner(in)**
pocket **die Tasche**
poison **das Gift**
Poland **Polen**
Pole **der/die Pole/Polin**
police **die Polizei**
police officer **der/die Polizist(in)**
police report **der Polizeibericht**
police station **das Polizeirevier**
Polish **polnisch**
politics **die Politik**
poor (adj) **arm**; (bad quality) **schlecht**
pop music **die Popmusik**
popsicle **das Eis am Stiel**
pork **das Schweinefleisch**
port (harbor) **der Hafen**
porter (hotel) **der Portier**
possible (adj) **möglich**
post **die Post**; (verb) **aufgeben**
postcard **die Postkarte**
postcode **die Postleitzahl**
poster **das Poster**
postman/postwoman **der/die Briefträger(in)**
post office **das Postamt**

potato **die Kartoffel**
pottery **die Töpferei**
poultry **das Geflügel**
pound (money, weight) **das Pfund**
powdered detergent **das Waschpulver**
pram **der Kinderwagen**
prawns **die Krabben** (f pl)
prefer: I prefer... **ich mag lieber...**
pregnant (adj) **schwanger**
prescription **das Rezept**
presentation **der Vortrag**
pretty (adj) (beautiful) **schön**; (quite) **ziemlich**; *pretty good* **recht gut**
price **der Preis**
priest **der/die Geistliche**
printer **der Drucker**
private (adj) **privat**
problem **das Problem**
professor **der/die Professor(in)**
profits **der Gewinn**
public (adj) **öffentlich**
public holiday **der Feiertag**
pull (verb) **ziehen**
pump (for water) **die Pumpe**
puncture **die Reifenpanne**; **der platte Reifen**; *have a flat tyre* **einen Platten haben**
purple (adj) **lila**
purse **das Portemonnaie**
push (verb) **drücken**
put (verb) **legen, stellen, setzen**

Q

quality **die Qualität**
quarter **das Viertel**
quay **der Kai**
question **die Frage**
queue **die Schlange**, (verb) **anstehen**
quick (adj) **schnell**
quiet (adj) **still, ruhig**
quite (fairly) **ziemlich**; (fully) **ganz**

R

rabbit **das Kaninchen**
radiator **der Heizkörper**; (car) **der Kühler**
radio **das Radio**
radish **der Rettich**; (small red) **das Radieschen**
railway **die Bahn**
rain **der Regen**
raincoat **der Regenmantel**
raisins **die Rosinen** (f pl)
rake **der Rechen**
rare (adj) (uncommon) **selten**; (steak) **blutig**
raspberries **die Himbeeren** (f pl)
rat **die Ratte**

razor blades **die Rasierklingen** (f pl)
read (verb) **lesen**
reading lamp **die Leselampe**
ready (adj) **fertig**
ready meals **die Fertiggerichte** (nt pl)
receipt **die Quittung**
reception **der Empfang**
receptionist **die Empfangsperson**
record (music) **die Schallplatte**; (sporting, etc) **der Rekord**
record shop **das Schallplattengeschäft**
red (adj) **rot**
refreshments **die Erfrischungen** (f pl)
registered mail **das Einschreiben**
relative **der Verwandte**
relax (verb) **sich entspannen**
religion **die Religion**
remember (verb) **sich erinnern**; *I don't remember* **ich erinnere mich nicht**
rent (verb) **mieten**
report **der Bericht**
research **die Forschungen**
reservation **die Reservierung**
rest (remainder) **der Rest**; (verb) **sich ausruhen**
restaurant **das Restaurant**
return (verb) (come back) **zurückkommen**; (give back) **zurückgeben**
return ticket **die Rückfahrkarte**
rhubarb **der Rhabarber**
rice **der Reis**
rich (adj) **reich**
right (adj) (correct) **richtig**; (direction) **rechts**
right side **die rechte Seite**
ring (jewelry) **der Ring**; (verb: to call) **anrufen**
ripe (adj) **reif**
river **der Fluss**
road **die Straße**
roasted (adj) **geröstet**
robbery **der Diebstahl**
rock (stone) **der Stein**; (music) **der Rock**
roll (bread) **das Brötchen**
roof **das Dach**
room (hotel) **das Zimmer**; (space) **der Raum**
room service **der Zimmerservice**
rope **das Seil**
rose **die Rose**
round (adj) (circular) **rund**
rubber (material) **der Gummi**
rubbish **der Abfall**
ruby (stone) **der Rubin**

rug (mat) **der Läufer**; (blanket) **die Wolldecke**
ruins **die Ruinen** (f pl)
ruler (for drawing) **das Lineal**
rum **der Rum**
run (verb) **laufen**
runway **die Start-und Landebahn**

S

sad (adj) **traurig**
safe (adj) **sicher**
safety pin **die Sicherheitsnadel**
sailboat **das Segelboot**
sailing **das Segeln**
salad **der Salat**
salami **die Salami**
sale (at lower prices) **der Schlussverkauf**
sales **der Absatz**
salmon **der Lachs**
salt **das Salz**
same: the same dress **das gleiche Kleid**; *same again please* **nochmal dasselbe, bitte**
sand **der Sand**
sandals **die Sandalen** (f pl)
sandwich **das Sandwich**
sanitary napkins **die Damenbinden** (f pl)
Saturday **Samstag**
sauce **die Soße**
saucepan **der Kochtopf**
saucer **die Untertasse**
sauna **die Sauna**
sausage **die Wurst**
say (verb) **sagen**; *what did you say?* **was haben Sie gesagt?**; *how do you say...?* **wie sagt man...?**
Scandinavia **Skandinavien**
scarf **der Schal**; (head) **das Kopftuch**
schedule **der Zeitplan**
school **die Schule**
scissors **die Schere**
Scotland **Schottland**
Scotsman **der Schotte**
Scotswoman **die Schottin**
Scottish (adj) **schottisch**
screen **der Bildschirm**
screw **die Schraube**
screwdriver **der Schraubenzieher**
sea **das Meer**
seafood **die Meeresfrüchte** (f pl)
seat **der Sitz**
seat belt **der Sicherheitsgurt**
second (time) **die Sekunde**; (in series) **zweiter**; *second class* **zweiter Klasse**

secretary **der/die Sekretär(in)**
see (verb) **sehen;** *I can't see*
 ich kann nichts sehen; *I*
 see **ich verstehe;** *see you*
 soon **bis bald;** *see you*
 tomorrow **bis morgen**
self-employed (adj)
 selbstständig
self-service laundry **der**
 Waschsalon
sell (verb) **verkaufen**
seminar **das Seminar**
separate (adj) **getrennt;**
 separated: we are
 separated **wir leben**
 getrennt
separately **getrennt**
September **September**
serious (adj) **ernst**
server (waiter/waitress)
 der/die Kellner(in)
seven **sieben**
seventeen **siebzehn**
seventy **siebzig**
several **mehrere**
sew (verb) **nähen**
shampoo **das Shampoo**
shave: to have a shave (verb)
 sich rasieren
shaving cream **die**
 Rasiercreme
shawl **das Umhängetuch**
she **sie**
sheet **das (Bett)laken**
shell **die Muschel**
shellfish (as food) **die**
 Schalentiere (nt pl)
sherry **der Sherry**
ship **das Schiff**
shirt **das Hemd**
shoelaces **die Schnürsenkel**
 (m pl)
shoe polish **die Schuhcreme**
shoe size **die Schuhgröße**
shoe shop **das**
 Schuhgeschäft
shoes **die Schuhe** (m pl)
shop **das Geschäft**
shopkeeper **der/die**
 Verkäufer(in)
shopping **das Einkaufen,**
 das Shoppen; (items
 bought) **die Einkäufe;**
 to go shopping (verb)
 einkaufen gehen
short (adj) **kurz**
shorts **die Shorts**
shoulder **die Schulter**
shower (bath) **die Dusche;**
 (rain) **der Schauer**
shower gel **das Duschgel**
shutter (camera)
 der Verschluss; (window)
 der Fensterladen
sick (adj: ill) **krank;** *I feel sick*
 mir ist übel; *to be sick*
 (verb: vomit) **sich**
 übergeben

side **die Seite;** (edge)
 die Kante
sidelights **das Standlicht**
sightseeing **die**
 Besichtigungen (f pl)
sign **das Schild**
silk **die Seide**
silver (metal) **das Silber;**
 (color) **silber**
SIM card **die SIM-Karte**
simple (adj) **einfach**
sing (verb) **singen**
singing **das Singen**
single (adj: one) **einziger;**
 (unmarried) **ledig, single**
single room **das**
 Einzelzimmer
single ticket **die einfache**
 Fahrkarte
sister **die Schwester**
sister-in-law **die Schwägerin**
six **sechs**
sixteen **sechzehn**
sixty **sechzig**
ski (verb) **Ski fahren**
ski binding **die Skibindung**
ski boots **die Skistiefel** (m pl)
skid (verb) **schleudern**
skiing **das Skifahren;** *to go*
 skiing (verb) **Skifahren**
 gehen
ski lift **der Skilift**
skin cleanser **der**
 Hautreiniger
ski resort **der Skiurlaubsort**
skirt **der Rock**
skis **die Skier** (m pl)
ski sticks **die Skistöcke** (m pl)
sky **der Himmel**
sledge **der Schlitten**
sleep **der Schlaf;**
 (verb) **schlafen**
sleeping bag **der Schlafsack**
sleeping pill **die**
 Schlaftablette
sleeve **der Ärmel**
slice of... **das Stück...**
slippers **die Pantoffeln** (m pl)
slow (adj) **langsam**
small (adj) **klein**
smell **der Geruch;**
 (verb) **riechen**
smile **das Lächeln;**
 (verb) **lächeln**
smoke **der Rauch;**
 (verb) **rauchen**
snack **der Imbiss**
sneakers **die Turnschuhe**
snow **der Schnee**
so **so;** *not so much* **nicht so**
 viel
soaking solution
 (for contact lenses) **die**
 Aufbewahrungslösung
soap **die Seife**
socks **die Socken** (f pl)
soda water **das Sodawasser**
sofa **die Couch, das Sofa**

soft (adj) **weich**
soil **die Erde**
somebody **jemand**
somehow **irgendwie**
something **etwas**
sometimes **manchmal**
somewhere **irgendwo**
son **der Sohn**
song **das Lied**
sorry! (apology) **Verzeihung!,**
 Entschuldigung!; *I'm*
 sorry **es tut mir leid;**
 sorry? (pardon) **wie bitte?**
soup **die Suppe**
south **der Süden**
South Africa **Südafrika**
souvenir **das Souvenir**
spa (town) **der Kurort;** (at a
 hotel) **das Spa**
spade (shovel) **der Spaten**
spades (cards) **Pik**
spanner **der**
 Schraubenschlüssel
spares **die Ersatzteile** (nt pl)
sparkplug **die**
 Zündkerze
speak **sprechen;** *do you*
 speak English? **sprechen**
 Sie Englisch?; *I don't*
 speak German **ich spreche**
 kein Deutsch
speed **die Geschwindigkeit**
spider **die Spinne**
spinach **der Spinat**
spoon **der Löffel**
sport **der Sport;** *sports*
 center **das Sportzentrum**
spring (mechanical)
 die Feder; (season)
 der Frühling
square (shape) **das Quadrat;**
 (in town) **der Platz**
stadium **das Stadion**
staircase **die Treppe**
stairs **die Treppe**
stamp **die Briefmarke**
stand **der Stand**
stapler **das Heftgerät**
star **der Stern;** (film) **der Star**
start **der Start, der Anfang;**
 (verb) **anfangen**
starters **die Vorspeisen** (f pl)
statement **die Aussage**
station **der Bahnhof;**
 (underground) **die Station**
statue **die Statue**
steak **das Steak**
steal (verb) **stehlen;** *it's*
 been stolen **es ist**
 gestohlen worden
steamed (adj) **gedämpft**
steamer (boat) **der**
 Dampfer; (cooking) **der**
 Dampfkochtopf
steering wheel **das Lenkrad**
stepdaughter **die Stieftochter**
stepfather **der Stiefvater**
stepmother **die Stiefmutter**

stepson **der Stiefsohn**
still water **Wasser ohne Kohlensäure, das Tafelwasser**
sting **der Stich**; (verb) **stechen**
stockings **die Strümpfe** (m pl)
stomach **der Bauch, der Magen**
stomach ache **die Bauchschmerzen** (m pl), **die Magenschmerzen** (m pl)
stop (bus stop) **die Haltestelle**; (verb) **anhalten**; *stop!* **halt!**
storm **der Sturm**
strawberries **die Erdbeeren** (f pl)
stream (water) **der Bach**
street **die Straße**
string (cord) **der Faden**; (guitar, etc.) **die Saite**
stroller **der Sportwagen**
strong (adj: person, drink) **stark**; (material) **stabil**; (taste) **streng**
student **der/die Student(in)**
stupid (adj) **dumm**
suburban train **S-Bahn**
suburbs **der Stadtrand**
sugar **der Zucker**
suit **der Anzug**; *it suits you* **es steht Ihnen**
suitcase **der Koffer**
sun **die Sonne**
sunbathe (verb) **sonnenbaden**
sunburn **der Sonnenbrand**
Sunday **Sonntag**
sunglasses **die Sonnenbrille**
sunny: it's sunny (adj) **es ist sonnig**
sunshade **der Sonnenschirm**
suntan: to get a suntan (verb) **braun werden**
suntan lotion **das Sonnenöl**
suntanned (adj) **braungebrannt**
superior **der/die Vorgesetzte**
supermarket **der Supermarkt**
supper **das Abendessen**
supplement **der Zuschlag**
suppository **das Zäpfchen**
sure (adj) **sicher**
sweat **der Schweiß**; (verb) **schwitzen**
sweatshirt **das Sweatshirt**
sweet (adj: not sour) **süß**; (confectionery) **die Süßigkeit, der Bonbon**
swim (verb) **schwimmen**
swimming **das Schwimmen**
swimming pool **das Schwimmbad**
swimsuit **der Badeanzug**
swim trunks **die Badehose**
Swiss **der/die Schweizer(in)**; (adj) **schweizerisch**

switch **der Schalter**
Switzerland **die Schweiz**
swivel chair **der Drehstuhl**
synagogue **die Synagoge**
syringe **die Spritze**
syrup **der Sirup**

T

table **der Tisch**
tablet **die Tablette**
taillights **die Rücklichter** (nt pl)
take **nehmen**
take-away **der Schnellimbiss**
takeout **der Abflug**
talcum powder **der Puder**
talk **das Gespräch**; (verb) **reden**
tall (adj) **groß**
tampons **die Tampons** (m pl)
tangerine **die Mandarine**
tap **der Hahn**
tapestry **der Wandteppich**
taxi **das Taxi**
taxi rank **der Taxistand**
tea **der Tee**; *black tea* **der schwarze Tee**; *tea with milk* **der Tee mit Milch**
teacher **der/die Lehrer(in)**
tea towel **das Geschirrtuch**
technician **der/die Techniker(in)**
telephone **das Telefon**
television **das Fernsehen**; *to watch television* (verb) **fernsehen**
temperature **die Temperatur**; (fever) **das Fieber**
ten **zehn**
tennis **das Tennis**
tent **das Zelt**
ten thousand **zehntausend**
tent peg **der Hering**
tent pole **die Zeltstange**
terminal **das Terminal**
terrace **die Terrasse**
than: bigger than **größer als**
thank (verb) **danken**; *thanks* **danke**; *thank you* **danke schön**
that: that man **dieser Mann**; *that woman* **diese Frau**; *what's that?* **was ist das?**; *I think that...* **ich denke, dass...**
the **der** (masculine singular); **die** (feminine singular); **das** (neuter singular); **die** (plural)
theater **das Theater**
their: their room **ihr Zimmer**; *their books* **ihre Bücher**; *it's theirs* **es gehört ihnen**
them: it's them **sie sind es**; *it's for them* **es ist für sie**; *give it to them* **geben Sie es ihnen**
then **dann**

there **da**; *there is/are... es gibt...; is/are there...?* **gibt es...?**
these **diese**
they **sie**
thick (adj) **dick**
thief **der Dieb**
thin (adj) **dünn**
think (verb) **denken**; *I think so* **ich glaube ja**; *I'll think about it* **ich überlege es mir**
third (adj) **dritter**
thirsty (adj) **durstig**; *I'm thirsty* **ich habe Durst**
thirteen **dreizehn**
thirty **dreißig**
this: this man **dieser Mann**; *this woman* **diese Frau**; *what's this?* **was ist das?**; *this is Mr....* **das ist Herr...**
those **diese da**; *those things* **die Dinge dort**
thousand **tausend**
three **drei**
three hundred **dreihundert**
throat **die Kehle**
throat lozenges **die Halstabletten** (f pl)
through **durch**
thunderstorm **das Gewitter**
Thursday **Donnerstag**
ticket **die Karte**; *ticket booth* **der Schalter**
tide: high tide **die Flut**; *low tide* **die Ebbe**
tie **die Krawatte**; (verb) **festmachen**
tight (adj) **eng**
tights **die Strumpfhose**
tile (floor, wall, etc.) **die Fliese**
time **die Zeit**; *what time is it?* **wie spät ist es?**
timetable (train, bus) **der Fahrplan**
tip (money) **das Trinkgeld**; (end) **die Spitze**
tire **der Reifen**
tired (adj) **müde**
tissues **die Taschentücher**
to: to England **nach England**; *to the station* **zum Bahnhof**; *to the doctor* **zum Arzt**
toast **der Toast**
tobacco **der Tabak**
toboggan **der Schlitten**
today **heute**
together **zusammen**
toilet **die Toilette**
toilet paper **das Toilettenpapier**
tomato **die Tomate**
tomato juice **der Tomatensaft**
tomorrow **morgen**
tongue **die Zunge**
tonic **das Tonic**
tonight **heute Abend**
too (also) **auch**; (excessively **zu**

tooth **der Zahn**
toothache **die Zahnschmerzen** (m pl)
toothbrush **die Zahnbürste**
toothpaste **die Zahnpasta**
torch **die Taschenlampe**
tour **die Rundreise**
tour guide **der/die Reiseleiter(in)**
tourist **der/die Tourist(in)**
tourist office **die Touristeninformation, das Fremdenverkehrsbüro**
towel **das Handtuch**
tower **der Turm**
town **die Stadt**
town hall **das Rathaus**
toy **das Spielzeug**
track suit **der Trainingsanzug**
tractor **der Traktor**
trade fair **die Handelsmesse**
tradition **die Tradition**
traffic **der Verkehr**
traffic jam **der Stau**
traffic lights **die Ampel**
trailer **der Anhänger**
train **der Zug**
trainee **der/die Auszubildende**
tram **die Straßenbahn**
translate **übersetzen**
translator **der/die Übersetzer(in)**
transmission **das Getriebe**
trash can liner **der Müllsack**
travel agency **das Reisebüro**
tray **das Tablett**
tree **der Baum**
trousers **die Hose**
truck **der Lastwagen**
true (adj) **wahr**
trunk (car) **der Kofferraum**
try (verb) **versuchen**
Tuesday **Dienstag**
tunnel **der Tunnel**
Turk **der/die Türke/Türkin**
Turkey **die Türkei**
Turkish **türkisch**
tweezers **die Pinzette**
twelve **zwölf**
twenty **zwanzig**
twin beds **die zwei Einzelbetten**
two **zwei**
typewriter **die Schreibmaschine**

U

ugly (adj) **hässlich**
umbrella **der (Regen)schirm**
uncle **der Onkel**
under... **unter...**
underground **die U-Bahn**
underpants **die Unterhose**
underskirt **der Unterrock**

understand **verstehen**; I don't understand **ich verstehe nicht**
underwear **die Unterwäsche**
United Kingdom **das Vereinigte Königreich**
United States **die Vereinigten Staaten** (m pl)
university **die Universität**
university lecturer **der/die Dozent(in)**
unleaded **bleifrei**
until **bis**
unusual **ungewöhnlich**
up **oben**; up there **da oben**
upward **nach oben**
urgent **dringend**
us: it's us **wir sind es**; it's for us **es ist für uns**; give it to us **geben Sie es uns**
use **der Gebrauch**; (verb) **gebrauchen**; it's no use **es hat keinen Zweck**
useful (adj) **hilfreich**
usual (adj) **gewöhnlich**
usually **gewöhnlich**

V

vacancy (room) **ein freies Zimmer**
vaccination **der Impftermin** (appointment); **die Impfung**
vacuum cleaner **der Staubsauger**
valley **das Tal**
valuables **die Wertsachen** (f pl)
valve **das Ventil**
vanilla **die Vanille**
vase **die Vase**
veal **das Kalbfleisch**
vegetable **das Gemüse**
vegetarian **der/die Vegetarier(in)**; (adj) **vegetarisch**
vehicle **das Fahrzeug**
very **sehr**
vest **das (Unter)hemd**
vet **der Tierarzt**
video (tape, film) **das Video**; video games **die Videospiele** (nt pl)
video recorder **der Videorecorder**; video tape **die Videokassette**
Vienna **Wien**
view **der Blick**
viewfinder **der Sucher**
villa **die Villa**
village **das Dorf**
vinegar **der Essig**
violin **die Geige**
visit **der Besuch**; (verb) **besuchen**
visiting hours **die Besuchszeit**

visitor **der/die Besucher(in)**
vitamin tablet **die Vitamintablette**
vodka **der Wodka**
voice **die Stimme**
voicemail **die Voicemail**

W

wait (verb) **warten**; wait! **warten Sie!**
waiter (server) **der Ober, der Kellner**
waiting room **das Wartezimmer**; (station) **der Wartesaal**
waitress (server) **die Kellnerin**
Wales **Wales**
walk **der Spaziergang**; (verb) **gehen**; to go for a walk (verb) **spazieren gehen**
wall (inside) **die Wand**; (outside) **die Mauer**
wallet **die Brieftasche**
war **der Krieg**
wardrobe **der Kleiderschrank**
warm (adj) **warm**
was: I was **ich war**; he/she/it was **er/sie/es war**
wash basin **das Waschbecken**
wasp **die Wespe**
watch **die (Armband)uhr**; (verb) **ansehen**
water **das Wasser**
waterfall **der Wasserfall**
water heater **das Heißwassergerät**
wave **die Welle**; (verb: with hand) **winken**
wavy (hair) **wellig**
we **wir**
weather **das Wetter**
website **die Webseite**
wedding **die Hochzeit**
wedding anniversary **Hochzeitstag**
Wednesday **Mittwoch**
weeds **das Unkraut**
week **die Woche**
welcome **willkommen**; you're welcome **keine Ursache**
well-behaved (adj) **brav**
well-done (steak) **durchgebraten**
wellingtons **die Gummistiefel**
Welsh **walisisch**
Welshman/woman **der/die Waliser(in)**
were: you were (singular informal) **du warst**; (plural informal) **ihr wart**; (singular and plural formal) **Sie waren**; we/they were **wir/sie waren**

west **der Westen**
wet (adj) **nass**
what? **was?**
wheel **das Rad**
wheelchair **der Rollstuhl**;
 wheelchair accessible (adj)
 rollstuhlgerecht;
 wheelchair user **der**
 Rollstuhlfahrer
when? **wann?**
where? **wo?**
whether **ob**
which? **welcher?**
whisky **der Whisky**
white (adj) **weiß**
who? **wer?**
why? **warum?**
wide (adj) **breit**
wife **die (Ehe)frau**
wind **der Wind**
window **das Fenster**;
 window box **der**
 Blumenkasten
windshield **die**
 Windschutzscheibe
wine **der Wein**
wine list **die Weinkarte**
wing **der Flügel**
with **mit**
without **ohne**
witness **der/die Zeuge/**
 Zeugin

woman **die Frau**
women's toilets **die**
 Damentoilette
wood (material) **das Holz**
wool **die Wolle**
word **das Wort**
work **die Arbeit**; (verb)
 arbeiten; (machine, etc)
 funktionieren
worse (adj) **schlechter**
worst (adj) **schlechtester**
wrapping paper **das**
 Packpapier; (for presents)
 das Geschenkpapier
wrist **das Handgelenk**
writing paper **das**
 Schreibpapier
wrong (adj) **falsch**

X , Y , Z

x-ray **die Röntgenaufnahme**
x-ray department **die**
 Röntgenabteilung
year **das Jahr**
yellow (adj) **gelb**
yes **ja**
yesterday **gestern**
yet: is it ready yet? **ist es**
 schon fertig?; not yet
 noch nicht
yogurt **der Jogurt**

you (singular informal) **du**;
 (plural informal) **ihr**;
 (singular and plural formal)
 Sie; for you **für dich/euch/**
 Sie; with you **mit dir/euch/**
 Ihnen
your (singular informal)
 dein/e; (plural informal)
 euer/eure; (singular and
 plural formal) **Ihr/e**; your
 shoes **deine/eure/Ihre**
 Schuhe
yours: is this yours?
 (singular informal) **gehört**
 das dir? (singular formal;
 plural) **gehört das Ihnen?**
youth hostel **die**
 Jugendherberge
zip **der Reißverschluß**
zoo **der Zoo**

Dictionary
GERMAN TO ENGLISH

The gender of German nouns listed here is indicated by the abbreviations *m* for masculine, *f* for feminine, and *nt* for neuter. Plural nouns are followed by the abbreviations *m pl*, *f pl*, and *nt pl*. The feminine form of most occupations and personal attributes is made by adding **-in** to the masculine form: **Buchhalter(in)** *accountant*, for example. Exceptions to this rule are listed separately. Adjectives and verbs are denoted by *adj* and *verb*.

A

Abend (m) *evening*
Abendessen (nt) *dinner, supper*
aber *but*
Abfahrt (f) *departure*
Abfall (m) *litter, trash*
Abfertigungsschalter (m) *check-in* (desk)
Abflug (m) *departures, take-off*; **Abflughalle** (f) *departure lounge*
Abführmittel (nt) *laxative*
Absatz (m) *heel* (shoe); *sales* (figures)
absichtlich *deliberately*
Abteil (nt) *compartment*
Abteilung (f) *department*
acht *eight*
achtzehn *eighteen*
achtzig *eighty*
Adapter (m) *adaptor*
Adresse (f) *address*
Aids *Aids*
Aktentasche (f) *briefcase*
Alkohol (m) *alcohol*
alle(s) *all, every*; **alle Straßen** *all the streets*; **das ist alles** *that's all*; **alles** *everything*
allein (adj) *alone*
allergisch (adj) *allergic*
Allgemeinarzt *general practitioner*
alt *old*; **wie alt sind Sie?** *how old are you?*
am *at, next to*; **am Bahnhof** *at the station*; **am Fenster** *next to the window*
Amerika *America*
Amerikaner(in) (m/f) *American* (person)
amerikanisch (adj) *American*
Ampel (f) *traffic lights*
Ananas (f) *pineapple*
andere *another* (different); **der/die/das andere...** *the other...*; **ein anderes Zimmer** *another room*; **das ist etwas anderes!** *that's different!*; **etwas anderes** *something else*;

andere (cont.) **jemand anders** *someone else*; **woanders** *somewhere else*; **ein andermal** *another time*
Anfang (m) *start*
anfangen (verb) *to start*
Anfänger (m) *beginner*
Angeln (nt) *fishing*; **Angeln gehen** (verb) *to go fishing*
angenehm (adj) *nice, pleasant*
anhalten (verb) *to stop*
Anhänger (m) *trailer*
ankommen (verb) *to arrive*
Ankunft (f) *arrivals*
Anrufbeantworter (m) *answering machine*
anrufen (verb) *to ring, call*
ansehen (verb) *to watch*
anstehen (verb) *to queue*
Antiquitätengeschäft (nt) *antiques shop*
Antiquitätenladen (m) *antique dealer*
Antiseptikum (nt) *antiseptic*
Antragsformular (nt) *application form*
Anzug (m) *suit*
Aperitif (m) *appetizer*
Apfel (m) *apple*
Apotheke (f) *chemist's, pharmacy*; **Apotheken-Notdienst** (m) *24-hour duty pharmacy*
Appetit (m) *appetite*
Aprikose (f) *apricot*
April *April*
Arbeit (f) *job, work*
arbeiten (verb) *to work*
Arbeitsfläche (f) *countertop*
arm (adj) *poor* (not rich)
Arm (m) *arm*
Armband (nt) *bracelet*
Armbanduhr (f) *watch*
Ärmel (m) *sleeve*
Ärmelkanal (m) *English Channel*
Arzt (m) *doctor*
Aschenbecher (m) *ashtray*
Asthma (nt) *asthma*
atmen (verb) *to breathe*

attraktiv (adj) *attractive*
auch *too* (also)
auf... *on/at/in...*; **auf der Post** *at the post office*; **auf Englisch** *in English*
Aufbewahrungslösung (f) *soaking solution* (for contact lenses)
aufgeben (verb) *to post*
aufstehen (verb) *to get up* (rise)
Aufzug (m) *elevator* (in building)
Auf Wiedersehen *goodbye*
Auge (nt) *eye*; **die Augen** *eyes*
Augenarzt/Augenärztin (m/f) *optician*
Augenbraue (f) *eyebrow*
August *August*
aus *out*
Ausflug (m) *excursion*
Ausgang (m) *exit*
ausgezeichnet (adj) *excellent*
Ausländer(in) (m/f) *foreigner*
Auspuff (m) *exhaust*
ausruhen: sich ausruhen (verb) *to rest*
Aussage (f) *statement*
außerhalb *outside*
aussteigen (verb) *to get off* (bus, etc.)
Ausstellung (f) *exhibition*
Auster (f) *oyster*
Australien *Australia*
Australier(in) (m/f) *Australian* (person)
australisch (adj) *Australian*
Ausweis (m) *passport*
Auszubildende (m/f) *trainee*
Auto (nt) *car*
Autobahn (f) *highway*
automatisch (adj) *automatic*

B

Baby (nt) *baby*
Bach (m) *stream* (water)
backen (verb) *to bake*
Bäcker(in) (m/f) *baker*
Bäckerei (f) *bakery*
Backofen (m) *oven*
Bad (nt) *bath*; **ein Bad nehmen** (verb) *to have a bath*

Badeanzug (m) *swimsuit*
Badehose (f) *swim trunks*
Badewanne (f) *bathtub*
Badezimmer (nt) *bathroom*
Bahn (f) *railway*
Bahnhof (m) *station*
Bahnsteig (m) *platform*
Balkon (m) *balcony*
Ball (m) *ball*
Ballett (nt) *ballet*
Banane (f) *banana*
Band (f) *band (musicians)*
Bank (f) *bank*
Banknoten (f pl) *(bank)notes*
Bar (f) *bar (drinks)*
Bargeld (nt) *cash*; **bar bezahlen** (verb) *to pay cash*
Bart (m) *beard*
Batterie (f) *battery*
Bauarbeiter(in) (m/f) *builder*
Bauch (m) *stomach*
Bauchschmerzen (m pl) *stomach ache*
Bauer (m) *farmer*
Bauernhof (m) *farm*
Baum (m) *tree*
Baumarkt (m) *hardware store*
Baumwolle (f) *cotton*
Bayern *Bavaria*
bedeutet: was bedeutet das? *what does this mean?*
behindert (adj) *disabled*
beide *both*; **wir beide** *both of us*
beige (adj) *beige*
bei Ihnen *at your place*
Bein (nt) *leg*; **Beinbruch** (m) *broken leg*
Beispiel (nt) *example*; **zum Beispiel** *for example*
beißen (verb) *to bite*
Belag (m) *filling (in sandwich)*
Belgien *Belgium*
Belgier(in) (m/f) *Belgian (person)*
belgisch (adj) *Belgian*
Belichtungsmesser (m) *light meter*
Benzin (nt) *gas*
Berater(in) (m/f) *consultant*
Berg (m) *hill, mountain*
Bericht (m) *report*
Berliner (m) *doughnut*
beschäftigt (adj) *busy (occupied)*
Bescheinigung (f) *certificate*
besetzt (adj) *engaged (occupied)*
Besichtigungen (f pl) *sightseeing*
besonders *especially*
Besprechung (f) *meeting*
besser (adj) *better*
Basteln (nt) *DIY*
bester *best*
bestreiten (verb) *to deny*

Besuch (m) *visit*
besuchen (verb) *to visit*
Besucher(in) (m/f) *visitor*
Besuchszeit (f) *visiting hours*
betrunken (adj) *drunk*
Bett (nt) *bed*
Bettlaken (nt) *sheet*
Bettwäsche (f) *bed linens*
bewegen (verb) *to move*
bezahlen (verb) *to pay*
Bezahlung (f) *payment*
BH (m) *bra*
Bibliothek (f) *library*
Bier (nt) *beer*
Bikini (m) *bikini*
Bildschirm (m) *screen, monitor*
billig (adj) *cheap*
bin: ich bin *I am*
Biochemie (f) *biochemistry*
Birne (f) *pear*
bis *until*; **bis Freitag** *by Friday*; **bis morgen** *see you tomorrow*;
bis bald *see you soon*
Biss (m) (verb) *bite (by dog, etc)*
bisschen *a little*; **es ist ein bisschen zu groß** *it's a little big*; **nur ein bisschen** *just a little*
bist: du bist *you are (informal)*
bitte *please*; **wie bitte?** *pardon?*
bitter (adj) *bitter*
Blase (f) *blister*
Blatt (nt) *leaf*
blau (adj) *blue*
blauer Fleck (m) *bruise*
bleichen (verb) *to bleach (hair)*
Bleichmittel (nt) *bleach*
bleifrei (adj) *unleaded*
Bleistift (m) *pencil*
Bleistiftspitzer (m) *pencil sharpener*
Blick (m) *view*
blind (adj) *blind (cannot see)*
Blindenhund (m) *guide dog*
Blinker (m) *indicator*
Blitz (m) *flash (camera)*
blond (adj) *blond*
Blume (f) *flower*
Blumenbeet (nt) *flowerbed*
Blumenkasten (m) *window box*
Blumenkohl (m) *cauliflower*
Blumenladen (m) *florist*
Blumenstecken (nt) *flower arranging*
Bluse (f) *blouse*
Blut (nt) *blood*
blutig (adj) *rare (steak)*
Blutprobe (f) *blood test*
Boden (m) *bottom, floor, ground*; **Bodenplane** (f) *groundsheet*
Bohnen (f pl) *beans*

Boiler (m) *boiler*
Bonbon (m) *sweet (candy)*
Boot (nt) *boat (small)*
Bordkarte (f) *boarding pass*
Botschaft (f) *embassy*
Boxen (nt) *boxing*
braten (verb) *fry*
Bratpfanne (f) *frying pan*
brauchen (verb) *to need*; **ich brauche...** *I need...*
braun (adj) *brown*; **braun werden** (verb) *to get a suntan*
braungebrannt *suntanned*
brav (adj) *well-behaved*
breit (adj) *wide*
Bremse (f) *brake*
bremsen (verb) *to brake*
brennen (verb) *to burn*
Bridge (nt) *bridge (game)*
Brief (m) *letter (mail)*
Brieffreund(in) (m/f) *pen pal*
Briefkasten (m) *mailbox*
Briefmarke (f) *stamp*
Brieftasche (f) *wallet*
Briefträger(in) (m/f) *postman/postwoman*
Brille (f) *eyeglasses*
britisch (adj) *British*
Brokkoli (m) *broccoli*
Brombeere (f) *blackberry*
Brosche (f) *brooch*
Broschüre (f) *brochure, leaflet*
Brot (nt) *bread*
Brötchen (nt) *bread roll*
Brücke (f) *bridge*
Bruder (m) *brother*
Brunnen (m) *fountain*
Brüssel *Brussels*
Brust (f) *chest (part of body)*
Buch (nt) *book*
buchen (verb) *to book*
Bücherei (f) *library*
Buchhalter(in) (m/f) *accountant*
Buchhandlung (f) *bookshop*
Buchstabe (m) *letter (alphabet)*
Budget (nt) *budget*
Bügeleisen (nt) *iron (for clothes)*
bügeln (verb) *to iron*
Burg (f) *castle*
Bürgersteig (m) *pavement*
Büro (nt) *office*
Bürste (f) *brush*
bürsten *to brush (verb: hair)*
Bus (m) *bus*
Busbahnhof (m) *bus/coach station*
Büstenhalter (m) *bra*
Butter (f) *butter*

C

Café (nt) *café*
Campinggas (nt) *camping gas*
Campingplatz (m) *campsite*

Campingplatzverwaltung (f) *campsite office*
Chips (m pl) *chips*
Compact-Disc (f) *compact disc*
Computer (m) *computer*
Couch (f) *sofa*
Creme (f) *cream (lotion)*
Curry (nt) *curry*

D

da *there*
Dach (nt) *roof*
Dachboden (m) *attic*
Dachrinne (f) *gutter*
Dame (f) *lady, woman*
Damenbinden (f pl) *sanitary napkins*
Damentoilette (f) *women's toilets*
Dampfer (m) *steamer (boat)*
Dampfkochtopf (m) *steamer (cooking)*
Däne (m) *Dane*
Dänemark *Denmark*
Dänin (f) *Dane*
dänisch *Danish*
danken (verb) *to thank;*
    danke *thanks;*
    danke schön *thank you*
dann *then*
das (nt) *the;*
    das ist Herr... *this is Mr....*
Dauerwelle (f) *perm*
Debit-Karte (f) *debit card*
Decke (f) *blanket; ceiling*
dein(e) *your (singular informal)*
Delegierte(r) (m/f) *delegate*
denken (verb) *to think*
Denkmal (nt) *monument*
Deodorant (nt) *deodorant*
der *the (masculine)*
deutsch (adj) *German;*
    Deutsch *German (language)*
Deutscher/Deutsche (m/f) *German (person)*
Deutschland *Germany*
Dezember *December*
Diabetiker(in) (m/f) *diabetic*
Diamant (m) *diamond (gem)*
dick (adj: person) *fat; thick*
die *the (feminine and plural)*
Dieb (m) *thief*
Diebstahl (m) *robbery*
Dienstag *Tuesday*
diese: diese Frau *that/this woman*
Diesel (m) *diesel*
dieser: dieser Mann *that/this man*
Dirigent (m) *conductor (orchestra)*
Dokument (nt) *document*
Dollar (m) *dollar*
dolmetschen (verb) *to interpret*
Dolmetscher(in) (m/f) *interpreter*

Dom (m) *cathedral*
Donau: die Donau *Danube*
Donnerstag *Thursday*
Doppelzimmer (nt) *double room*
Dorf (nt) *village*
dort drüben *over there*
Dose (f) *can (container);*
    Dosenöffner (m) *can opener*
Dozent(in) *university lecturer*
Drahtseilbahn (f) *cable car*
Drehstuhl (m) *swivel chair*
drei *three*
dreihundert *three hundred*
dreißig *thirty*
dreizehn *thirteen*
dringend *urgent*
dritter *third*
drücken (verb) *to push*
Drucker (m) *printer*
du *you (singular informal)*
dumm (adj) *stupid*
dunkel (adj) *dark*
dünn (adj) *thin*
durch *through*
Durchfall (m) *diarrhea*
durchgebraten (adj) *well-done (meat)*
Durst (m) *thirst;* **ich habe Durst** *I'm thirsty*
durstig (adj) *thirsty*
Dusche (f) *shower*
Duschgel (nt) *shower gel*

E

E-Mail (f) *email;* **E-Mail-Adresse** (f) *email address*
Ebbe (f) *low tide*
Ecke (f) *corner*
Ehefrau (f) *wife*
Ehemann (m) *husband*
ehrlich (adj) *honest*
Ei (nt) *egg*
Eile: ich bin in Eile *I'm in a hurry*
Eimer (m) *bucket*
Einbrecher (m) *burglar*
einchecken (verb) *to check in*
einer von beiden *either of them*
einfach (adj) *simple;* **einfache Fahrkarte** (f) *single ticket*
Einfahrt (f) *driveway*
Eingang (m) *entrance*
Einkäufe (m pl) *shopping (items bought)*
Einkaufen (nt) *shopping (activity);* **einkaufen gehen** (verb) *to go shopping*
Einladung (f) *invitation*
einlösen (verb) *to cash*
eins *one (number);*
    ein Bier/eine Wurst *one beer/one sausage*

Einschreiben (nt) *registered mail*
einsteigen (verb) *to get on (bus, etc)*
Eintrittskarte (f) *entrance ticket*
Eintrittspreis (m) *admission charge*
Einwegwindeln (f pl) *disposable diapers*
Einzelzimmer (nt) *single room*
einziger *single (one)*
Eis (nt) *ice, ice cream;*
    Eiscreme (f) *ice cream;*
    Eis am Stiel (nt) *popsicle*
Eisen (nt) *iron (metal)*
elastisch (adj) *elastic*
Elektriker(in) (m/f) *electrician*
elektrisch (adj) *electric*
elf *eleven*
Ellbogen (m) *elbow*
Eltern *parents*
Empfang (m) *reception*
Empfangsperson (m/f) *receptionist*
Ende (nt) *end*
endlich! *at last!*
eng (adj) *narrow, tight*
England *England*
Engländer(in) (m/f) *Englishman/Englishwoman*
englisch (adj) *English;*
    Englisch *English (language)*
Enkel (m) *grandson*
Enkelin (f) *granddaughter*
Entschuldigung! *excuse me!, sorry!*
entweder... oder... *either... or...*
entwickeln (verb) *to develop (film)*
Entzündung (f) *infection*
Epileptiker(in) (m/f) *epileptic*
er *he*
Erbsen (f pl) *peas*
Erdbeeren (f pl) *strawberries*
Erde (f) *soil*
Erdgeschoss (nt) *ground floor*
Erdnüsse (f pl) *peanuts*
Erfrischungen (f pl) *refreshments*
erinnern: sich erinnern *to remember;* **ich erinnere mich nicht** *I don't remember*
Erkältung (f) *cold (illness);* **ich bin erkältet** *I have a cold*
Ermäßigungen (f pl) *discounts*
ernst (adj) *serious*
Ersatzteile (nt pl) *spares*
Erste Hilfe (f) *first aid*
erster *first;* **erster Klasse** *first class;* **erster Stock** (m) *first floor*
es *it*
Essen (nt) *food, meal;*
    essen (verb) *to eat*

Essig (m) *vinegar*
Esszimmer (nt) *dining room*
Etikett (nt) *label*
etwa: etwa 16 *about 16*
etwas *something*
euer/eure *your* (plural informal)
Eurotunnel (m) *Channel Tunnel*

F

Faden (m) *string* (cord)
Fahne (f) *flag*
Fähre (f) *ferry*
fahren (verb) *to drive, to go* (travel)
Fahrer(in) (m/f) *driver*
Fahrgast (m) *passenger*
Fahrplan (m) *timetable* (train, bus)
Fahrpreis (m) *fare*
Fahrrad (nt) *bicycle*
Fahrt (f) *journey*
Fahrzeug (nt) *vehicle*
fair (adj) *fair* (just)
falsch (adj) *wrong*
Familie (f) *family*
Fan (m) *fan* (enthusiast)
fantastisch (adj) *fantastic*
Farbe (f) *color, paint*
Farbfilm (m) *color film*
fast *almost*
faul (adj) *lazy*
Februar *February*
Feder (f) *spring* (mechanical)
Fehler (m) *mistake*
Feiertag (m) *public holiday*
Feige (f) *fig*
Feinkostgeschäft (nt) *delicatessen*
Feld (nt) *field*
Fenster (nt) *window*
Fensterladen (m) *shutter*
Ferien *holiday*
Fernsehen (nt) *television*
fernsehen *to watch television*
Ferse (f) *heel* (foot)
fertig (adj) *ready*;
    Fertiggerichte (nt pl) *ready meals*
festmachen (verb) *to tie*
Fett (nt) (adj) *fat*
feucht (adj) *damp*
Feuer (nt) *fire*
Feuerlöscher (m) *fire extinguisher*
Feuerwehr (f) *fire department*
Feuerwerk (nt) *fireworks*
Feuerzeug (nt) *lighter*
Feuerzeugbenzin (nt) *lighter fuel*
Fieber (nt) *temperature, fever*
Film (m) *film, movie*
Filter (m) *filter*
Filterpapier (nt) *filter papers*
Finger (m) *finger*
Fisch (m) *fish*

Fischgeschäft (nt) *fishmonger's*
flach (adj) (level) *flat*
Flasche (f) *bottle*
Flaschenöffner (m) *bottle opener*
Fleisch (nt) *meat*
Fliege (f) *fly* (insect)
fliegen (verb) *to fly*
Fliese (f) *tile* (floor, wall, etc.)
Floh (m) *flea*
Flohspray (nt) *flea spray*
Flöte (f) *flute*
Flug (m) *flight*
Flügel (m) *wing*
Flughafen (m) *airport*
Flughafenbus (m) *airport bus*
Fluglinie (f) *airline*
Flugnummer (f) *flight number*
Flugsteig (m) *gate* (at airport)
Flugticket (nt) *flight ticket*
Flugzeug (nt) *aircraft*
Fluss (m) *river*
Flut (f) *high tide*
Flyer (m) *leaflet, flyer*
Fön (m) *hair dryer*
Forschungen (f pl) *research*
Foto (nt) *photograph*
Fotograf (m) *photographer*
fotografieren (verb) *to photograph*
Fotokopierer (m) *photocopier*
Frage (f) *question*
Frankreich *France*
Franzose (m) *Frenchman*
Französin (f) *Frenchwoman*
französisch (adj) *French*
Frau *Mrs.*
Frau *Ms.*
Frau (f) *woman, wife*
frei (adj) *free*
Freitag *Friday*
Fremdenverkehrsbüro (nt) *tourist office*
Freund(in) (m/f) *friend*
freundlich (adj) *friendly*
freut mich *pleased to meet you*
Friedhof (m) *cemetery*
Friseur (m) *hairdresser's*
Friseursalon (m) *ladies' hairdresser's*
Fritten *French fries*
froh (adj) *glad*
Frost (m) *frost*;
Frucht (f) *fruit*; **Fruchtsaft** (m) *fruit juice*
früh (adj) *early*
Frühling (m) *spring* (season)
Frühstück (nt) *breakfast*
fühlen *to feel* (verb: touch)
Führerschein (m) *driver's license*
Führung (f) *guided tour*

Füllung (f) *filling* (in tooth, cake)
Fundbüro (nt) *lost property*
fünf *five*
fünfzehn *fifteen*
fünfzig *fifty*
funktionieren (verb) *to work* (machine, etc.)
für *for*; **für mich** *for me*; **wofür?** *what for?*; **für eine Woche** *for a week*
furchtbar (adj) *awful*
Fuß (m) *foot*; **Füße** (m pl) *feet*
Fußball (m) *football*
Fußboden (m) *floor* (ground)
Fußgänger (m) *pedestrian*;
Fußgängerzone (f) *pedestrian zone*

G

Gabel (f) *fork*
Gang (m) *aisle*
ganz *quite* (fully)
Garage (f) *garage* (for parking)
Garantie (f) *guarantee*
garantieren (verb) *to guarantee*
Garten (m) *garden*
Gartenarbeit (f) *gardening*
Gartencenter (nt) *garden center*
Gärtner(in) (m/f) *gardener*
Gaspedal (nt) *accelerator*
Gast (m) *guest*
Gastgeber(in) (m/f) *host*
Gasthaus (nt) *inn*
Gebäck (nt) *pastry*
Gebäude (nt) *building*
geben (verb) *to give*
Gebiet (nt) *field of work*
Gebiss (m) *dentures, false teeth*
geboren *to be born*: **ich bin in... geboren** *I was born in...*
gebraten (adj) *fried*
Gebrauch (m) *use*
gebrauchen (verb) *to use*
gebrochen *broken* (arm, etc.)
Geburtstag (m) *birthday*; **Herzlichen Glückwunsch!** *happy birthday!*
Geburtstagsgeschenk (nt) *birthday present*
Geburtstagskarte (f) *birthday card*
gedämpft (adj) *steamed*
gefährlich (adj) *dangerous*
Geflügel (nt) *poultry*
Gefrierschrank (m) *freezer*
gegen *against*
gegenüber *opposite*
gegrillt (adj) *grilled*
Geheimnummer (f) *PIN* (number)
gehen (verb) *to go, to walk*; **gehen Sie weg!** *go away!*

Geige (f) *violin*
Geisteswissenschaften
(f pl) *humanities*
Geistlicher/Geistliche (m/f)
priest
gekocht (adj) *boiled*
Gel (nt) *gel* (hair)
gelb (adj) *yellow*
Geld (nt) *money*
Geldautomat (m)
cash machine (ATM)
Geldschein (m) *banknote*
gelegentlich *occasionally*
Gemüse (nt) *vegetable*
Genehmigung (f) *license*
genug (adj) *enough*
Gepäck (nt) *luggage*
Gepäckablage (f) *luggage rack*
Gepäckausgabe (f)
baggage claim
Gepäckschließfach (nt)
left luggage locker
Gepäckwagen (m) *luggage cart*
gerade *just;* **es ist gerade angekommen** *it's just arrived*
gerecht (adj) *fair* (just)
gern: ich schwimme gern
I like swimming
geröstet (adj) *roasted*
Geruch (m) *smell*
Geschäft (nt) *business, shop*
Geschäftsführer(in)
(m/f) *manager*
Geschenk (nt) *gift;*
Geschenkpapier (nt)
wrapping paper
Geschichte (f) *history*
geschieden (adj) *divorced*
Geschirrspülmaschine (f)
dishwasher
Geschirrspülmittel (nt)
dishwashing liquid
Geschirrtuch (nt)
tea towel
geschlossen (adj) *closed*
Geschmack (m) *flavor*
Geschwindigkeit (f) *speed*
Gesicht (nt) *face*
Gespräch (nt) *talk*
gestern *yesterday*
Getränk (nt) *drink*
getrennt (adj) *separate(ly);*
wir leben getrennt
we are separated
Getriebe (nt) *transmission*
Gewehr (nt) *gun* (rifle)
Gewinn (m) *profits*
Gewitter (nt) *thunderstorm*
gewöhnlich (adj) *ordinary, usual, usually*
gibt: es gibt… *there is/are…;*
gibt es…? *is/are there…?*
Gift (nt) *poison*
Gin (m) *gin*
Gitarre (f) *guitar*

Glas (nt) *glass*
glaube: ich glaube ja
I think so
gleiche *the same;* **das gleiche Kleid** *the same dress*
Gleis (nt) *platform*
Glocke (f) *bell* (church)
Glück (nt) *luck;* **viel Glück!**
good luck!
glücklich *happy*
Glühbirne (f) *light bulb*
Gold (nt) *gold*
Golf (nt) *golf*
Grafiker(in) (m/f) *designer*
Gras (nt) *grass*
gratis (adj) *free* (no charge)
grau (adj) *gray*
grell (adj) *loud* (colour)
Grenze (f) *border*
Grill (m) *barbecue, grill*
groß (adj) *big, large, tall;*
größer als *bigger than*
Großbritannien *Great Britain*
Großeltern *grandparents*
Großmutter (f)
grandmother
Großstadt (f) *city*
Großvater (m) *grandfather*
grün (adj) *green*
Grund (m) *bottom* (sea)
Gruppe (f) *party* (group)
Gummi (m) *rubber*
(material)
Gummiband (nt) *elastic band*
Gummistiefel (m pl)
wellingtons
Gurke (f) *cucumber*
Gürtel (m) *belt*
gut (adj) *good;* **mir ist nicht gut** *I don't feel well*
gut aussehend (adj)
handsome
Guten Abend *good night*
guten Tag *hello, good day*

H

Haar (nt) *hair*
Haarschnitt (m) *haircut*
Haarspray (nt) *hair spray*
Haarspülung (f) *conditioner*
haben (verb) *to have;* **ich habe… I** *have…;* **haben Sie…?** *do you have…?*
Hafen (m) *harbor, port*
Hahn (m) *tap*
Hähnchen (nt) *chicken*
(cooked)
halb *half;* **eine halbe Stunde**
half an hour
Halbbruder (m) *half-brother*
Halbpension (f) *half board*
Halbschwester (f) *half-sister*
hallo *hello* (on phone); *hi*
Hals (m) *neck*
Halsband (nt) *collar*
Halskette (f) *necklace*

Halstabletten (f pl)
throat lozenges
halt! *stop!*
Haltestelle (f) *stop* (bus stop)
Hamburger (m) *hamburger*
Hammer (m) *hammer*
Hamster (m) *hamster*
Hand (f) *hand*
Handbremse (f) *handbrake*
Händedruck (m) *handshake*
Handelsmesse (f) *trade fair*
Handgelenk (nt) *wrist*
Handgepäck (nt) *carry-on bag*
Handschuhe (m pl) *gloves*
Handtasche (f) *handbag*
Handtuch (nt) *towel*
Handy (nt) *cell phone*
hart (adj) *hard*
hässlich (adj) *ugly*
Hauptgericht (nt) *main course*
Hauptstraße (f) *main road*
Haus (nt) *house;*
zu Hause *at home*
Haushaltshilfe (f) *cleaner*
Haushaltswaren (f pl)
household products
Hausmeister(in) (m/f)
caretaker
Haustiere (nt pl) *pets*
Hautreiniger (m) *skin cleanser*
Hecke (f) *hedge*
Heftgerät (nt) *stapler*
Heftzwecke (f) *thumbtack*
heiß (adj) *hot;* **mir ist heiß**
I feel hot
heißen (verb) *to be called;*
wie heißt das? *what's it called?;* **wie heißen Sie?**
what's your name?
Heißwassergerät (nt)
water heater
Heizgerät (nt) *heater*
Heizkörper (m) *radiator*
Heizung (f) *heating*
helfen (verb) *to help*
hell (adj) *light* (not dark)
Hemd (nt) *shirt*
herauskommen (verb)
to get out
Herd (m) *cooker*
hereinkommen (verb)
to come in
Hering (m) *tent peg*
Herr *Mr.*
Herrenfriseur (m) *barber's*
Herrentoilette (f)
men's toilets
herunter *down*
Herz (nt) *heart, hearts*
(cards); **ich bin herzkrank**
I have a heart condition
herzlichen Glückwunsch!
congratulations!
Heuschnupfen (m) *hay fever*
heute *today;* **heute Abend** *tonight*

Hilfe (f) *help*
hilfreich (adj) *useful*
Himbeeren (f pl) *raspberries*
Himmel (m) *sky*
hinter... *behind...*
HIV-positiv (adj) *HIV-positive*
Hobby (nt) *hobby*
hoch (adj) *high*
Hochzeit (f) *wedding*
Hochzeitsreise (f) *honeymoon*
Hochzeitstag (m) *wedding anniversary*
Höhle (f) *cave*
holen (verb) *to get, to fetch*
Holland *Holland*
Holz (nt) *wood (material)*
Homöopathie (f) *homeopathy*
Honig (m) *honey*
hören (verb) *to hear*
Hörgerät (nt) *hearing aid*
Horn (nt) *horn (animal)*
Hose (f) *pants*
Hosenträger (m pl) *suspenders*
Hotelpersonal (nt) *housekeeping*
hübsch *nice (adj: attractive)*
Huhn (nt) *chicken (animal)*
Hummer (m) *lobster*
Hund (m) *dog*
hundert *hundred*
Hunger (m) *hunger;* **ich habe Hunger** *I'm hungry*
Hupe (f) *horn (car)*
husten (verb) *to cough;* **Husten** (m) *cough*
Hut (m) *hat*

I

ich *I;* **ich bin** *I am*
ihr *you (plural informal)*
ihr(e) *their/her;* **Ihr(e)** *your (singular and plural formal)*
im: im Hotel *in the hotel*
Imbiss (m) *snack*
immer *always*
Impftermin (f) *vaccination (appointment)*
Impfung (f) *vaccination*
in *in;* **in der Nacht** *at night*
induktive Höranlage (f) *hearing loop*
Infektion (f) *infection*
Information (f) *information*
Ingenieur(in) (m/f) *engineer*
Infusion (f) *intravenous drip*
Ingwer (m) *ginger (spice)*
Insekt (nt) *insect*
Insektenmittel (nt) *insect repellent*
Insel (f) *island*

interessant (adj) *interesting*
Internet (nt) *Internet*
Ire (m) *Irishman*
irgendwie *somehow*
irgendwo *somewhere*
Irin (f) *Irishwoman*
irisch (adj) *Irish*
Irland *Ireland*
ist *is;* **er/sie/es ist...** *he/she/it is...*
Italien *Italy*
Italiener(in) (m/f) *Italian*
italienisch (adj) *Italian*

J

ja *yes*
Jacke (f) *jacket*
Jahr (nt) *year*
Jahrmarkt (m) *fair, carnival*
Jalousie (f) *blinds*
Januar *January*
Jazz (m) *jazz*
Jeans (f) *jeans*
jeder *each, every, everyone*
jemand *somebody*
jetzt *now*
joggen (verb) *to jog;* **joggen gehen** (verb) *to go for a jog*
Jogurt (nt) *yogurt*
Jucken (nt) *itch*
Jugendherberge (f) *youth hostel*
Juli *July*
Junge (m) *boy*
Juni *June*
Juwelier (m) *jeweler*
Juweliergeschäft (nt) *jeweler's*

K

Kabelfernsehen (nt) *cable TV*
Kaffee (m) *coffee;* **Kaffee ohne Milch** *black coffee*
Käfig (m) *cage*
Kai (m) *quay*
Kalbfleisch (nt) *veal*
kalt (adj) *cold;* **mir ist kalt** *I am cold*
Kamera (f) *camera*
Kamm (m) *comb*
Kanada *Canada*
Kanadier(in) (m/f) *Canadian (person)*
kanadisch (adj) *Canadian*
Kanal (m) *canal*
Kaninchen (nt) *rabbit*
kann ich... haben? *can I have...?*
Kante (f) *side (edge)*

Kanu (nt) *canoe*
kaputt *broken (adj: machine, etc.)*
Karo *diamonds (cards)*
Karotte (f) *carrot*
Karte (f) *card, ticket;*
Kartenspiel (nt) *pack of cards*
Kartoffel (f) *potato*
Käse (m) *cheese*
Kasse (f) *box office, checkout*
Kassette (f) *cassette*
Kassettenrekorder (m) *cassette player*
Kassierer(in) *cashier* (m/f)
Kater (m) *hangover*
Katze (f) *cat*
kaufen (verb) *to buy*
Kaufhaus (nt) *department store*
Kaugummi (m) *chewing gum*
Kaution (f) *deposit*
Kehle (f) *throat*
kehren (verb) *to sweep*
Keilriemen (m) *fan belt*
kein *not any;* **ich habe kein Geld** *I don't have any money*
keine Ursache *you're welcome*
Keller (m) *cellar*
Kellner(in) (m/f) *server, waiter/waitress*
kennen *to know (to be acquainted with)*
Kerze (f) *candle*
Kilo (nt) *kilo*
Kilometer (m) *kilometer*
Kind (nt) *child*
Kinder *children*
Kinderbett (nt) *cot*
Kindersitz (m) *car seat*
Kinderstation (f) *children's ward*
Kinderwagen (m) *stroller*
Kino (nt) *movie theater*
Kirche (f) *church*
Kirmes (f) *fair, carnival*
Kirsche (f) *cherry*
Kissen (nt) *cushion*
klar (adj) *clear*
Klasse (f) *class*
klassische Musik (f) *classical music*
Klavier (nt) *piano*
Kleid (nt) *dress*
Kleiderbügel (m) *coat hanger*
Kleidergröße (f) *clothes size*
Kleiderschrank (m) *wardrobe*
Kleidung (f) *clothes*
klein (adj) *little, small*
Kleingarten (m) *allotment*
Kleingeld (nt) *change (money)*
kleinschneiden (verb) *to chop, to cut*
Klempner(in) (m/f) *plumber*
Klimaanlage (f) *air-conditioning*

Klingel (f) *(door) bell*
Klinke (f) *handle (door)*
Klub (m) *club*
klug (adj) *clever*
Knie (nt) *knee*
Knoblauch (m) *garlic*
Knöchel (m) *ankle*
Knochen (m) *bone*
Knopf (m) *button*
Koch/Köchin (m/f) *cook*
kochen (verb) *to boil, to cook*
Kochtopf (m) *saucepan*
Köder (m) *bait*
Koffer (m) *suitcase;*
Kofferraum (m) *trunk (car)*
Kohl (m) *cabbage*
Kohlrabi (m) *kohlrabi*
Kolben (m) *piston*
Köln *Cologne*
komisch (adj) *funny*
kommen (verb) *to come;* **ich komme aus…** *I come from…;* **kommen Sie her!** *come here!*
Kommode (f) *chest of drawers*
kompliziert (adj) *complicated*
Konditorei (f) *cake shop*
Kondom (nt) *condom*
Konferenz (f) *conference*
Konferenzzimmer (nt) *conference room*
Konfitüre (f) *jam*
können Sie…? *can you…?*
Konsulat (nt) *consulate*
Kontaktlinsen (f pl) *contact lenses*
kontaktloses Bezahlen *contactless payment*
Konzert (nt) *concert*
Kopf (m) *head*
Kopfhörer (m) *headphones*
Kopfkissen (nt) *pillow*
Kopfsalat (m) *lettuce*
Kopfschmerzen (m pl) *headache*
Kopftuch (nt) *headscarf*
Korb (m) *basket*
Korken (m) *cork*
Korkenzieher (m) *corkscrew*
Körper (m) *body*
Korridor (m) *corridor*
Kosmetika (nt pl) *cosmetics*
kosten (verb) *to cost;* **was kostet das?** *what does it cost?*
kostenlos (adj) *free (no charge)*
Kostenvoranschlag (m) *estimate*
Kotelett (nt) *chop (food)*
Krabbe (f) *crab*
Krabben (f pl) *shrimp*
Kragen (m) *collar*
Krampf (m) *cramp*
krank (adj) *ill, sick*
Krankenhaus (nt) *hospital*
Krankenpfleger (m) *nurse*
Krankenschwester (f) *nurse*

Krankenwagen (m) *ambulance*
Krawatte (f) *tie*
Krebs (m) *crayfish*
Kreditkarte (f) *credit card*
Kreuz *clubs (cards)*
Kreuzfahrt (f) *cruise*
Krieg (m) *war*
Krücken (f pl) *crutches*
Küche (f) *kitchen*
Kuchen (m) *cake*
kühl (adj) *cool*
Kühler (m) *radiator (car)*
Kühlschrank (m) *fridge*
Kunde (m) *client*
Kunst (f) *art*
Kunstgalerie (f) *art gallery*
Künstler(in) (m/f) *artist*
Kupplung (f) *clutch*
Kurort (m) *spa (town)*
kurz (adj) *short*
Kusine (f) *cousin*

L

Lächeln (nt) *smile;* **lächeln** (verb) *to smile*
lachen (verb) *to laugh*
Lachs (m) *salmon*
Ladegerät (nt) *charger (for mobiles)*
Ladekabel (nt) *charging cable*
Ladesäule (f) *charging station*
Ladestecker (m) *charger (for electric vehicles)*
Lagerfeuer (nt) *campfire*
Lamm (nt) *lamb (animal)*
Lammfleisch (nt) *lamb (meat)*
Lampe (f) *lamp*
Lampenschirm (m) *lampshade*
Land (nt) *country, land*
landen (verb) *to land*
Landkarte (f) *map (of country)*
lang (adj) *long*
Länge (f) *length*
langsam (adj) *slow*
langweilig (adj) *boring*
Laptop (m) *laptop (computer)*
Lastwagen (m) *truck*
Lauch (m) *leek*
laufen (verb) *to run*
Läufer (m) *rug (mat)*
laut (adj) *loud, noisy*
Leben (nt) *life*
Lebensmittelgeschäft (nt) *grocery*
Lebensmittelvergiftung (f) *food poisoning*
Leber (f) *liver*
lecker (adj) *nice (to eat)*
Leder (nt) *leather*
ledig (adj) *single (unmarried)*

leer (adj) *empty*
Leerung (f) *collection (postal)*
legen (verb) *to put*
Lehrer(in) *teacher*
Leiche (f) *body (corpse)*
leicht (adj) *easy, light (not heavy)*
leid: es tut mir leid *I'm sorry*
leihen (verb) *to hire*
Leim (m) *glue*
Leine (f) *lead*
Lektor(in) (m/f) *editor*
Lenkrad (nt) *steering wheel*
lernen (verb) *to learn*
Leselampe (f) *reading lamp*
lesen (verb) *to read*
letzter *last (final);* **letzte Woche** *last week*
Leute *people*
Licht (nt) *light*
lieb (adj) *dear (person)*
Liebe (f) *love*
lieben (verb) *to love*
lieber mögen (verb) *to prefer;* **ich mag lieber…** *I prefer…*
Lied (nt) *song*
Lieferung (f) *delivery*
Liegestuhl (m) *deck chair*
Likör (m) *liqueur*
lila (adj) *purple*
Limette (f) *lime (fruit)*
Limonade (f) *lemonade*
Lineal (nt) *ruler (for drawing)*
links *left (not right);* **linke Seite** *left side*
Linse (f) *lens*
Lippen-Fettstift (m) *lip balm*
Lippenstift (m) *lipstick*
Liste (f) *list*
Liter (m) *liter*
Literatur (f) *literature*
Locken (f pl) *curls*
Löffel (m) *spoon*
Lounge (f) *lounge (in hotel)*
Luft (f) *air*
Luftmatratze (f) *air mattress*
Luftpost (f) *airmail*
Lutscher (m) *lollipop*
Luxemburg *Luxembourg*

M

machen (verb) *to make;* **macht nichts** *it doesn't matter*
Mädchen (nt) *girl*
Magen (m) *stomach;* **Magenschmerzen** (m pl) *stomachache;* **Magenverstimmung** (f) *indigestion*
Mai *May*
Make-up (nt) *makeup*
Maler(in) (m/f) *decorator*

Manager(in) (m/f) *executive*
manchmal *sometimes*
Mandarine (f) *tangerine*
Mann (m) *man, husband*
Männer (m pl) *men*
Manschettenknöpfe (m pl) *cuff links*
Mantel (m) *coat*
Margarine (f) *margarine*
Markt (m) *market*
Marmelade (f) *jam*
Marmor (m) *marble*
März *March*
Mascara (f) *mascara*
Maske (f) *face mask*
Matratze (f) *mattress*
Mauer (f) *wall (outside)*
Maurer(in) (m/f) *bricklayer*
Maus (f) *mouse*
Mechaniker(in) (m/f) *mechanic*
Medikamente (nt pl) *medication*
Medizin (f) *medicine*
Meer (nt) *sea*; **Meeresfrüchte** (f pl) *seafood*
Mehl (nt) *flour*
mehr *more*; **Mehrgepäck** (nt) *excess baggage*
mehrere *several*
mein(e) *my*
Melone (f) *melon*
Messe (f) *mass (church)*
Messer (nt) *knife*
Metzgerei (f) *butcher's*
mieten (verb) *to rent*
Mikrowelle (f) *microwave*
Milch (f) *milk*
Milchprodukte (nt pl) *dairy products*
Million *million*
eine Million *one million*
Mineralwasser (nt) *mineral water*
Minute (f) *minute*
mir: es gehört mir *it's mine*
mit *with*
Mittag (m) *noon (midday)*
Mittagessen (nt) *lunch*
Mitte (f) *center, middle*; **in der Mitte** *in the middle*
Mitternacht (f) *midnight*
Mittwoch *Wednesday*
Möbel (nt pl) *furniture*
Mobiltelefon (nt) *cell phone*
möchten Sie...? *would you like...?*
Mode (f) *fashion*
Modem (nt) *modem*
moderne Architektur (f) *modern architecture*
möglich (adj) *possible*; **so bald wie möglich** *as soon as possible*
Möhre (f) *carrot*
Monat (m) *month*
Mond (m) *moon*
Monitor (m) *monitor*

Montag *Monday*
Moped (nt) *moped*
Morgen (m) *morning*; **am Morgen** *in the morning*; **morgen** *tomorrow*
Motor (m) *engine (motor)*
Motorboot (nt) *motorboat*
Motorhaube (f) *hood (car)*
Motorrad (nt) *motorbike*
Mountainbike (nt) *mountain bike*
müde (adj) *tired*
Müllsack (m) *trash can liner*
Mülltonne (f) *dustbin*
München *Munich*
Mund (m) *mouth*
Münze (f) *coin*
Muschel (f) *shell*
Muscheln (f pl) *mussels*
Museum (nt) *museum*
Musik (f) *music*;
Musikanlange (f) *music system*; **Musikinstrument** (nt) *musical instrument*
Musiker(in) (m/f) *musician*
müssen (verb) *to have to (must)*; **ich muss...** *I must...*
Mutter (f) *mother; nut (for bolt)*
Mütze (f) *cap (hat)*

N

nach *after, toward*; **nach England** *to England*
Nachname (m) *surname*
Nachricht (f) *message*
Nachrichten *news*
nächster *next*;
nächste Woche *next week*
Nacht (f) *night*
Nachthemd (nt) *nightgown*
Nachtisch (m) *desserts*
Nachtclub (m) *nightclub*
Nachtportier (m) *night porter*
Nachttisch (m) *bedside table*
Nadel (f) *needle*
Nagel (m) *nail (metal, finger)*; **Nagelfeile** (f) *nail file*; **Nagellack** (m) *nail polish*; **Nagelzwicker** (m) *nail clippers*
nah *close, near*; **nahe der Tür** *near the door*; **in der Nähe von London** *near London*
nähen (verb) *to sew*
Name (m) *name*
Nase (f) *nose*
nass (adj) *wet*
Nebel (m) *fog*
neben *beside*
Neffe (m) *nephew*
Negativ (nt) *negative (photo)*
nehmen (verb) *to take*
nein *no (response)*
neu (adj) *new*

neun *nine*
neunzehn *nineteen*
neunzig *ninety*
Neuseeland *New Zealand*
Neuseeländer(in) (m/f) *New Zealander*
nicht *not*;
nicht so viel *not so much*; **nicht viele** (adj) *not many*
Nichte (f) *niece*
nichts *nothing*
nie *never*
Niederlande: die Niederlande *the Netherlands*; **Niederländer(in)** (m/f) *Dutchman/Dutchwoman*
niederländisch (adj) *Dutch*
niedrig (adj) *low*
Niere (f) *kidney*
nirgendwo *nowhere*
noch ein *another one*;
noch einen Kaffee, bitte *another coffee, please*
nochmal *again*;
nochmal dasselbe, bitte *same again, please*
noch nicht *not yet*
Nockenwelle (f) *camshaft*
Norden (m) *north*
Nordirland *Northern Ireland*
Nordsee: die Nordsee *North Sea*
Notausgang (m) *emergency exit*
Notbremse (f) *emergency brake*
Notfall (m) *emergency*
nötig: das ist nicht nötig *there's no need*
Notizblock (m) *notepad*
Notizbuch (nt) *notebook*
notwendig (adj) *necessary*
November *November*
Nudeln (f pl) *pasta*
Nummer (f) *number*;
Nummernschild (nt) *number plate*
nur *just, only*
Nuss (f) *nut (fruit or seed)*

O

ob *whether*
oben *up*;
nach oben *upward*; **da oben** *up there*
Ober (m) *waiter*
Obst (nt) *fruit*
oder *or*
offen (adj) *open*
öffentlich (adj) *public*
öffnen (verb) *to open*
Öffnungszeiten (f pl) *opening times*
oft *often*
ohne *without*

ohnmächtig werden
(verb) to faint
Ohr (nt) ear;
Ohren (nt pl) ears
Ohrhörer earphones (m pl)
Ohrringe (m pl) earrings
okay OK
Oktober October
Öl (nt) oil
Olive (f) olive
Omelette (nt) omelet
Onkel (m) uncle
Online-Karten online maps
Oper (f) opera
Operation (f) operation
Operationssaal (m)
operating room
Orange (f) orange (fruit)
orange (adj) orange (color)
Orangenmarmelade (f)
marmalade
Orangensaft (m)
orange juice
Orchester (nt) orchestra
Ort (m) place (town, etc.)
Osten (m) east
Österreich Austria
Österreicher(in) (m/f)
Austrian (person);
österreichisch
(adj) Austrian
Ostsee (f) Baltic Sea

P

Paar (nt) pair
Packpapier (nt) wrapping
paper
Paket (nt) package, packet,
parcel
Palast (m) palace
Panne (f) breakdown (car)
Pantoffeln (m pl) slippers
Papier (nt) paper
Paprika (m) pepper
(red/green)
Paraffin (nt) paraffin
Parfüm (nt) perfume
Park (m) park
parken (verb) to park;
Parken verboten
no parking
Parkplatz (m) car park
Partei (f) party (political,
celebration)
Pass (m) passport
Passagier (m) passenger
passen Sie auf! be careful!
Passkontrolle (f)
passport control
Passwort (nt) password
peinlich (adj) embarrassing
Penizillin (nt) penicillin
perfekt (adj) perfect
Perle (f) pearl
Petersilie (f) parsley
Pfannkuchen (m) pancake
Pfeffer (m) pepper (spice)

Pfefferminzbonbons
(m pl) peppermints
Pfeife (f) pipe (for smoking)
Pfirsich (m) peach
Pflanze (f) plant
Pflaster (nt) adhesive
bandage (for cut)
Pforte (f) gate (garden gate)
Pfund (nt) pound
(money, weight)
Picknick (nt) picnic
Pik spades (cards)
Pilot(in) (m/f) pilot
Pilz (m) mushroom
Pinsel (m) paintbrush
Pinzette (f) tweezers
Pistole (f) gun (pistol)
Plastik (nt) plastic
Plastiktüte (f) plastic bag
platter Reifen (m) flat tire,
puncture; **einen Platten
haben** have a flat tire,
puncture
Platz (m) place, square
(in town)
Plätzchen (nt) biscuit
Pole (m) Pole
Polen Poland
Polin (f) Pole
Politik (f) politics
Polizei (f) police
Polizeibericht (m)
police report
Polizeirevier (nt)
police station
Polizist(in) (m/f)
police officer
polnisch Polish
Pommes chips
Popmusik (f) pop music
Porree (m) leeks
Portemonnaie (nt) purse
Portier (m) porter (hotel)
Portwein (m) port (drink)
Porzellan (nt) china
Post (f) mail
Postamt (nt) post office
Poster (nt) poster
Postkarte (f) postcard
Postleitzahl (f) postcode
Preis (m) price
prima! (adj) great!
privat (adj) private
pro per; **pro Nacht** per night
Problem (nt) problem
Professor(in) (m/f)
professor
prost! cheers!
Prothese (f) dentures,
false teeth
Puder (m) powder (cosmetics),
talcum powder
Pullover (m) sweater
Pulver (nt) powder
Pulverkaffee (m) instant
coffee
Pumpe (f) pump (for water)
Puppe (f) doll

Q, R

Quadrat (nt) square (shape)
Qualität (f) quality
Qualle (f) jellyfish
Quittung (f) receipt
Rad (nt) wheel
radfahren (verb) to cycle
Radiergummi (m)
rubber (eraser)
Radieschen (nt) radish
Radio (nt) radio
Rang (m) circle
Rasen (m) lawn
Rasenmäher (m) lawnmower
Rasiercreme (f) shaving
cream
rasieren: sich rasieren
(verb) to shave
Rasierklingen (f pl)
razor blades
Rasierwasser (nt) aftershave
Rathaus (nt) town hall
Ratte (f) rat
Rauch (m) smoke
rauchen (verb) to smoke
Raum (m) room (space)
Rechen (m) rake
Rechner (m) calculator
Rechnung (f) bill, invoice
recht (gut) fairly (good)
rechts right (direction);
rechte Seite (f) right side
**Rechtsanwalt/
Rechtsanwältin** (m/f)
lawyer
reden (verb) to talk
Regen (m) rain
Regenmantel (m) raincoat
Regenschirm (m) umbrella
Regierung (f) government
reich (adj) rich
reif (adj) ripe
Reifen (m) tire
Reifenpanne (f) flat tire,
puncture
Reinigung (f) dry cleaner
Reis (m) rice
Reise (f) journey
Reisebüro (nt) travel agency
Reiseführer (m) guide,
guidebook
Reiseleiter(in) (m/f)
tour guide
Reißnagel (m) thumbtack
Reißverschluß (m) zip
Rekord (m) record (sporting,
etc)
Religion (f) religion
Reservierung (f) reservation
Rest (m) rest (remainder)
Restaurant (nt) restaurant
Rettich (m) radish
Rezept (nt) prescription
Rhabarber (m) rhubarb
richtig (adj) right (correct)
riechen (verb) to smell; **das
riecht gut** that smells good

Riegel (m) *bolt* (on door)
Rindfleisch (nt) *beef*
Ring (m) *ring* (jewelry)
Rock (m) *skirt; rock* (music)
Rohr (nt) *pipe* (for water)
Rollstuhl (m) *wheelchair;*
   Rollstuhlfahrer (m)
   wheelchair user;
   rollstuhlgerecht (adj)
   wheelchair accessibler
Rolltreppe (f) *escalator*
Roman (m) *novel*
Röntgenabteilung (f)
   x-ray department
Röntgenaufnahme (f) *x-ray*
rosa (adj) *pink*
Rose (f) *rose*
Rosinen (f pl) *raisins*
rot (adj) *red*
Rubin (m) *ruby* (gem)
Rücken (m) *back* (body)
Rückfahrkarte (f)
   return ticket
Rücklichter (nt pl) *taillights*
Rucksack (m) *backpack*
Rückseite (f) *back* (not front)
rufen (verb) *to shout*
ruhig (adj) *quiet*
Ruinen (f pl) *ruins*
Rum (m) *rum*
rund (adj) *round* (circular)
Rundreise (f) *tour*

S

S Bahn (f) *suburban train*
sagen (verb) *to say;*
   was haben Sie gesagt?
   what did you say?;
   wie sagt man…?
   how do you say…?
Sahne (f) *cream*
   (for cake, etc.)
Saite (f) *string* (guitar, etc.)
Salami (f) *salami*
Salat (m) *salad*
Salbe (f) *ointment*
Salz (nt) *salt*
Sammlung (f) *collection*
   (stamps, etc.)
Samstag *Saturday*
Sand (m) *sand*
Sandalen (f pl) *sandals*
Sandwich (nt) *sandwich*
Satellitenfernsehen (nt)
   satellite TV
satt: ich bin satt *I'm full* (up)
sauber (adj) *clean*
Sauna (f) *sauna*
Schach *chess*
Schachtel (f) *box, packet*
Schachtel Pralinen (f)
   box of chocolates
Schaffner (m) *conductor* (bus)
Schal (m) *scarf*
Schalentiere (nt pl) *shellfish*
Schallplatte (f) *record*
   (music)

Schallplattengeschäft (nt)
   record shop
Schalter (m) *switch; ticket*
   booth
Schaltknüppel (m) *gear lever*
Schauer (m) *shower* (rain)
Schaumfestiger (m) *mousse*
   (for hair)
Scheck (m) *check*
Scheckheft (nt) *checkbook*
Scheckkarte (f) *debit card*
Scheinwerfer (m pl) *headlights*
Scheitel (m) *parting* (hair)
Schere (f) *scissors*
Schiff (nt) *boat, ship*
Schild (nt) *sign*
Schinken (m) *ham*
Schlaf (m) *sleep*
Schlafanzug (m) *pajamas*
schlafen (verb) *to sleep*
Schlaflosigkeit (f) *insomnia*
Schlafsack (m) *sleeping bag*
Schlaftablette (f) *sleeping pill*
Schlafzimmer (nt) *bedroom*
Schlange (f) *queue*
Schlauch (m) *inner tube*
schlecht (adj) *bad, poor*
   (quality)
schlechter (adj) *worse*
schlechtester (adj) *worst*
schleudern (verb) *to skid*
schließen (verb) *to close*
Schlitten (m) *sledge, toboggan*
Schlittschuhe *ice skates;*
Schlittschuh laufen gehen
   (verb) *to go ice-skating*
Schloss (nt) *castle*
Schlüssel (m) *key*
Schlussverkauf (m) *sale*
   (at reduced prices)
Schmerz (m) *ache, pain*
Schmerztablette (f)
   painkiller
Schmuck (m) *jewelry*
schmutzig (adj) *dirty*
Schnee (m) *snow*
schnelden (verb) *to cut*
schnell (adj) *fast, quick*
Schnellimbiss (m) *takeout*
Schnitt (m) *cut*
Schnuller (m) *pacifier*
   (for baby)
Schnupfen (m) *cold* (illness);
   ich habe Schnupfen *I*
   have a cold
Schnurrbart (m) *moustache*
Schnürsenkel (m pl)
   shoelaces
Schokolade (f) *chocolate*
schon *already, yet;*
   ist es schon fertig?
   is it ready yet?
schön (adj) *beautiful, pretty*
Schornstein (m) *chimney*
Schotte (m) *Scotsman*
Schottin (f) *Scotswoman*
schottisch (adj) *Scottish*
Schottland *Scotland*

Schrank (m) *cupboard*
Schraube (f) *screw*
Schraubenschlüssel (m)
   wrench
Schraubenzieher (m)
   screwdriver
Schrebergarten (m)
   allotment
schrecklich (adj) *horrible*
Schreibmaschine (f)
   typewriter
Schreibpapier (nt)
   writing paper
Schreiner(in) (m/f) *carpenter*
Schublade (f) *drawer*
Schuhcreme (f) *shoe polish*
Schuhe (m pl) *shoes*
Schuhgröße (f) *shoe size*
Schuhgeschäft (nt) *shoe*
   store
Schule (f) *school*
Schulter (f) *shoulder*
Schüssel (f) *bowl*
Schwager (m) *brother-in-law*
Schwägerin (f) *sister-in-law*
schwanger (adj) *pregnant*
schwarz (adj) *black*
schwarze Johannisbeere (f)
   black currant
Schwarzwald (m) *Black Forest*
Schweinefleisch (nt) *pork*
Schweiß (m) *sweat*
Schweiz: die Schweiz
   Switzerland
Schweizer(in) (m/f)
   Swiss (person)
schweizerisch (adj) *Swiss*
schwer *heavy, hard*
   (adj: difficult)
Schwester (f) *sister*
schwierig (adj) *difficult*
Schwimmbad (nt)
   swimming pool
Schwimmen (nt)
   swimming; **schwimmen**
   (verb) *to swim*
Schwimmflossen (f pl) *flippers*
schwitzen (verb) *to sweat*
schwul (adj) *gay* (homosexual)
sechs *six*
sechzehn *sixteen*
sechzig *sixty*
See (m) *lake*
Segelboot (nt) *sailboat*
Segeln (nt) *sailing*
sehen (verb) *to see;* **ich kann**
   nichts sehen *I can't see*
sehr *very*
Seide (f) *silk*
Seife (f) *soap*
Seil (nt) *rope*
sein(e) *his*
Seite (f) *page, side*
Sekretär(in) (m/f) *secretary*
Sekunde (f) *second* (time)
selbstständig (adj) *self-*
   employed
selten *rare* (uncommon)

Seminar (nt) *seminar*
Senf (m) *mustard*
September *September*
Serviette (f) *napkin*
Sessel (m) *armchair*
setzen (verb) *to put*
Shampoo (nt) *shampoo*
Sherry (m) *sherry*
Shoppen (nt) *shopping* (activity)
Shorts (f) *shorts*
sicher (adj) *safe, sure*
Sicherheitsgurt (m) *seat belt*
Sicherheitsnadel (f) *safety pin*
Sie *you* (singular and plural formal)
sie *she/they*
sieben *seven*
siebzehn *seventeen*
siebzig *seventy*
Silber (nt) *silver* (metal);
silber *silver* (color)
SIM-Karte (f) *SIM card*
sind: wir/sie/Sie sind;
we/they/you (formal) *are*
Singen (nt) *singing*; **singen** (verb) *to sing*
Sirup (m) *syrup*
Sitz (m) *seat*
Skandinavien *Scandinavia*
Skibindung (f) *ski binding*
Skier (m pl) *skis*
Ski fahren (verb) *to ski*;
Skifahren gehen (verb) *to go skiing*
Skilift (m) *ski lift*
Skistiefel (m pl) *ski boots*
Skistöcke (m pl) *ski sticks*
Skiurlaubsort (m) *ski resort*
Smaragd (m) *emerald*
so *like this, so*
Socken (f pl) *socks*
Sodawasser (nt) *soda water*
Sofa (nt) *sofa*
sofort *immediately*
Sohn (m) *son*
Sonderangebot (nt) *bargain*
Sonne (f) *sun*
sonnenbaden (verb) *to sunbathe*
Sonnenbrand (m) *sunburn*
Sonnenbrille (f) *sunglasses*
Sonnenöl (nt) *suntan lotion*
Sonnenschirm (m) *sunshade*
sonnig (adj) *sunny*
Sonntag *Sunday*
sorgfältig (adj) *careful*
Soße (f) *sauce*
Souvenir (nt) *souvenir*
sowohl... als auch...
both... and...
Spa (m) *spa* (at a hotel)
spät (adj) *late*
Spaten (m) *spade* (shovel)
später (adj) *later*
spazieren gehen (verb) *to go for a walk*
Spaziergang (m) *walk* (stroll)
Speck (m) *bacon*

Speisekarte (f) *menu*
Spiegel (m) *mirror*
Spiel (nt) *match* (sport)
spielen (verb) *to play*
Spielzeug (nt) *toy*
Spinat (m) *spinach*
Spinne (f) *spider*
Spitze (f) *lace; tip* (end)
Sport (m) *sport*;
Sportzentrum (nt) *sports center*
Sportwagen (m) *stroller*
Sprache (f) *language*
Sprachführer (m) *phrase book*
sprechen (verb) *to speak*;
sprechen Sie Englisch? *do you speak English?*;
ich spreche kein Deutsch *I don't speak German*
Spritze (f) *injection, syringe*
sprudelnd (adj) *fizzy*
Sprung (m) *leap, dive*
Sprungbrett (nt) *diving board*
Spülbecken (nt) *basin* (sink)
stabil *strong, stable* (adj: material)
Stadion (nt) *stadium*
Stadt (f) *town, city*
Stadtplan (m) *town plan, map*
Stadtrand (m) *suburbs*
Stadtzentrum (nt) *city/city center*
Stand (m) *stand*
Standlicht (nt) *sidelights*
Star (m) *star* (film)
stark (adj) *strong* (person, drink)
Start (m) *start*
Start-und Landebahn (f) *runway*
Station (f) *station* (underground)
Statue (f) *statue*
Stau (m) *traffic jam*
Staubsauger (m) *vacuum cleaner*
Staubtuch (nt) *duster*
Steak (nt) *steak*
stechen (verb) *to bite, to sting* (insect)
Stecker (m) *plug* (electrical)
Stecknadel (f) *pin*
stehlen (verb) *to steal*; **es ist gestohlen worden** *it's been stolen*
steht: es steht Ihnen *it suits you*
Stein (m) *rock* (stone)
stellen (verb) *to put*
Steppdecke (f) *duvet*
sterben (verb) *to die*
Stern (m) *star*
Stich (m) *bite, sting* (by insect)
stickig (adj) *close* (stuffy)
Stiefel (m) *boot* (footwear)
Stiefmutter (f) *stepmother*
Stiefsohn (m) *stepson*

Stieftochter (f) *stepdaughter*
Stiefvater (m) *stepfather*
Stift (m) *pen*
still (adj) *quiet*
stillhalten! *don't move!*
Stimme (f) *voice*
Stock (m) *floor* (story)
Stoff (m) *material* (fabric)
Stöpsel (m) *plug* (sink)
Stoßstange (f) *bumper*
Strand (m) *beach*
Straße (f) *road, street*
Straßenbahn (f) *tram*
Streichholz (nt) *match* (light)
streng *strong* (adj: taste)
stricken (verb) *to knit*
Strickwaren (f pl) *knitwear*
Strom (m) *electricity*
Stromanschluss (m) *electrical hook-up*
Strümpfe (m pl) *stockings*
Strumpfhose (f) *tights*
Stück (nt) *piece, slice, play* (theater); **fünf Euro das Stück** *five euros each*
Student(in) (m/f) *student*
Stuhl (m) *chair*
Stunde (f) *hour, lesson*
Sturm (m) *storm*
Sucher (m) *viewfinder*
Südafrika *South Africa*
Süden (m) *south*
Supermarkt (m) *supermarket*
Suppe (f) *soup*
süß *sweet* (adj: not sour)
Süßigkeit (f) *sweet* (candy)
Sweatshirt (nt) *sweatshirt*
Synagoge (f) *synagogue*

T

Tabak (m) *tobacco*
Tablett (nt) *tray*
Tablette (f) *pill, tablet*
Tafel Schokolade (f) *bar of chocolate*
Tafelwasser (nt) *still water*
Tag (m) *day*
Tagebuch (nt) *personal diary*
Tagesdecke (f) *bedspread*
Tagesordnung (f) *agenda*
Tal (nt) *valley*
Tampons (m pl) *tampons*
Tankstelle (f) *gas station*
Tante (f) *aunt*
Tanz (m) *dance*
tanzen (verb) *to dance*
Tasche (f) *pocket, bag*
Taschendieb (m) *pickpocket*
Taschenlampe (f) *flashlight*
Taschenmesser (nt) *penknife*
Taschentücher (nt pl) *tissues*
Tasse (f) *cup*
Tastatur (f) *keyboard*
taub (adj) *deaf*
tauchen (verb) *to dive*
tauschen, umtauschen (verb) *to exchange*

tausend *thousand*
Taxi (nt) *taxi*
Taxistand (m) *taxi stand*
Technik (f) *engineering*
Techniker(in) (m/f)
technician
Tee (m) *tea*; **schwarzer Tee**
black tea; **Tee mit Milch**
tea with milk
Teilchen (nt) *danish pastry*
Telefon (nt) *telephone*
Telefonbuch (nt) *directory*
telefonieren (verb)
to call (on the phone)
Telefonkarte (f) *phonecard*
Telefonzelle (f) *phone booth*
Teller (m) *plate*
Temperatur (f) *temperature*
Tennis (nt) *tennis*
Teppich (m) *carpet*
Termin (m) *appointment*
Terminal (nt) *terminal*
Terminkalender (m)
appointments diary
Terrasse (f) *terrace*
Tesafilm (m) *clear adhesive
tape*
teuer (adj) *expensive*
Theater (nt) *theater*
tief (adj) *deep*, (voice) *low*
Tiefkühlkost (f) *frozen foods*
Tierarzt (m) *vet*
Tierpass (m) *pet passport*
Tinte (f) *ink*
Tisch (m) *table*
Toast (m) *toast*
Tochter (f) *daughter*
Toilette (f) *toilet*
Toilettenpapier (nt) *toilet paper*
Tomate (f) *tomato*
Tomatensaft (m) *tomato juice*
Tonic (nt) *tonic*
Töpferei (f) *pottery*
Tor (nt) *gate*
tot (adj) *dead*
Tourist(in) (m/f) *tourist*
Touristeninformation (f)
tourist office
Tradition (f) *tradition*
Tragetasche (f) *plastic bag*
trainieren (verb) *to train,
to coach*
Trainingsanzug (m) *track
suit*
Traktor (m) *tractor*
trampen (verb) *to hitchhike*
Trauben (f pl) *grapes*
traurig (adj) *sad*
Treffen (nt) *meeting*
Treppe (f) *stairs, staircase*
trinken (verb) *to drink*
Trinkgeld (nt) *tip* (money)
Trinkwasser (nt) *drinking water*
trocken (adj) *dry*
Tropfen (m pl) *drops*
Truhe (f) *chest* (furniture)
tun (verb) *to do*
Tunnel (m) *tunnel*

Tür (f) *door*
Türke (m) *Turk*
Türkin (f) *Turk*
Türkei: die Türkei *Turkey*
türkisch (adj) *Turkish*
Turm (m) *tower*
Turnschuhe (m pl) *sneakers*

U

U-Bahn (f) *underground, metro*
U-Bahnstation (f)
metro station
übel: mir ist übel *I feel sick*
über *over, across, more than*
überall *everywhere*
Überführung (f) *flyover*
überfüllt (adj) *crowded*
übergeben: sich übergeben
(verb) *to be sick* (vomit)
überholen (verb) *to overtake*
Überlandbus (m) *coach*
übersetzen (verb) *to translate*
Übersetzer(in) (m/f)
translator
Überzelt (nt) *flier*
Uhr (f) *clock, watch*
um 3 Uhr *at 3 o'clock*
Umschlag (m) *envelope*
Umhängetuch (nt) *shawl*
umziehen *to move* (verb:
house)
umziehen: sich umziehen
to change (verb: clothes)
und *and*
undeutlich (adj) *faint
(unclear), pale*
Unfall (m) *accident*
Unfallstation (f)
emergency department
ungewöhnlich (adj) *unusual*
Universität (f) *university*
Universitätsklinikum (nt)
*hospital attached to a
university*
Unkraut (nt) *weeds*
unmöglich (adj) *impossible*
unser/e *our*
unten *down*; **hier unten**
down here
unter... *below..., under...*
Untergeschoss (nt) *basement*
Unterhaltung (f) *entertainment*
Unterhemd (nt) *vest*
Unterhose (f) *underpants*
Unterkunft (f) *accommodations*
Unterrock (m) *underskirt, slip*
Untertasse (f) *saucer*
Unterwäsche (f) *underwear*
Urlaub (m) *holiday*

V

Vanille (f) *vanilla*
Vase (f) *vase*
Vater (m) *father*
Vegetarier(in) (m/f)
vegetarian (person)

vegetarisch (adj) *vegetarian*
Ventil (nt) *valve*
Ventilator (m) *fan* (ventilator)
Verband (m) *bandage*
Verbrennung (f) *burn*
Vereinigtes Königreich (nt)
United Kingdom
Vereinigte Staaten (m pl)
United States
Vergaser (m) *carburetor*
vergessen (verb) *to forget*
Vergrößerung (f)
enlargement
verheiratet (adj) *married*
Verhütungsmittel (nt)
contraceptive
verkaufen (verb) *to sell*
Verkäufer(in) (m/f) *shopkeeper*
Verkehr (m) *traffic*
Verlängerungsschnur (f)
extension lead
Verletzung (f) *injury*
verlobt *engaged* (adj: couple)
Verlobter/Verlobte (m/f)
fiancé(e)
Vermittlung (f) *operator*
verriegeln (verb) *to bolt*
verrückt (adj) *mad*
verschieden (adj) *different*
Verschluss (m) *cap* (bottle),
shutter (camera)
Versicherung (f) *insurance*
verspätet (adj) *delayed*
**Verspätung: der Bus hat
Verspätung** *the bus
is late*
verstehen (verb) *to
understand*; **ich verstehe**
I see/I understand; **ich
verstehe nicht** *I don't
understand*
versuchen (verb) *to try*
Vertrag (m) *contract*
Vertreter (m) *agent*
Verwandter/Verwandte
(m/f) *relative*
Verzeihung! *sorry!* (apology)
Vetter (m) *cousin*
Video (nt) *video*;
Videokassette (f) *video tape*;
Videorecorder (m) *video
recorder*; **Videospiele** (nt
pl) *video games*
viel (adj) *a lot, much*
vielleicht *maybe, perhaps*
vier *four*
Viertel (nt) *quarter*
vierter *fourth*
vierzehn *fourteen*
vierzig *forty*
Villa (f) *villa*
Visitenkarte (f)
business card
Vitamintablette (f)
vitamin tablet
Vogel (m) *bird*
Voicemail (f) *voicemail*
Volksmusik (f) *folk music*

voll (adj) *busy* (bar, etc.), *full*
Vollpension (f) *full board*
von *of*
vor... *before..., in front of...*
vorbei *over* (finished)
Vorgesetzter/Vorgesetzte (m/f) *superior*
Vorhang (m) *curtain*
Vorhängeschloss (nt) *padlock*
Vorlesungssaal (m) *lecture hall*
Vorname (m) *first name*
Vorspeisen (f pl) *appetizer*
Vortrag (m) *presentation*

W

Wächter (m) *guard*
Wagen (m) *carriage* (train)
wahr (adj) *true*
während *during*
Wald (m) *forest*
Wales *Wales*
Waliser(in) (m/f) *Welshman/ Welshwoman*
walisisch (adj) *Welsh*
Wand (f) *wall* (inside)
Wandern (nt) *hiking*
Wandteppich (m) *tapestry*
wann? *when?*
war *was*; **ich war** *I was*; **er/sie/es war** *he/she/it was*
waren *were*; **wir/sie waren** *we/they were*; **Sie waren** (singular and plural formal) *you were*
warm (adj) *warm*
warst *were*; **du warst** (singular informal) *you were*; **ihr wart** (plural informal) *you were*
warten (verb) *to wait*; **warten Sie!** *wait!*
Wartesaal (m) *waiting room* (station)
Wartezimmer (nt) *waiting room*
warum? *why?*
was? *what?*; **was ist das?** *what's that/this?*
Waschbecken (nt) *wash basin*
Wäsche (f) *laundry* (dirty clothes)
Wäscheklammer (f) *clothespin*
Wäscherei (f) *laundry* (place)
Waschpulver (nt) *powdered detergent*
Waschsalon (m) *self-service laundry*
Wasser (nt) *water*;
Wasser mit Kohlensäure, das Sprudelwasser *fizzy water*; **Wasser ohne Kohlensäure** *still water*
Wasserfall (m) *waterfall*
Wasserkessel (m) *kettle*

Watte (f) *cotton ball*
Webseite (f) *website*
Wechselkurs (m) *exchange rate*
wechseln (verb) *to change* (money)
Wechselstube (f) *bureau de change*
Wecker (m) *alarm clock*
weder... noch... *neither... nor...*
Weg (m) *path*
weich (adj) *soft*
Weihnachten (nt) *Christmas*
weil *because*
Wein (m) *wine*;
Weinkarte (f) *wine list*
Weinbrand (m) *brandy*
weinen *to cry* (verb: weep)
weiß (adj) *white*
weit (adj) *far*; **wie weit ist es?** *how far is it?*; **ist es weit von hier?** *is it far away?*
welcher? *which?*
Welle (f) *wave*
wellig *wavy* (adj: hair)
weniger (adj) *less*
wenn *if*
wer? *who?*
Werkstatt (f) *car repairs, garage*
Wertsachen (f pl) *valuables*
Wespe (f) *wasp*
Westen (m) *west*
Wetter (nt) *weather*
Whisky (m) *whisky*
wie? *how?*; **wie heißen Sie?** *what's your name?*; **wie spät ist es?** *what's the time?*
Wien *Vienna*
willkommen *welcome*
Wimperntusche (f) *mascara*
Wind (m) *wind*
Windel (f) *diaper*
Windschutzscheibe (f) *windshield*
winken (verb) *to wave*
wir *we*
wissen (verb) *to know* (a fact); **ich weiß nicht** *I don't know*
Witz (m) *joke*
wo? *where?*
Woche (f) *week*
Wodka (m) *vodka*
Wohnmobil (nt) *camper van*
Wohnung (f) *apartment*
Wohnwagen (m) *caravan*
Wohnzimmer (nt) *living room*
Wolldecke (f) *rug* (blanket)
Wolle (f) *wool*
Wort (nt) *word*
Wörterbuch (nt) *dictionary*
Wurst (f) *sausage*

Z

Zahl (f) *number*
Zahlen (f pl) *figures*
Zahn (m) *tooth*
Zahnarzt (m) *dentist*
Zahnbürste (f) *toothbrush*
Zahnpasta (f) *toothpaste*
Zahnschmerzen (m pl) *toothache*
Zäpfchen (nt) *suppository*
Zaun (m) *fence*
zehn *ten*
zehntausend *ten thousand*
Zeit (f) *time*
Zeitplan (m) *schedule*
Zeitschrift (f) *magazine*
Zeitung (f) *newspaper*
Zeitungskiosk (m) *newsagent's* (shop)
Zelt (nt) *tent*
Zeltboden (m) *groundsheet*
Zeltstange (f) *tent pole*
Zentrale (f) *head office*
Zentralheizung (f) *central heating*
zerbrochen *broken* (adj: vase, etc.)
Zeuge/Zeugin (m/f) *witness*
ziehen (verb) *to pull*
ziemlich (adj) *fairly, quite*
Zigarette (f) *cigarette*
Zigarre (f) *cigar*
Zimmer (nt) *room*
Zimmerservice (m) *room service*
Zitrone (f) *lemon*
Zoll (m) *Customs*
zollfrei (adj) *duty-free*
Zoo (m) *zoo*
zu *too* (excessively)
Zucker (m) *sugar*
Zug (m) *train*
zum *to*; **zum Bahnhof** *to the station*
Zündkerze (f) *spark plug*
Zündung (f) *ignition*
Zunge (f) *tongue*
zurückgeben (verb) *to return* (give back)
zurückkommen (verb) *to return* (come back)
zusammen *together*
Zusammenbruch (m) *nervous breakdown*
Zuschlag (m) *supplement*
zwanzig *twenty*
Zweck (m) *purpose*; **es hat keinen Zweck** *it's no use*
zwei *two*;
zwei Einzelbetten *twin beds*;
zwei Wochen *fortnight*
Zweigstelle (f) *branch*
zweiter *second* (in series);
zweiter Klasse *second class*
Zwiebel (f) *onion*
zwischen... *between...*
zwölf *twelve*

Acknowledgments

FOURTH EDITION (2023)

For this edition, the publisher would like to thank Ankita Gupta for editorial assistance; Nunhoih Guite and Manpreet Kaur for picture research assistance; Ute Heek and Lukas Joas for the editorial review; Karen Constanti for assistance with artwork commissioning; and Andiamo! Language Services Ltd. for foreign language proofreading.

THIRD EDITION (2018)

Senior Editors Angeles Gavira, Christine Stroyan
Project Art Editor Vanessa Marr
DTP Designer John Goldsmid
Jacket Design Development Manager Sophia MTT
Jacket Designer Juhi Sheth
Pre-Producer David Almond
Senior Producer Ana Vallarino
Associate Publisher Liz Wheeler
Publishing Director Jonathan Metcalf

FIRST EDITION (2005)

The publisher would like to thank the following for their help in the preparation of this book: Edith and Dieter Gollnow for the organization of location photography in Germany; Die Bahn DB, Deutsche Bahn AG, Hannover; Üstra Hannoversche Verkehrsbetriebe AG, Hannover; Raustaurant: Der Gartensaal im Neuen Rathaus, Hannover; Sprengel-Museum Hannover; Polizei-Direktion Hannover; Café An der Martkirche, Hannover; Teestübchen Am Ballhof; Europa-Apotheke, Hannover; Wochenmarkt Gretchenstraße; Magnet Showroom, Enfield; MyHotel, London; Kathy Gammon; Juliette Meeus and Harry.

Produced for Dorling Kindersley by Schermuly Design Co
Language content for Dorling Kindersley by g-and-w publishing
Managed by Jane Wightwick
Editing and additional input Sam Fletcher, Christopher Wightwick
Additional design assistance Lee Riches, Fehmi Cömert, Sally Geeve
Additional editorial assistance Paul Docherty, Mary Lindsay, Lynn Bresler
Picture research Louise Thomas

PICTURE CREDITS

The publisher would like to thank the following for their kind permission to reproduce their photographs.

Key: a-above; b-below/bottom; c-centre; f-far; l-left; r-right; t-top

1 Getty Images / iStock: chrisinthai. **2 Alamy Stock Photo:** Renee McMahon (br). **Dreamstime.com:** Andreas Prott (tr). **3 Dreamstime.com:** Arne9001 (br); Sergey Novikov (bl). **Getty Images / iStock:** Global_Pics (tr); Madeleine_Steinbach (tl). **8 Getty Images / iStock:** 4x6 (c, cr). **9 Getty Images:** Maskot (tl). **10 Dreamstime. com:** Fizkes (bl). **Getty Images / iStock:** E+ / Morsa Images (cr). **11 Getty Images / iStock:** pixdeluxe (tl). **12 Getty Images / iStock:** stocknroll (cr). **13 Dreamstime.com:** Monkey Business Images (br). **Getty Images / iStock:** E+ / kali9 (cla); monkeybusinessimages (cl). **14 Dreamstime.com:** Nyul (crb/woman). **Getty Images / iStock:** Prostock-Studio (crb). **15 Dreamstime.com:** Arne9001 (cla). **Getty Images / iStock:** agrobacter (cl); nd3000 (tl). **Ingram Image Library:** (cbl, bl). **17 Getty Images / iStock:** E+ / Morsa Images (bl); pixdeluxe (ca). **18-19 Getty Images / iStock:** Madeleine_Steinbach (c). **18 Getty Images / iStock:** lutavia (cb). **19 Alamy Stock Photo:** Foodfolio (c); nito (cb). **21 Getty Images:** DigitalVision / 10'000 Hours (tl). **22 Getty Images / iStock:** gmevi (crb). **23 DK Images:** Dave king (tcl). **24 Dreamstime.com:** Charlieaja (br). **Getty Images:** Stuart Snelling / EyeEm (cr). **25 Ingram Image Library:** (tl). **Getty Images / iStock:** monkeybusinessimages (clb, bl); ShotShare (cl). **26 Dreamstime.com:** Monkey Business Images (crb). **Getty Images / iStock:** kuppa_rock (tr); Madeleine_Steinbach (br); lutavia (bc). **27 Getty Images / iStock:** gmevi (tl). **28 Dreamstime.com:** Robert Kneschke (br). **29 Alamy Stock Photo:** PhotoAlto / Michele Constantini (bl). **Shutterstock.com:** Africa Studio (clb); by-studio (cl). **30 DK Images:** (cr), (bcr). **31 DK Images:** Andy Crawford (cla). **Getty Images / iStock:** E+ / AsiaVision (cl).

32 Getty Images / iStock: E+ / kupicoo (cr). **33 Getty Images / iStock:** Moon Safari (tl, cla, cl, clb). **34–35 Dreamstime.com:** Jiri Hera (ca). **34 Dreamstime.com:** Roman Egorov (c). **Getty Images:** fStop / Halfdark (cr). **Shutterstock.com:** Araddara (cb). **35 Dreamstime.com:** Oleg Dudko (cl). **36–37 Dreamstime.com:** Jiri Hera (t). **36 Dreamstime.com:** Oleg Dudko (tr); Roman Egorov (tc). **37 Getty Images:** Stuart Snelling / EyeEm (bl); fStop / Halfdark (cla). **Ingram Image Library:** (c). **38 Alamy Stock Photo:** Jochen Eckel / Sddeutsche Zeitung Photo (cr). **39 Getty Images / iStock:** tommaso79 (tl). **40 Getty Images / iStock:** chrisinthai (cr); Sjo (bl). **41 Getty Images / iStock:** FooTToo (bl); frankpeters (cla). **42 Alamy Stock Photo:** Michael Klinec (cr). **43 Alamy Stock Photo:** Renee McMahon (cl). **Dreamstime.com:** Elena Elisseeva (cla). **Getty Images / iStock:** frankpeters (cb); Filip Viranovski (tl). **44–45 Shutterstock.com:** Nerthuz (c). **46–47 Alamy Stock Photo:** Michael Klinec (c). **46 Alamy Stock Photo:** Takatoshi Kurikawa (cra). **Getty Images / iStock:** chrisinthai (br); Sjo (ca). **Shutterstock.com:** Nerthuz (tc). **47 Alamy Stock Photo:** Jochen Eckel / Sddeutsche Zeitung Photo (bl). **48–49 Dreamstime.com:** Sebastian Czapnik (c). **48 Dreamstime.com:** Biserko (br); Sergey Novikov (bc); Dmitry Naumov (cb). **Shutterstock.com:** Mo Photography Berlin (cb/Museum). **49 Dreamstime.com:** A1977 (bl). **50–51 Shutterstock.com:** Sharkshock (c). **50 Alamy Stock Photo:** Chromorange / Ralph Peters (cb). **52 Getty Images / iStock:** krblokhin (cr). **53 Alamy Stock Photo:** Image Farm Inc. / James Dawson (cla); Matthew Ashmore / Stockimo (cla/toilet). **Getty Images / iStock:** brightstars (tl). **54 Alamy Stock Photo:** Moodboard Stock Photography (cr). **Getty Images / iStock:** E+ / martin-dm (cla). **DK Images:** Andy Crawford (br). **55 Dreamstime.com:** Vinicius Tupinamba (cla). **Getty Images / iStock:** E+ / xavierarnau (tl). **56–57 Shutterstock.com:** Nerthuz (b). **56 Dreamstime.com:** A1977 (c); Sergey Novikov (tr); Sebastian Czapnik (cr); Dmitry Naumov (tc); Biserko (ca). **Getty Images / iStock:** Filip Viranovski (ca/Cathedral). **Shutterstock.com:** Mo Photography Berlin (tc/Museum). **58 Dreamstime.com:** David Brooks (cla). **Getty Images / iStock:** E+ / zeljkosantrac (crb/Family). **59 Dreamstime.com:** Denys Kovtun (tl). **Getty Images / iStock:** 0802290022 (clb). **60 Getty Images / iStock:** Global_Pics (bl); surachetsh (cb). **Shutterstock.com:** Sarymsakov Andrey (cr). **61 Alamy Stock Photo:** Cultura Creative RF / ISO07 (cla). **Dreamstime.com:** Piotr Adamowicz (bl). **Getty Images / iStock:** yipengge (tl). **Ingram Image Library:** (cl). **62–63 Dreamstime.com:** Jennifer Thompson (c). **64 Dreamstime.com:** Andreas Prott (crb). **65 Ingram Image Library:** (tl). **Alamy Stock Photo:** Arcaid Images / Richard Bryant (clb/Bathroom). **Dreamstime.com:** Apiwan Borrikonratchata (cla/woman); Vitalyedush (cla). **Getty Images / iStock:** piovesempre (clb). **Shutterstock.com:** Sarymsakov Andrey (cl). **66 Alamy Stock Photo:** Arcaid Images / Richard Bryant (ca). **Dreamstime.com:** Jennifer Thompson (b). **67 Ingram Image Library:** (bl). **68 Dreamstime.com:** Arne9001 (cr, c). **Getty Images / iStock:** E+ / alvarez (crb); PK-Photos (cb). **Shutterstock.com:** Weho (cra). **69 Alamy Stock Photo:** ImagesEurope (clb). **Dreamstime.com:** Marcel De Grijs (cl). **Getty Images / iStock:** nastya_ph (tl). **70–71 Getty Images / iStock:** KenWiedemann (c). **71 Ingram Image Library:** (cr). **72 Getty Images / iStock:** E+ / Janine Lamontagne (bl). **73 Alamy Stock Photo:** imageBROKER / Harald Theissen (cla/wine). **Dreamstime.com:** Charlieaja (tl); Konstantin Iliev (clb). **Getty Images / iStock:** E+ / Drazen_ (cla). **74 Getty Images:** beyond fotomedia / Alessandro Ventura (r). **75 Getty Images / iStock:** leolintang (bl). **76 Alamy Stock Photo:** ImagesEurope (crb). **Dreamstime.com:** Arne9001 (fbr); Marcel De Grijs (fcrb). **Getty Images / iStock:** KenWiedemann (cra); PK-Photos (bc). **Shutterstock.com:** Weho (br). **79 Getty Images / iStock:** E+ / shapecharge (tl, cla, cl, clb). **Shutterstock.com:** Zhu Difeng (bl). **80 Dreamstime.com:** Robert Kneschke (cra). **82 Alamy Stock Photo:** Momentum Creative / John Sykaluk (cr). **Ingram Image Library:** (cr). **Getty Images / iStock:** Bim (crb). **Shutterstock.com:** Gorodenkoff (cra). **83 Alamy Stock Photo:** wildphotos.com (cla). **84–85 Shutterstock.com:** Pressmaster (c). **84 Shutterstock.com:** Ground Picture (bl). **85 Getty Images / iStock:** PeopleImages (tc). **Shutterstock.com:** Drazen Zigic (c). **Ingram Image Library:** (crb). **89 Getty Images / iStock:** Damir Khabirov (tl). **DK Images:** David Jordan (cla); Stephen Oliver (cl). **Ingram Image Library:** (clb). **91 Dreamstime.com:** Sebnem Ragiboglu (cla). **92 Getty Images / iStock:** E+ / FatCamera (cr). **93 Dreamstime.com:** Roman Egorov (cb); Prostockstudio (tl). **94 Getty Images / iStock:** E+ / Morsa Images (cra); E+ / Tempura (b). **95 DK Images:** Stephen Oliver (tl).**Dreamstime.com:** Shawn Hempel (clb). **Getty Images / iStock:** seb_ra (cl). **97 Dreamstime.com:** Prostockstudio (b). **Getty Images:** beyond fotomedia / Alessandro Ventura (t). **98 Getty Images / iStock:** sl-f (bl). **98–99 Getty Images / iStock:** MediaProduction (c). **99 Alamy Stock Photo:** Itsik Marom (tc). **Getty Images / iStock:** E+ / CreativaStudio (c); Santje09 (ca). **Shutterstock.com:** Gajus (tl). **100 Dreamstime.com:** Draftmode (cb). **Getty Images / iStock:** sihuo0860371 (cr). **102 Getty Images / iStock:** cjp (cr). **102–103 Getty Images / iStock:** DigiStu (b). **103 Dreamstime.com:** Welcomia (cla). **Ingram Image Library:** (cr). **Getty Images / iStock:** Imagesines (cl). **104–105 DK Images:** Paul Bricknell tc(2); Geoff Dann tc(1); Max Gibbs tc(5); Frank Greenaway tc(4); Dave King tc(3); TracyMorgan tc(6). **104 DK Images:** Jane Burton (bcr). **105 DK Images:** dave King (cla). **106 Dreamstime.com:** Draftmode (bc). **Getty Images / iStock:** sihuo0860371 (br). **107 Alamy Stock Photo:** Itsik Marom (cl). **Getty Images / iStock:** DigiStu (bl). **108 Dreamstime.com:** Naumenkoaleksandr (crb). **109 Getty Images / iStock:** mediaphotos (cla). **110 Getty Images / iStock:** Biserka Stojanovic (cr). **111 Dreamstime.com:** Welcomia (cla). **112 Getty Images / iStock:** E+ / freemixer (cr). **DK Images:** Steve Shott (b). **113 Getty Images / iStock:** RossHelen (tl). **Shutterstock.com:** Evgeny Atamanenko (clb). **114 Dreamstime.com:** Amsis1 (br); Brett Critchley (crb). **Getty Images / iStock:** Ridofranz (cr). **115 Dreamstime.com:** Roman Egorov (br); Ulianna19970 (cla). **Getty Images / iStock:** Tatsiana Volkava (cl); Wicki58 (clb/X2). **116 Dreamstime.com:** Naumenkoaleksandr (crb); Welcomia (cra). **Getty Images / iStock:** mediaphotos (br); Santje09 (ca). **117 Getty Images / iStock:** Tatsiana Volkava (ca). **118–119 Dreamstime.com:** Vladwitty (b). **119 Dreamstime.com:** Prostockstudio (cb). **120 Dreamstime.com:** Sergeyoch (bc); Wavebreakmedia Ltd (cr); Skypixel (cb); Volkop (bc/Racket). **121 Getty Images / iStock:** E+ / AscentXmedia (cla). **122–123 Alamy Stock Photo:** Tony Tallec (c). **123 Getty Images / iStock:** nastya_ph (cla). **124–125 DK Images:** Paul Bricknell tc(2); Geoff Dann tc(5); Max Gibbs tc(3); Frank Greenaway tc(4); Dave King tc(1); TracyMorgan tc(6). **124 Dreamstime.com:** Sergeyoch (crb); Wavebreakmedia Ltd (bc); Skypixel (cb); Volkop (cb/Racket). **128 Getty Images / iStock:** Mariha-kitchen (tl).

All other images © Dorling Kindersley